Texas Road Trip

Texas Road Trip

stories from across the great state
and a few personal reflections

Bryan Woolley

TCU PRESS   TCU   FORT WORTH

for

TED, PAT, AND CHRIS

great road companions

Copyright © 2004, Bryan Woolley

Library of Congress Cataloging-in-Publication Data

Woolley, Bryan.
     Texas road trip : stories from across the great state and a few personal
     reflections / by Bryan Woolley.— 1st ed.
        p. cm.
     ISBN 0-87565-291-3
     1. Texas—Description and travel—Anecdotes. 2. Texas—Social life
and customs—Anecdotes. 3. Texas—Biography—Anecdotes. 4. Woolley,
Bryan—Travel—Texas—Anecdotes. 5. Automobile travel—Texas—Anecdotes.
I. Title.
F391.2.W655 2004
976.4—dc22

                                                          2004004694

Design: Shadetree Studio

Printed in Canada

Introduction

Among the pleasures of my life is driving. Moving through the landscape thrills me. More than 300,000 miles of paved streets and highways crisscross Texas. They range from cross-country interstates to narrow farm-to-market roads. Some, like Route 66 and U.S. 80, are fractured remnants of an earlier time. Branching off from rural pavements, thousands of dusty, rocky private roads head into pinewoods or mesquite flats. Texas is a fine place to drive.

Except for Interstate 35, which the North American Trade Agreement has turned into a clog of trucks spewing diesel smoke and danger, even the superhighways are good routes to ride. Better, though, are the sparsely traveled farm-to-markets and the old highways that used to connect the little towns before the interstates bypassed them. On those roads, men wearing western hats mosey slowly toward town or home in pickup trucks. They lift a finger or two in greeting to everyone they encounter. Sometimes, when they meet somebody they know, they stop in the road and visit. The road is part of the community. Time moves slowly here. No one is in a hurry.

The best roads are the dusty, unpaved traces that leave so-called "civilization" entirely behind and disappear into nature and silence. To travel these, you must open a gate or cross a cattle guard into somebody's private domain, but the "No Trespassing" sign on the fence means what it says. Driving the little roads beyond the fences is a privilege. The people at the end of them had better be your friends. Or you had better have asked permission to come. Else you might be told politely but firmly to leave.

A few stories in this book are about people in Dallas and Austin and other cities. But most are about people I met on road trips through the Texas that lies beyond the interstates. I met them in little towns and the rural countryside in every region, from the Panhandle to the Gulf, from the Piney Woods to the mountains in the West. The stories were published in *The Dallas Morning News*, which gave me permission to collect them here. I also have included a few personal ruminations. I think of this book as the story of my own life as I have roamed the land I love.

After many years moving across the land, I continue to marvel at the grace, the kindness, and the generosity I have found among the people of Texas, whatever their region, race, gender, or economic situation.

They are my people. I am grateful to them all.

Bryan Woolley
Dallas
May 2004

Rider

Most people would say Joel Nelson breaks horses, but he doesn't care for that term. What he does, he says, is start colts.

"I take two- or three-year-old colts that haven't been broke to ride, and I start handling them, saddling them up, getting on them," he says. "I put the first thirty to sixty days on them. From that point, a ranch cowboy who has any kind of talent for horses can take him and go on with him. But the first thirty to sixty days, they're pretty unpredictable and inexperienced."

Mr. Nelson, who followed his father into his profession, is the complete American cowboy. Over the past thirty years he has started colts and worked cattle on ranches all over Texas, from the King Ranch in South Texas to the Nail on the Brazos to the o6 in the Trans-Pecos. He has ridden for the Parker Ranch in Hawaii and handled packhorses for an outfitter in Montana. He has built saddles at the Big Bend Saddlery in Alpine.

He writes poems about his work and other matters and is invited to recite them at cowboy poetry gatherings all over the West. He has brought out a CD called *The Breaker in the Pen,* on which he recites a dozen of his poems in his rich drawl. The long title piece describes the ancient contest that begins when a man steps into a corral and attempts to assert his will over a powerful beast that outweighs him by eight to ten times.

> *At times he thinks he's crazy,*

one of the verses goes,

> *Other times he knows for sure.*
> *But centaur blood pumps through his veins,*
> *And there isn't any cure.*

"Normally, you try to ride six or eight head a day. Just short rides for short periods of time," he says. "A horse can learn quite a little bit with an hour or so of handling every day.

"They're as different as people. There'll be slow learners and fast learners. It's the colt starter's responsibility to adjust himself to fit each horse, so that each can progress at his own level. Some horses feel like they've got to buck. Some horses aren't at all inclined to. I try to get things done with them as easily as possible, so they don't get pressured up to the point where they feel they have to buck. If you present things to them in an understandable way, they're pretty forgiving and will try to get along with you. You can make a lot faster progress on them if you don't get them on the fight."

> He's not high on riding buckers,
> And disdains the use of quirt.
> He's eaten quite a little more
> Than his fair share of dirt.

But no matter how patient and respectful a man is, from time to time he's bound to encounter a nightmare. Mr. Nelson met his a little over a year ago.

He was starting some colts on a ranch at Seymour, the town where he grew up, near Wichita Falls. He was only on the second day of the job. Among the horses was a very big three-year-old thoroughbred.

"I had saddled him the day before and let him wear it, and he kind of had gotten OK with that," Mr. Nelson says. "So the second day I was trying to get him accustomed to my stepping up and down in my stirrup. That was bothering him. He was blowing up and bucking. But I got him to the point where he could stand me stepping up. The weight shift, tipping that saddle a little bit to the side, sometimes puts a bit of a bind on a horse. They're unused to that feel and get pretty upset sometimes. That's where he was.

"I had stepped up in the stirrup and was standing there. I hadn't swung my leg over the saddle. And I thought, 'This is better. He's accepting this. It's time I quit on him. I'll just step down and call it a day.' About the time my foot touched the ground, he blew straight up in the air and spun and kicked me in the face.

"I heard this explosion in my face when his foot hit. It broke everything. My eye orbits, my forehead, my cheeks, my upper jaw. It flattened my nose and spread it all over my face.

"I didn't feel anything, and I didn't pass out. They took me to the hospital in Seymour and then to one in Wichita Falls. They looked at me and didn't want anything to do with me. So they put me in a helicopter and took me to Parkland Hospital in Dallas. They kept me there four days so the swelling could subside, then had me in surgery for eleven-and-a-half hours, reconstructing my face.

"That helicopter ride cost $10,000. Since they didn't work on me for four days, I could have hitchhiked to Dallas and saved that money."

Because an infection developed, the doctors had to remove one of the plates they had installed in his face. He returned to Parkland in early June to have it put back in. Later, he'll undergo eye surgery to correct the double vision that the thoroughbred's hoof precipitated.

Mr. Nelson is eager to get rid of the black patch he now must wear on his left eye. It's a hot thing to have on in the West Texas summertime.

The ride might end with two as one,
Just like it all began;
Else the breaker finds the wherewithal
To rise and ride again.

When he was a student at Seymour High School, Joel had two literature teachers—Miss Anita Welsh and Miss Annalena Kessler—who instilled a love of poetry in him.

Miss Welsh was young and pretty, and Joel had a crush on her. When she assigned her students twenty or thirty lines of poetry to memorize and recite before the class, Joel memorized Edgar Allan Poe's "The Raven," which goes on for pages. "I wanted so much to impress her," he says.

Miss Kessler, he says, was an older lady, a very stern teacher. "She clomped around in big high-heeled lace-up shoes and wore flower-print dresses. She really loved poetry. I remember she came into class crying one day because Carl Sandburg had passed away. She was in tears for two or three days. Later on, I really appreciated that. She had a big influence on me. I can still recite poems I learned back in high school."

But when he went off to Stephen F. Austin State University in Nacogdoches, he majored in forestry and range management. After graduation, he worked for a short while for the U.S. Forest Service in East Texas and Northern Idaho. In 1969 he was drafted.

"I served fourteen months in Vietnam with the 101st Airborne Division," he says. "I was with a reconnaissance outfit, Echo Company. About twelve of those months, I was working with six-man recon teams up in the DMZ on the Laotian border. I would never want to be in a situation like that again, but I'm really happy that I was able to experience that and come out OK. War is a learning and growing experience."

Some of the letters he wrote to his family were in verse, his first attempt at poetry. But he had been back home for fifteen years before he began writing poems more or less regularly. Among those he recites frequently at the cowboy poetry gatherings are several that deal with war and what it means to be a soldier.

An especially powerful one is "Shady Valleys." It begins:

> The horseman was a soldier.
> Word had it none was bolder.
> Hence the orders in the folder
> Sent him with the Light Brigade.
> In the ghastly scene that followed
> Was the gallant unit swallowed,
> Where in bloody grass they wallowed,
> There in the valley shade.

"At the time, I had a really patriotic outlook toward the war," Mr. Nelson says. "I was really gung-ho. I thought we were 100 percent right in what we were doing. In retrospect, though, I see the futility of it, at least in the way we approached it. I have a lot of regrets now that we had to become involved in it.

"And I can sympathize and empathize with those who were highly opposed to it. I thought they were wrong at the time, but now I can understand their feelings. I had friends who evaded the draft, and I never did have a problem with that, even then. And I still don't have a problem with it."

Then the lucky who were spared
Rode back where no one cared,
Determined shoulders squared,
But somewhat wiser now.
These descendents of the knighted,
Who in their quests delighted
At the wrongs that they had righted.
Yet it seemed a waste somehow.

He's sitting in his living room in his little house on a Davis Mountains hillside fifteen miles south of Alpine, within sight of a border patrol highway checkpoint. On a small table lie Yevgeny Yevtushenko's *Selected Poems* and *This House of Sky* by Ivan Doig and *The Perfect Storm* by Sebastian Junger. On a wall hang several bridles and hackamores, tools of his trade, and a glassed frame displaying arrowheads. There are Mexican blankets and a saddle on a stand. A thick, much-Scotch-taped *Webster's New World Dictionary* is by the window. The jungles and rice paddies of Vietnam couldn't be farther away. But Mr. Nelson's bare eye begins to cloud as he speaks of battle and the men he knew there and the ones who died.

"I didn't have a sweetheart at home when I went to 'Nam. And I'm really grateful for that," he says. "I saw guys go through a lot of hardship over there for that reason. The separation was hard. And I had a few good friends who got Dear John letters. And I had some good friends who didn't make it back. That must have been hard for the sweethearts back home."

One would deem it somewhat strange
That in all of hist'ry's range
There is noted little change.
When sounds the battle call

And, fighting gallantly as told
At the urging of the old,
The youthful and the bold
Become names upon a Wall.

He returned from Vietnam in September 1970. "I had contracted malaria," he says. "For two months I was in the hospital over there. I recovered from that, but shortly after I got back I came down with a relapse and was down for another month or two. When I finally recovered, I went straight to work on ranches as a cowboy. And that's pretty much what I've done ever since. I was going back to what my dad did. He was a ranch cowboy and a peace officer for a lot of his life."

About a year after Mr. Nelson's return from Vietnam, he married. During their early post-war days he and his wife, Barney, drifted about, working on a ranch near Marfa, then one near Alpine, then to a camp on the Nail Ranch in Shackleford County, then back to Alpine. He built saddles at the saddlery for a while.

"One day in the summer of 1978," he says, "Chris Lacy from the o6 came in the shop and told me he had a camp open. He wanted me to move to Willow Spring, which is about thirteen miles up north of Alpine. He told me I could continue to build all the saddles I wanted to out there. So I thought, 'Well, I'll try it for a year and see how it works out.' I moved out there and stayed for fourteen years. It was the greatest place I ever worked. And the Lacys are the greatest people I ever worked for."

The o6 comprises a huge swatch of the beautiful Davis Mountains country. Chris Lacy, who runs it now, is the nephew of the late Herbert Kokernot, Jr., who was beloved throughout the Big Bend for his philanthropy and his love of baseball and his love of the land.

"The o6 is still pretty much an old-school type ranch, and that's one of the things I enjoyed about it," Mr. Nelson says. "When Mr. Kokernot died [in 1986], we had a very small funeral at the ranch and buried him in the shipping trap north of the headquarters. There's no headstone, no fence around the grave. Three years later, we buried Mrs. Kokernot right beside him.

"I remember riding by Mr. Kokernot's grave a couple of weeks after we buried him. The mound of dirt was still fairly fresh, nothing was growing on it. But an old Hereford cow was laying on the ground up against it, chewing her cud. And I thought, 'Boy, that's just the way Herbert would want it, right there.' And that's the way it has stayed.

"Chris is a lot like Herbert. He let me take care of my camp. He very seldom showed up, very seldom suggested that I do a certain thing, very seldom asked what I was doing. He pretty much left me alone, and we had a good working relationship."

The Nelsons' daughter, Carla, grew up alongside the Lacys' children. "We were all kind of like family," Mr. Nelson says.

But in 1991, Joel and Barney's marriage ended, and he decided he needed a change of scenery. That's when he went to Hawaii for the first time, to start colts for the big Parker Ranch. But he has always loved the Big Bend mountain ranges, and he returned. Now fifty-six, he still will help out a rancher who needs an experienced hand and works on roundups now and then. But starting colts is where he makes his living.

Near sundown, as the day is cooling, he's atop one of the four horses now residing in his pens, teaching the animal how to maneuver so that the rider can open a gate without dismounting.

"After about three weeks, when they're relaxed, I start teaching them little jobs they can do," Mr. Nelson says. "It gives them a purpose for the drills I teach them. It gives them something to concentrate on that makes their work a little more meaningful to them, and less boring."

A red pickup is pulling up at the house. It's Carla and her cowboy husband, Chris Spencer, and their nineteen-month-old son, Riley. They live on a ranch nearby. Carla and Chris' second child is due in August.

"My grandson has really changed my life," Mr. Nelson says. "I never knew I would have such attachment for a little one. I couldn't imagine being that excited and hung up on a little kid."

He walks up the hill and greets his family. He takes the little boy's hand, and they go together to see the horses.

One of them, a trim little sorrel, will someday be Riley's, a gift. Mr. Nelson lifts the child, so that he can stroke the colt's soft nose. When the sorrel is old enough to start, Mr. Nelson will be the breaker in the pen.

There's a poem that Mr. Nelson loves to recite more than any of his own. It's called "Anthem." It's the work of a friend, Buck Ramsey, a cow-boy who died.

And in the morning I was riding
Out through the brakes of that long plain
And leather creaking on the quieting
Would sound with trot and trot again.
I lived in time with horse hoof falling.
I listened well and heard the calling
The earth, my mother, bade to me
Though I would still ride, wild and free.
And as I flew out on the morning
Before the bird, before the dawn,
I was the poem, I was the song. . . .

Charlie

People talking about Charlie Smith always use the same words. Tough. Strong. Dependable. Loyal. Proud. Stubborn. "Charlie's a mountain of a man," says his stepfather-in-law, Marshall Pyburn. "There's nothing he couldn't do or accomplish. Two years ago, he could whip a grizzly bear."

Charlie is six foot four and good-looking. His dark eyes are keen and bright. They engage the attention of anyone in his company. Two years ago, he weighed about 240. He was twenty-five years old then.

At Mullin High School, where he graduated in 1996, Charlie was Mr. Everything: quarterback of the school's championship six-man football team, most valuable player, homecoming king three years running, Christmas prince, basketball and track star. He has boxes full of medals and ribbons and certificates and newspaper clippings. He made pretty good grades.

"He was a smart kid," says Marlene Shelton, who was the Mullin school superintendent in those days. "But like a lot of other boys, he probably could have done more if he'd wanted to."

As its motto, Charlie's class chose "Living life to the fullest." Everybody says that's what Charlie always did. It required ingenuity.

In Mills County, about thirty miles south of Comanche, Mullin is one of those dried-up little railroad towns that dot the Texas landscape. It peaked around 1910, when its population was 750. Cotton used to be the cash crop. Now it's livestock. Trains still scream through several times a day, but no longer stop. Most of the 175 people still living in Mullin are natives whose families have been in the town and the hilly country around it for many generations. A lot of them are kin.

"We rode the dirt roads," says Charlie's cousin and best friend, Travis Wilson. "You can go millions of miles in this county and never touch pavement. As soon as we'd get out of school until way up in the morning, if we wasn't footballing on Friday night, we was on the roads.

"We rode 600 and 700 miles a night sometimes, raising Cain, and never touching pavement. We'd chase down a coon and skin it. We'd build a fire. We'd go fishing in the bayou. Sometimes we'd drink a little beer. We had a lot of fun."

Charlie, Travis says, was the leader of the group. "He's natural-born to it. You could bring people in from nine different states and put them in a bunch, and Charlie would get in the middle of them and he would listen to them and he would make stuff work. He's just like that."

For Charlie and Travis, living the full life also meant working. Hard manual labor was expected in Mullin. It was part of being a man. "Our dads and our uncles, they would come get us," Travis says. "One day we'd be building fence. The next morning we'd be out here gathering cows and penning bulls. The next day after that, somebody else would gather us up and take us to a job somewhere. Charlie and me, we was always working. If we wasn't riding tractors, we was hauling hay or picking up rocks. We chased down an emu that got out of a man's pasture. If somebody wasn't getting hurt or bleeding, we wasn't having no fun."

Charlie's parents, Jim and Jennetta, traveled the rodeo circuit. She was a champion barrel racer. He was a pick-up man for the bronc riders. They divorced about the time Charlie graduated. Jennetta remarried and moved away from Mullin. Jim drives a "bull wagon," hauling cattle, and is on the road nearly all the time.

Once when Charlie was a little boy, Jim tied his spurs together with baling wire under the belly of a calf. "You're going to stay on him until you break him!" he said. Later, when Charlie was a football star, his father roamed the sidelines at the games. "You damn pansies!" he would shout. "You look like cheerleaders out there!"

"The older men, they made us tough," Travis says. "They'd say, 'Don't baby them boys around. If they're hurt, get them fixed up and make them go on.' That's the way it was. If you was really hurt, you was hurt. But if you was just banged up a little bit, you'd better get up and go on. The worst thing in the world was disappointing your old man."

Tears are in Travis' eyes now. "Charlie's a good man," he says. "He's stubborn. He'll fight it out. He ain't scared of it."

★

One day in the spring of 2002, Charlie stepped out of the tractor-trailer rig he was driving for Mills County Stone Co. and slipped and fell on his back. Those who saw him laughed about it. But during the following weeks, Randy Holland, a driver who worked with Charlie, began to notice something strange.

"Whenever Charlie would go to turn around, he would fall," Randy says. "I just thought it was a little clumsiness. Well, it got to where when he set down, his leg would jump up and down, just quiver and move."

Charlie's cousin Travis saw differences, too. "There was something eerie about him when he would get out of his truck," he says. "He was kind of stumbling." He once saw Charlie fall, too.

"I never did say nothing. Used to, when Charlie and me would see each other, we would lock horns, you know, kind of fighting. He would throw me around like a rag doll. He got to where he wouldn't do that anymore. He would just kind of back away. He wasn't as stout as he used to be. But if he wanted me to know, he would tell me.

"And then he did. He told me something was wrong with him and he didn't know what it was."

In his twenty-five years, Charlie had been to a doctor twice: once when he cut his lip on an old trashcan, and when he blew out his knee in a football game and rode to a hospital in an ambulance.

Now he was married to Rémy, a girl from Comanche he had dated since he was eighteen and she was fifteen. They lived in the small frame house in Mullin where Charlie grew up, a few blocks from the school where he was a hero. They had an infant daughter, Kyra. Rémy was pregnant again. She was worried about Charlie.

"My back pain really started progressing, almost like a kidney hurt," Charlie says. "Rémy made me go. I went first to a chiropractor. I thought it might be a pinched nerve. He took some x-rays and said he couldn't do nothing for me. He told me to go see a neurologist in Abilene. I said, 'I ain't going to do that. Ain't nothing wrong.' But slowly and surely the pain progressed, and we did go.

"We went there two or three months. They ran every kind of test in the world. Drawed blood until I thought I'd go dry. They told me it could be tick fever because we was always down by the river, always out in the woods. Then the doctor said he was going to recommend me to Dallas."

In October 2002, doctors at UT-Southwestern Medical School told Charlie right off that they thought he had amyotrophic lateral sclerosis (ALS), a disease that weakens the body's muscles, then paralyzes them, then eventually kills the victim. In this country it's known commonly as Lou Gehrig's disease. Among the bad things that can happen to people, not many are worse.

The disease usually strikes people in their fifties or older. Victims often die within three to five years. Those who go on a respirator sometimes live much longer, but are paralyzed and often bedridden. Cases among young people are rare. The younger the victim is, the faster the disease progresses. Charlie was twenty-five.

"They said I was the youngest person they'd diagnosed with ALS in Dallas," Charlie says. "They said I might have three to six months, maybe a year. They told me I was going to have to have a respirator and a hospital bed.

"My stomach just dropped. I was in awe that they would say something like that in front of my wife and kid. It made me ball up inside. I wanted to ask, 'Where did you come from, to tell me how long I'm going to last?' I wanted to say 'I ain't going nowhere. I'll be back here in ten years to kick your ass.'"

Soon he had to climb down for good from the truck he had driven to Houston and San Antonio and Dallas, delivering landscaping stone. He went on Social Security, receiving a monthly $700 disability check, and Medicaid.

Bills were piling up. "I couldn't see going up there and spending 200-and-something dollars a pop for a hotel room and then setting in that office for six-and-a-half hours just so a doctor and a bunch of medical students could parade in and test my reflexes," Charlie says. "That was all they was doing. They run us through like cattle. And every time I went there, they took money out of what we've got each month to live on. They was taking nearly half of that."

A fundraiser fish fry in Comanche brought in about $5,000. Charlie and Rémy caught up on their bills. When Charlie Jr. was born last May, they had stem cells saved from his umbilical cord and spent $2,500 of the fish fry money to have them frozen and stored in a facility in California.

They had heard of stem cell research that someday might help victims of ALS and other diseases. They hoped the baby's cells might provide hope for his father.

"The doctors in Dallas told us they didn't know nothing about that research," Charlie says. "They said all the Internet stuff on it was from over in Europe, that it's illegal here because they were taking cells from aborted babies. But we took them from little Charlie's umbilical cord. And we thought they might be a possible solution. They might give me another three years, four or five years. You never know."

After four or five trips to Dallas, Charlie and Rémy quit going.

"They couldn't understand why I was so hardheaded," Charlie says. "But I'd rather sit right here and watch my babies go and laugh and have fun and go outside and watch the dog run around," he says. "The way I was raised up, you don't give up, no matter what. And if you don't let something get you, it won't get you."

Travis Wilson and another high school football buddy, Marshall Craker, have stopped by Charlie's house. They're talking about the old days, the games, the nights roaming the dirt roads, the huge catfish they used to catch out of Pecan Bayou.

Charlie is sitting in his big lounge chair in a corner of the living room. In the opposite corner, CNN is flashing on the big TV screen, muted. Nobody is watching it. Travis and Marshall are making Charlie laugh. He's enjoying their visit and joins in with his own version of their common memories.

His speech is slow and slurred. His fingers are curled in toward his palms and stiff. He has trouble fishing a cigarette out of the pack on the table beside him. Travis flicks the lighter for him.

Charlie is telling a couple of visiting strangers about the football team. "We played together from the fourth grade until we was seniors," he says. "It was like playground football with your brothers. Everybody knew what everybody was going to do. Everybody flowed smooth."

Most of his buddies moved away from Mullin after high school. But Travis lives in Zephyr and Marshall Craker, in Santa Anna, nearby towns.

They and a few others drop in from time to time, to chew the fat. "Every other month, we have a houseful two weekends running," Charlie says. "Everybody piles in." Randy Holland, Charlie's older truck driver friend, lives only about a block away. He's usually available when Charlie and Rémy need help.

Rémy's stepfather, Marshall Pyburn, and her mother, LaQuitta, who is a nurse, are pillars of the beleaguered young family, even though they live in Comanche. They drive to Mullin, do whatever they can. Charlie trusts them, and likes them.

But Rémy, a pretty young woman with shoulder-length brown hair and a nice smile, bears nearly all the load. She's twenty-three years old. Kyra is two years old. Charlie Jr. is only nine months, still in diapers. "I'm all right," Rémy says. "I don't have it that bad."

Travis introduced Charlie and Rémy long ago, it seems now, at a basketball game. They fell for each other even though both were dating others at the time. "Rémy's a good girl," Travis says. "She hangs in there. She takes care of the house and her kids. She's always been like one of the guys, too."

But weariness tugs at the corners of her eyes and mouth. Her parents worry about her.

"Charlie has disintegrated to the point where it takes him ten minutes to walk from his chair to the bedroom," Marshall Pyburn says. "He may fall once a week; he may fall every day. He's bullheaded. He won't give up. If it means falling, he'll fall. He laid on the floor once for two hours. He wouldn't let Rémy help him up. He told her he would get up on his own. He's careful of the children. He still weighs about 180. If he was to fall on one of them, it would be terrible.

"I take my hat off to Rémy. She's my hero. She has stood by Charlie and loved him heart and soul. She and Charlie have been through more than ten people should have to go through in a lifetime. I keep telling her, 'God's in your pocket. You'll come out of this a better person.' I really believe that."

The doctors prescribed Rilutek for Charlie. It's the only drug that's supposed to somehow help ALS victims. The cost of the prescription was $2,000 a month, and Charlie says it "messed with my heart and gave me kidney cramps." He never finished the first bottle.

The doctors gave him prescriptions for painkillers, which Charlie doesn't take. "I'd rather feel some pain and deal with it and be myself than be all doped up," he says. "My old man always said, 'If you ain't feeling some pain, you ain't living.'"

The doctors gave him a walker, which he doesn't use. And he turned away a physical therapist because, his friends say, he didn't want a stranger to see him having trouble getting around.

"There are lots of people out there who have it twice as bad as I do," he says. "I'm not going to mope around and feel sorry for myself. Don't ever think you're at the end of the world. That's the way I was raised."

But to his cousin Travis, it's all a cruel puzzle. Talking about Charlie is too hard. He shoves his hat away from his forehead.

"Charlie's illness is the kind of thing that ain't supposed to happen here," he says. "You're supposed to grow old here in Mullin, you know. Most people do."

Sky-Vue

When Sam Kirkland was ten years old, he went to work at the Sky-Vue Drive-In out on Highway 87, picking up trash, serving up Cokes, doing whatever needed to be done. He loved the place. He worked there all through high school. Then he went off to college for a while, then worked on jobs here and there around West Texas.

By the time he moved back to Lamesa in 1979, Sam had a wife and four kids and a job pumping wells for an oil company. The Sky-Vue was closed. People from Lamesa and the smaller towns around it had been going to the picture show there since 1948, but now it was a wreck. Weeds stood as high as the speaker poles. The asphalt ramps were cracked and crumbling. The snack bar was filthy and full of junk.

Sam couldn't stand it. He went and had a talk with Skeet Noret, who had built the Sky-Vue and still owned it. "I asked him if I could clean it up," Sam says. "I didn't want to see it looking the way it did. I had worked there all those years. Some things just grow on you."

Skeet gave his permission. So every day after he got home from the oil fields, Sam would take his lawnmower out to the theater and mow the ramps and try to tidy up the place. Sometimes his wife, Carolyn, and the kids would help him. It took sixteen weeks.

Then Skeet came out and had a look. "Hey, Sam," he said. "Why don't you open it up for the summer?"

"That was the summer of 1980," Sam says. "We were poor as church mice back then. Carolyn and I figured if we could make $50 a weekend, it would really help our family. We opened it up. Our kids helped us, and we had two hired help. That summer has lasted for twenty-one years. We're still here. Business gets better and better."

In 1987, Sam and Carolyn bought the Sky-Vue from Skeet. They show first-run movies on Friday, Saturday, and Sunday nights all year, and on

Wednesday nights in the summer. Normally, they change the movie every week. But sometimes the distributor requires them to keep a big movie like *Planet of the Apes* or *Jurassic Park III* for two weeks. When that happens, Sam shows a double feature during the second week.

"You can't expect people to come back the second week to see the same movie again," Sam says. "But, if I add a second feature, a lot of them will return. Tonight we're giving them a John Wayne movie on top of *Jurassic Park III*. We just throw that in. *Big Jake*. There's no cost to it."

Three-quarters of the crowd on this Saturday night will be from out of town, Sam says. They'll drive fifty miles from Midland, sixty miles from Lubbock, seventy from Odessa, and from all the little towns between.

"They do it for nostalgia," Sam says. "They're trying to get back something they used to have or something they wish they had. They could see *Jurassic Park III* in Lubbock or Odessa or Midland. But they would have to go to one of them multiplexes and spend $7.25 a head and a whole bunch of money for popcorn and Cokes. Here we charge $4 to get in. Our snack bar has great food at great prices. Mom and Dad don't have to hire a babysitter. Kids under six get in free. We *want* them to bring the kids. And we give them *Big Jake* for nothing."

At a drive-in theater, he says, freedom is the number-one thing. "You can sit there in your lawn chair and gab all you want to. You can smoke if you want to. The kids can go to the playground and play during the movie. You can move around and visit with your neighbors. You can't do any of that at a multiplex."

In 1954, there were 388 drive-in theaters in Texas. Even the small towns had them. Now about a dozen remain. Lubbock and Midland and Odessa don't have one. Lamesa, population 12,000, does.

It's the only place on the South Plains where you can watch John Wayne and eat a Chihuahua at the same time.

The Chihuahua is a sandwich. Skeet Noret's daddy invented it in 1951. "He was a good cook and liked to experiment with food," Sam says. "He made this unusual new sandwich, and him and Skeet was standing there tasting it and trying to think of a name for it. They thought they might call it the Monterrey. Then some Spanish girls walked by. One of them had on some real tight jeans. Two Spanish boys was walking behind them, and one of them looked at that girl and said, *'Aaii, Chihuahua!'*"

"Skeet's dad said, 'That's it! That's what we'll name this sandwich!'"

The Norets liked the name so much they registered it as a trademark. The Chihuahua is served in a special sack with a picture of a pretty girl wearing a sombrero. The only place on earth you can buy one is at the Sky-Vue.

"We have specially made corn tortillas," Sam says. "We fry them hard and crisp and flat. Then we put our special chili on one of them, and onions, if you like onions. Then we take raw cabbage and grate it and put it on there. Then we take our special pimento cheese and spread it on the other tortilla. Then we put the tortillas together. And we put a jalapeno pepper in the sack with it."

"You keep it in the sack while you're eating it," Carolyn says. "If you don't, it falls apart and grease slides down your arms."

The regulars usually buy a side order of jalapeno corn fritters or pop-pers—jalapeno peppers stuffed with cheese and fried in a batter—to fill out their meal.

The Chihuahua has long been the most popular item at the snack bar. It sells for $1.95. Carolyn and her ten snack bar helpers move about 500 of them a night. Sometimes they sell 100,000 in a year. "When Sam and I reopened the drive-in," Carolyn says, "everybody asked us, 'Are y'all going to have Chihuahuas again?' It's the Lamesa crowd that loves them. The out-of-town people don't eat Chihuahuas much."

They go for the box dinners of chicken strips, steak fingers, fried cod, or shrimp, served with fries, a corn fritter, toast, and a pickle. Or corn dogs or nachos or cheese sticks or giant dill pickles or funnel cakes or char burgers. Plus popcorn and soft drinks and candy. Nothing on the menu costs more than $4.75 (the cod or shrimp box lunch), and some of the gum is a nickel.

Sam leaves the house at six-forty-five A.M. for his day job in the oil fields. At about nine-thirty, Carolyn drives to the Sky-Vue and puts the chili on the stove. She lights the steam table, cuts the cabbage for the Chihuahuas, then goes to the store for the corn fritter and funnel cake ingredients.

"The next thing you know, it's two-thirty," she says. "I get my char patties started and set things up. Sam gets here about three-thirty and helps with the cooking and or whatever else needs to be done." That includes running the projector, patrolling the crowd, and mopping the snack bar floor at closing time. On double-feature nights, he doesn't get home till twelve-thirty or one A.M.

At six P.M. in the summertime there's still three hours of daylight left on the South Plains, but one of the hired help opens the box office. Sky-Vue Drive-In food is so popular that some people come to eat and don't stay for the movie. Sam doesn't charge them admission, so they have to enter the theater via a special lane and park in a designated fenced-in spot in front of the snack bar, isolated from the movie area. Sam keeps a watchful eye. They have to leave the theater as soon as they get their food.

By seven, the movie crowd is arriving. Drivers back their pickups onto the ramps and arrange folding aluminum lawn chairs and chaise longues in the beds. Others set up their chairs on the ground with their ice chests and food sacks alongside. Others sit inside their cars, doors open, chatting with their neighbors. A small brown dog moves among them, greeting all.

Justin Wood and Tara Bynum have come down from Lubbock in the new red Dodge pickup that Justin got for high school graduation last spring. He and Tara are students at Texas Tech and thought a night at the old drive-in would be a fun date. But they forgot that the movie can't start until the sun is down.

"We arrived in Lamesa way too early," Tara says. "We drove all around town, but there isn't much to see. So we found the Dollar General Store and bought some coloring books and crayons to occupy our time."

She shows off her work. She's one of those people who colors within the lines.

Juanice Hirst, Janie New, and Kay Sherill are sitting in the bed of the pickup next to Justin's. Garry Smith is standing beside the truck. Kay is Janie's sister, and Jaunice is Garry's sister. They've come down from Lubbock, too, Garry's treat.

"When we was young," Janie says, "the greatest thing was seeing how many people we could get in the trunk of our car and sneak them into the drive-in."

"Why, we would have them in the trunk and down on the floor," Juanice says. "We could get a whole crew in for the price of two or three people."

"Lots of good memories," Garry says.

The sun is sinking. Rays beam through purple clouds. A cool breeze has sprung up. Fifty kids or more are on the old steel-and-wood merry-go-round and the swings and the jungle gym, their reedy voices distinct and sweet in the fading light. Adults stand and sit in little bunches, visiting, as if they're at a huge family reunion. Jerry and Brenda Randall and their friend Amber Appleton arrive from Lubbock on their big Harleys and park on the back row. Eric and Melissa Price have come in from their farm to celebrate their second wedding anniversary at the Sky-Vue. They recently moved back to the Plains from North Carolina and are happy to be home. "North Carolina's nice," Eric says, "but it's got so many trees you can't see anything." The food line inside the snack bar already stretches to the door. It won't shorten for hours.

Jackie and Darla Stidham have driven over from O'Donnell in a perfect black 1955 Ford Crown Victoria that belongs to Darla's dad. Their son Gary and his wife, Teresa, and Jackie's mother, Katherine, have come along. Jackie and Darla have been married for twenty-seven years. They've been coming to the Sky-Vue since they were teenagers.

"When we was dating, we parked on the back row and didn't watch the movies," Jackie says. "Now we park up here on the front and we watch them."

Darla smiles.

"They used to have double features here all the time," Jackie says, "and in between the movies we would play bingo for money. And a long time ago, they used to get a band up on top of the snack bar and have live music."

Sometimes the music was supplied by a skinny high school kid from Lubbock named Buddy Holly and a couple of friends he called the Crickets.

At eleven minutes before nine o'clock, Sam cranks up the projector, and *Jurassic Park III* begins. A bigger, badder dinosaur chases people through the jungle. It's a short movie. By ten-fifteen it's done. Early leavers start their engines and steer toward the exit. Car lights flicker across the screen.

By ten-thirty the intermission crowd is thinning out of the snack bar, but Sam Lujan still waits his turn at the counter. He's from Seminole. The opening credits of *Big Jake* are moving on the screen. Sam Lujan is watching them through the door.

"I never thought I'd get to see John Wayne on the big screen at a drive-in theater," he says. "This is the reason I came tonight."

An older man looks at him in amazement. It's true. At thirty-five, Sam Lujan is too young to have seen the Duke on anything bigger than a TV tube. The older man shakes his head. This is probably why the world has gone to hell.

On the screen, a rancher and his cowhands are about to lynch a humble sheepherder. They've laid the noose around the man's neck. But Big Jake is riding. He's coming to the rescue.

"I love John Wayne," Sam Lujan says. "My boys love John Wayne, too."

Big Jake is riding. He's a big man. His horse is big. The theme music is big western music with lots of French horns. The Sky-Vue screen is eighty feet tall and 120 feet long. Tonight Big Jake is as big as he was meant to be.

Pack Rat

When strangers walk into a museum in a little West Texas town, they expect to see rusty branding irons, saddles, thumb-buster six-shooters, and barbed wire. Especially when the sign on the door says it's the OS Ranch Museum.

"We don't have any of that," says Giles McCrary. "A lot of people get surprised. Some of them are disappointed."

Mr. McCrary is the founder of the OS Ranch Museum and owner of the ranch it's named for. It doesn't bother him that his museum has nothing to do with ranching. It's just the way things turned out. He wanted to call it simply the OS Museum, but another museum somewhere already had that name. So his is the OS Ranch Museum.

It's upstairs over the OS Ranch Supply, a fancy gift shop that has nothing to do with the museum or the ranch or ranch supplies. "The people who have the store asked me if they could use the name," Mr. McCrary says. "I said fine."

The shop and the museum occupy a sturdy two-story dark-brick building at the corner of Main Street and Avenue I in Post, a cattle-and-oil town at the edge of the High Plains. The building once housed the company offices of C.W. Post, the cereal king—Post Toasties, Post Raisin Bran, and all that—who founded the town and named it after himself.

What visitors see when they go up the stairs or the elevator to Mr. McCrary's museum depends on the season. In winter, the big glass display cases are full of nativity scenes and Santa Clauses. Hundreds of them from all over the world. Some are of exquisite, delicately painted glass or porcelain, created for the wealthy. Some are carved of wood or horn, some crafted by poor folk from such humble materials as paper and sardine cans.

In spring the Christmas exhibits are packed away and Easter items are set up: gorgeous eggs from several continents, including replicas of five of

Fabergé's fabulous jeweled ones. Devised for the amusement of aristocrats, each of M. Fabergé's creations opens up to reveal a bouquet of precious gems or a jeweled brooch or some such breathtaking geegaw. There's also a replica Fabergé miniature of the Russian czar's carriage, decorated with emeralds, diamonds, rubies, and sapphires.

"The Fabergés are the stars of the Easter exhibit," says Marie Neff, the museum director. "People come from everywhere to see them. They're so rare in this part of the world." There are also paintings, sculptures, and weavings relating to spring and Easter.

"Then in summer it's sort of a mishmash," Mr. McCrary says. "Summer is our chance to put out the things we don't get to show the rest of the year."

These may include artifacts he brought home from visits with Indonesian headhunters or pieces of carved ivory from Japan and India. Or carved jade from China. Or Mr. McCrary's specially commissioned replicas of swords that belonged to Christopher Columbus, Robert E. Lee, Alexander the Great, and other famous men. Or specimens from his collection of chess sets. "I don't play the game," he says, "but I'm told I have some sixty-odd sets. From very crude, primitive ones to some extremely fine ones."

In his office, down a hallway from the main museum room, Mr. McCrary displays large porcelain figures of American Indians, a rosewood bowl from the South Pacific, a Lalique water buffalo from France, a porcelain Jesus and disciples in a porcelain fishing boat on a porcelain Sea of Galilee, made in Spain. And stuff from the Vatican and Mexico City. Behind glass is part of his large collection of ivory from Africa and China and Tibet and Alaska, some of it very old. And a plastic Big Billy Bass that sings "Don't Worry, Be Happy" and "Take Me to the River," which Mr. McCrary bought at the Dollar General Store.

Arranged in his building's various rooms also are bronzes and paintings by western artists Lincoln Fox, Jim Hamilton, Wayne Baize, Mike Scoval, Gary Carter, and Henriette Wyeth Hurd. There's a large bronze by Glenna Goodacre, originally from Lubbock, who also did the Vietnam War women's monument in Washington. There's an intricately detailed model of Lord Nelson's ship, H.M.S. *Victory*, built by a Texas A&M professor named Robert E. Stewart and purchased from his widow. And a nineteenth-century pump organ that was ox-carted to Erath County, Texas, then into Oklahoma Territory, then back to Erath County. There's a huge nineteenth-century Chinese jade statue of a herd of eight horses carved from a single stone, and an even larger nineteenth-century Chinese city carved from ivory, with birds, people, trees, and boats, in its own rosewood-and-glass case.

"I'm not really a collector, I'm a pack rat," Mr. McCrary says. "I've got a little of everything and not much of anything. As I'm walking along, I glance out of the corner of my eye, and if nothing grabs me, I keep moving. If something grabs me, I stop and look."

And he buys. Ms. Neff estimates that his collection contains more than 10,000 items, many of them not yet seen by the public. "I've got them stashed," Mr. McCrary says.

He was born in Fort Worth eighty-one years ago into a wealthy family. His banker grandfather, W.E. Connell, had bought ranches all over West Texas. In 1901 he bought the OS spread near Post. "I used to come out from Fort Worth on the train to visit when I was little," Mr. McCrary says. "At that time, the big pasture was 100 sections [64,000 acres]. It used to take ten days just to round up that pasture."

In 1949 he was sent out to run the place. "I've been in Post a little over fifty years, and I'm still looked on with suspicion as a newcomer," he says. Nevertheless, he was mayor for twenty-two years.

The town isn't much older than he is. C.W. Post, the Michigan cereal tycoon, bought 200,000 acres of Garza County land in 1907 and organized the Double U Company to build a model town called Post City. Today it's called Post and has about 4,000 residents. It's nestled at the foot of the Caprock, that long, high limestone bluff that marks the boundary between the High Plains to the west and the Rolling Plains to the east. Mr. Post brought in Scottish stonemasons to build the town. He sold and leased farms and built a textile plant.

"He envisioned growing cotton and manufacturing it and marketing it all in the same place," Mr. McCrary says. "But as it turned out, the cotton here had short staple, so it wasn't suitable for better-quality sheets and pillow cases."

The rough, broken country was OK for cattle, though. And, as wild-catters later discovered, it had oil under it. Mr. McCrary has done well. He was content in Garza County, taking care of his cattle, oil, and investments and doing philanthropic things in Post and in Lubbock, forty miles away. He had never traveled outside the country. Then in 1980 he made a trip to the Middle East. It changed his life.

"I was with the nicest couple from Denver for three or four days," he says. "He was slightly handicapped. He had had a light stroke. He had a limp and had to walk with a cane. He was in his late sixties, maybe mid-seventies. We were out in the desert in Jordan and we were going into these old palaces with lots of steps and no light, and he was having a difficult time. He fell several times.

"That's when it occurred to me how foolish it is to wait until 'the time is right' to do what you want to do. Because who knows what's going to happen mañana? So I started traveling wherever I wanted to go."

He travels two or three times a year. Most of his trips last four to eight weeks, some for as long as four months. "It costs more to go and come back than to stay," he says. He has been on every continent more than once and has visited more than 100 countries. Louise, his wife of sixty years, usually stays home. "She'll go to Europe or some place like that," Mr. McCrary says, "but she runs out of steam. So I go alone."

He has been in Europe many times. He has had a personal audience with the pope. But he prefers out-of-the-way destinations where tourists don't go. He tells stories of South American jungles, African savannahs, headhunters in Papua, New Guinea, street violence in Peru. "I never tire of seeing something new," he says. He has seen five of the seven major waterfalls of the world. He has been to Antarctica three times. He especially loves the remote islands of the South Pacific.

"Some of them are so small, so isolated, that they're not even on the maps," he says. "The only way to get there is to drop anchor out in the deep water, take a small boat in as close as you can get, and then make a wet landing. They don't have docking facilities and they don't have strangers coming ashore."

He's drawn to such hidden places, he says, "because the people are real. When you go to Dallas, those are not real people. New York, Chicago,

London are the same. A city is a city anywhere in the world. Once you've seen one, you've seen them all. They're confusion. A lot of traffic, a lot of congestion, a lot of pushing and pulling."

He carries a microcassette recorder and talks into it along the way. He brings the tapes home and has them transcribed and bound in blue binders. There are several shelves full of these volumes in one of the rooms. Shelves that cover another wall are filled with albums containing his collection of postage stamps.

"Whenever I'm in another country," he says, "I go to the local post office and say, 'I want two of every stamp you've got.' A time or two, I thought I was going to have to call the bank.

"I pick up stuff wherever I go. I don't shop, and I'm not looking for any particular item. I'm not particularly interested in the quality. I'm interested in what appeals to me personally. And I've never sold or traded anything. Once I acquire it, it's here. I've still got everything I ever bought."

In February 1991, he hired Ms. Neff to inventory his collection. "My job was to find out what he had under the bed and in the closets," she says. "When we found it all, he decided he had better build a museum."

Mr. McCrary created the OS Ranch Foundation to fund the place and pay its three full-time employees. "I have an uncle who encouraged me to do it. His name is Sam," he says. "Are you familiar with him?"

The museum opened in August 1991. Since then, 7,000 to 10,000 visitors a year have entered its doors. "They come from all over West Texas," Ms. Neff says. "Midland, Odessa, San Angelo, Abilene. A surprising number come from Dallas and Fort Worth. Some of them come every time we change the exhibit." Many come from some of the foreign countries that its creator has visited.

"We're in the perfect spot," Ms. Neff says, "because everybody has to stop at the traffic light at the intersection of Highway 84 and Highway 380. It's the only traffic light between Amarillo and Dallas. When they stop, they realize they're tired. Then they see the museum sign and decide it would be a good place to rest a few minutes."

On the other hand, says Mr. McCrary, it's a rare day when a resident of Post darkens his door.

"I don't know why the local people don't come," he says. "Post is a small town. Maybe they think I'm showing off."

42

Frank Lancaster learned the game down on the Colorado River while fishing. "We had put our lines in the water, and we was playing 42 on the bank," he says.

He thinks that was sometime in the 1920s. He was about sixteen. "I've been playing some seventy-five years now," he says.

"Well, I've got a question for you," says his friend Terry Stephens. "When are you going to learn to play correctly?"

The other men at the table laugh. Mr. Lancaster shows a small smile, then spits a stream of tobacco juice into the Styrofoam coffee cup he keeps beside him. "That's a good question," he says.

It's a typical morning at Stephens Feed & Fertilizer, headquarters of the DeLeon daily 42 crowd. At the table with Mr. Lancaster are Billy Carruth and Bill Barnes, who graduated from DeLeon High School together in 1941, and Robert Hudson, a much younger man. Mr. Stephens, who owns the store, and one of his employees, Ernest Escomilla, are sitting behind the players, watching. So are Mr. Hudson's younger brother, Tommy, and Charlie Crawford. When the present game ends, two of the watchers will team up to challenge the winners.

The men at the table finish the hand and turn the dominoes dots-down in the middle of the table. Mr. Lancaster shuffles them, moving them clockwise several times. Then each player drags seven dominoes to his side of the table, stands them on edge, and looks them over.

Mr. Barnes begins the bidding. "Thirty!" he says. "Two!" says Mr. Hudson. "Three!" says Mr. Barnes' partner, Mr. Carruth. "Take it!" says Mr. Lancaster.

"It's always interesting to see what Bill is going to be wearing when he comes here in the morning," Mr. Stephens says. "Sometimes he wears his own glasses. Sometimes he wears his wife's."

"They claim I don't play good with any of them," Mr. Barnes says.

Having won the bid, Mr. Carruth slides the double four to the center of the table. "There's your trump," he says.

This simple ritual has been repeated at Stephens Feed & Fertilizer hundreds of times almost every day for two decades. Between breakfast and dinnertime, twenty or more peanut farmers, ranchers, and retired old men will drop into the store and play a few hands of what has been called "the national game of Texas." Some older players, such as Mr. Lancaster, come early and stay most of the day, taking time out only for lunch and a nap. Others drop in just to drink a Dr Pepper from Mr. Stephens' vending machine and watch the play for a while.

Some arrive as early six A.M. and play a few hands of straight dominoes before they go to work. "Then them that don't do nothing start coming in," says Mr. Stephens. "They get up late. Frank sleeps till about eight. Billy, he'll get up and feed, put out some hay and everything before he comes to town. Then the 42 starts."

"Thirty!" "Thirty-one" "Try two!" "Come out!"

Billy Carruth is a rancher. Donald Nowlin is a peanut farmer. Johnny Chupp raises cantaloupes. Charlie Crawford worked at the store before he retired. Billy Jack Cottrell is a retired welder. Tommy Hudson works for an electrician. Robert Hudson feeds cows. Mr. Lancaster, says Mr. Stephens, "has been retired from Mobil longer than he worked for them. But he still lives by hisself, and he still drives." They're typical of the players who show up in the course of a day. Their ages range from Tommy Hudson's thirty to Mr. Lancaster's ninety-one.

The routine had its genesis one winter morning when the stock tanks froze. The ranchers and farmers had to rise early and chop holes in the ice so their livestock could drink.

"After they chopped the ice, they had nothing else to do with the day," says Mr. Stephens. "They came in here. I had a deck of dominoes, so we set up a table and started playing. We had about fourteen days of freezing. What year was it we chopped ice, Billy?"

"I don't remember when it was, but it was a cold dude," replies Mr. Carruth. "A December."

"After that, we would play during cold weather and then put it up," says Mr. Stephens. "Then, after while it got so that we never put it up."

He and Mr. Escomilla are two-time winners of the 42 tournament that's played at the high school every year as part of the DeLeon Peach and Melon Festival. Thirty or forty teams show up from all over the area. Mr. Carruth is another regular tournament contestant. He guesses he has played 42 for maybe sixty-five of his seventy-seven years. "I learned by watching my parents," he says. "They would go over to the neighbors' house and play it every Friday night. I just picked it up. That's the way most people learn it. They just pick it up on their own."

Tommy Hudson says he has picked up a lot of pointers just by hanging out at the feed store. "These old fellers can give you a world of education," he says. "I've learned a lot from playing with them."

Their table stands near an entrance to the store, in front of high shelves laden with fire ant killers, septic tank treatments, pinkeye medicine, poultry waterers, and calf feeders. Ranged along the walls and on other shelves down the center of the long room are saddle cinches, ropes, bridles, ax handles, fencing wire, fence pliers, welding masks, emery wheels, work gloves, and other goods that one might need in Comanche County.

"Thirty-one!" "Five!" "Whoa! Pass." "Six!"

The table is square and came from a local restaurant that went out of business. The top was white Formica. But over the years, the slide and shuffle of the dominoes across its surface has worn through to the brown fiberboard underneath. Even the fiberboard is worn so slick and shiny that it reflects the dominoes sitting on it.

Lots of talk and loud laughter accompany the play. The men rag each other with that insulting Texan humor that strangers find so puzzling. They make fun of each other's looks, their habits and foibles, their ages and infirmities, and the incompetence with which their partners and opponents play.

Tommy Hudson says he and his brother Robert never dare play as partners. "If you've got brothers, you know what the hell that means," he says. "We'd argue the whole time."

But later in the day the brothers break their rule and somehow wind up as partners. Of course, Robert makes a costly mistake. "Now you see why we don't play together," Tommy says. "Dumb-ass moves like that."

An hour later, Robert asks Tommy to partner with him again. But Tommy hasn't forgotten. "No, no, no, hell no, no," he replies.

The other men laugh.

☆

It's our national game, says Dennis Roberson, because it's played in every city, small town, hamlet, farmhouse, and bunkhouse in Texas and almost nowhere else.

"People in Texas are smart enough to know they don't want to go anywhere else," he says. "That's why 42 never left. The only other places you'll find 42 players are Oklahoma, New Mexico, and sometimes Louisiana. Why? Because they used to live in Texas, or their family is in Texas. For instance, my wife was born in Oklahoma, but her folks knew 42 because they had come from Texas."

The game was invented in the hamlet of Trappe Spring, now called Garner, in Parker County, just off the road between Weatherford and Mineral Wells. Mr. Roberson tells the story in his book, *Winning 42: Strategy & Lore of the National Game of Texas,* which he believes is the only book ever devoted entirely to 42.

One spring Sunday afternoon in 1887, Mr. Roberson tells it, twelve-year-old William Thomas and fourteen-year-old Walter Earl were discovered playing cards in a hayloft. Their fathers whipped them and burned their cards. Because in Baptist Texas in those days—and for many years afterward—a deck of cards was regarded as one of Satan's most potent instruments, as cannily designed to lead young folks onto the hellward path as (shudder) billiards or (gasp) dancing. Playing any card game—whether poker, bridge, whist, spades, or old maid—was a grave sin. Why? Because it was played with cards, the faithful reasoned. End of discussion.

On the other hand, the righteous could play dominoes until Gabriel blew his horn and the Lord didn't care, as long as no wagering occurred. So William and Walter, being clever young fellows, invented a card game to be played with dominoes.

Much too simply described, it's a bidding game, less complex than bridge, bearing a resemblance to old-fashioned whist, somewhat like the games of spades or hearts. There are forty-two points to be won in each hand, thus the name. Each player bids the number of points between thirty and forty-two that he thinks he and his partner can make with the dominoes they hold, and the winning bidder tries to make at least the number of points he has bid. If he and his partner fail to make their points, their opponents get them.

William and Walter taught their parents how to play their game, the parents taught the neighbors, and soon 42 was spreading through and beyond Parker County like hoof-and-mouth disease.

"The game became popular at a time when the country was poor, and people depended on their families and their neighbors for their entertainment," says Mr. Roberson. "It was extremely popular during the Depression because it didn't cost anything. Within fifty years after it was invented, it had spread to every corner of Texas. During World War II, my dad and a lot of other Texas G.I.s took their dominoes with them to war, and they would try to teach 42 to their buddies from other states. But it didn't really catch on. It didn't really spread."

Most Texans have moved to the cities since then and don't socialize with their families and neighbors as often as they did then. Our homes are full of TV sets, stereos, computers, and video games to occupy our leisure hours. Nevertheless, says Mr. Roberson, 42 remains alive and robust. Like bridge, it has become a tournament sport. Towns such as DeLeon, Mineral Wells, Weatherford, and Irving have large contests every year that attract players from all over the state. Temple is host to an annual competition for players over fifty years old. The official Texas State Championship of 42 tournament is every March in Hallettsville.

"And a lot of families still play it at their reunions," says Vaughn Roberson, father of Dennis. "Once a year, our family meets in Austin, rents a hotel suite, sets up 42 tables and watches a Texas football game. Last year we had thirty-four people. We played 42 all weekend."

The elder Roberson, a professor of 42, teaches courses in it for Tarrant County College and for members of the American Association of Retired Persons. He also plays in a couple of church groups every month.

"Dennis and I are partners in several tournaments every year, and sometimes my wife and I just invite him and his wife over, and maybe a few others, and set up a table or two. I must play about forty hours a month.

"It's hard to interest young people in 42 these days because there are so many other things they can do. But a lot of them will take it up when they get older."

☆

Well, maybe not everywhere.

A sign in the window of the Garner Store & Cafe reads: "Garner, Texas, where the domino game of 42 was invented." Brent Butler put the sign there soon after he moved down from Mineral Wells and bought the place.

"I thought I was going to get 42 going again around here," he says, his voice full of rue. "I put on a tournament in '99. It was going to be an annual event. I bought a plaque with spaces for the winners' names for twelve years. I set up two tables and put dominoes on them. It turned out real good. We had ten teams. Some people came from Fort Worth, one from Granbury.

"But I couldn't get anybody to play day in and day out. They just wanted to set around and drink coffee. The tables and dominoes sat there for a year, collecting dust. Then I sent out invitations for the annual tournament in 2000, and just four people responded. I ended up canceling it. I was disappointed.

"So I took out the 42 tables and put in a pool table. The kids like that better than dominoes."

The Garner Store & Cafe Annual 42 Tournament plaque still is hanging on the wall near the cash register. Don Johnson and Joyce Pence won in 1999. Theirs are the only names on the plaque. Mr. Butler says they're likely to remain so.

Sister

The Sacred Heart Children's Home is a cluster of beige brick buildings on top of a hill on the edge of Laredo, on the right side of the highway to Zapata. A chain link fence runs along one side of the property. On the other side of the fence is the Rio Grande, a narrow brown stream flowing lazily through a thicket of mesquite. On the other side of the river is Mexico.

The U.S. Border Patrol keeps a close watch along this stretch of the river with video cameras hidden among the mesquite and with officers sitting in pale green border patrol vehicles near the most often used crossing points. Other officers roam up and down the Zapata highway, looking for Mexicans who somehow made it across.

Despite all the surveillance, there are times when children from Mexico wade across the river, climb the fence, and steal laundry from the Sacred Heart clotheslines.

"They are very quick," says Sister Yolanda Fernández. "They take our girls' shorts and T-shirts and then they're back over the fence in no time. They know we see them, but they just laugh."

Sister Yolanda laughs, too, telling of it. She's a small, smiling woman. She speaks softly, matter-of-factly. Stolen clothes are a small matter on the Texas-Mexico border, an international boundary that isn't really a boundary except in the minds of Washington politicians and bureaucrats.

The federal minions—the border patrol, the customs service, the FBI, the DEA—try to do their duty, but Texans and Mexicans move between the countries with ease, legally and illegally, some with good in their hearts, some with evil. Extended families live on both sides, as they have for generations. Spanish is the first language on both banks of the river.

Except on the maps, the border has never been either Mexican or American on either side. It's a third country, long and slender, spread along the river from Brownsville to El Paso, with its own music, food, customs and culture, and plenty of poverty and trouble.

Sister Yolanda is fifty-seven years old. She entered the Order of the Servants of the Sacred Heart of Jesus and the Poor when she was twenty. It's a Mexican order, founded in Guanajuato in 1885. Its mother house, where Sister Yolanda took her vows, is in Puebla. But she has spent nearly all of her almost four decades as a nun in Laredo at the Sacred Heart Children's Home, which her order established in 1907.

"In the beginning, the children were usually orphans or children with only one parent," she says. "But the children we have here now are from broken families, children whose families are in jail, children whose parents are sick in a hospital or in a psychiatric unit, children whose mothers abandoned them and whose fathers have to work, children whose parents are very poor."

There's no hand-wringing in her voice, no attempt to solicit pity, no effort to elicit shock or even surprise at the miseries that find their way to the Sacred Heart door. "Some of the children stay here for many years," she says, "and others just until a problem gets solved. We've had children who came here when they were five and stayed until they were seventeen or eighteen and married here in our chapel. We've had children who stayed only a year or two. It depends on the problem they have at home."

Criotina Vásquez, who married in the Sacred Heart chapel in 1988 and is now expecting her fourth child, says she was typical of the children who move in and out of the home. "My parents were separated. My mother lived in Nuevo Laredo, and my dad was over here. So my grandmother was taking care of us. Every time my mother would get mad with my dad, she would take us across to Nuevo Laredo."

So, when she was nine years old, her grandmother took Criotina and her sister Patricia and her brother Juan into Sacred Heart.

"It was so my mother couldn't be taking us out of school," says Mrs. Vásquez. "It was the best thing that ever happened to me. I loved it there."

Fifty-seven children are living at the home now. Twenty-one of them are boys, ages five to ten. The rest are girls, five years old and up.

The sisters can't keep the boys long. If a lad can't rejoin his family by the time he's ten, he's sent to Boys Town at Omaha, Nebraska, where he finishes his growing up. "This year, we have sent six or seven boys up there," Sister Yolanda says. "Once in a while, we send them a little candy or something so they will know that we are here, that they still are a part of us. And some of them spend their Christmas holidays here."

But the girls may stay at Sacred Heart until they're grown. The oldest current resident is sixteen.

Most of the children are from Laredo, but some come from San Antonio and the Rio Grande Valley and even from Nuevo Laredo, the larger city just across the river. These are children of American citizens who live in Mexico.

The children are cared for by seventeen members of the Order of the Servants of the Sacred Heart of Jesus and the Poor—who, unlike many nuns these days, still wear the black-and-white habit of their order—and three young women who are planning to become sisters.

Like the hundreds who have been in her care over the years, Sister Yolanda was also a child of the borderlands, born in El Paso and reared in Ciudad Juárez across the river.

"My parents felt very sad when I entered the order," she says. "They had an erroneous view of the religious life. My father kept telling me that I couldn't drink Cokes or eat candies anymore after I became a sister."

Years later, he would spend his last days at the Sacred Heart Children's Home. "My mother died first," Sister Yolanda says, "and when my father was dying, my brother was living in California and I didn't have any sisters to care for him. So I asked my community to give me permission to go and take care of him. They told me, 'No, we need you. Bring your dad and take care of him here.' So my father died here in Laredo in the same room where I was living."

When she came to Sacred Heart in 1965, Sister Yolanda was only a little older than some of the girls were. Except for two years in San Antonio earning a degree in social work and two brief stints working at another home that her order runs in Chihuahua, she has spent her life on the hill beside the highway to Zapata.

She was a child-care worker with the little boys, then with teenage girls. Then she became the administrator. In 1996, after years running the home, she was named secretary to her order's regional superior, who is headquartered at Sacred Heart but is also in charge of two homes in El Paso and one in Juárez.

"The need is everywhere, not just on the border," Sister Yolanda says. "A lot of parents are involved in drugs. There's a lot of divorces, a lot of children born out of wedlock. Some of them, their parents have married again, and the children aren't accepted by the new parents. They don't pay any attention to them. They don't care about them. Or they don't know how to handle them. Children who are born of parents who use drugs or are alcoholics usually have problems themselves. And the parents don't know how to handle those problems.

"It's really sad that children are put in situations like that. It's not their fault. Sometimes I wonder whose fault it is. It's like a chain. It keeps on going. Children who never really had any parents then have their own children. They've never experienced what a family is. They have their boyfriends and they have their children and they don't know how to take care of them.

"We try to keep in contact with those parents, so the children don't get too separated from them. We encourage the parents to come here on the weekends. We like them to take their children home for a day or two. But sometimes they can't come because they're in jail or out of town or in the hospital. If the parents can't come, maybe the grandmothers can come? Or the aunts and uncles?"

But it's the nuns who rear the children. "Sister Yolanda would be like a mother to us," says Mrs. Vásquez. "She was very nice. She would take time to talk to us."

"It's why I went into the order," Sister Yolanda says. "The children. Their need. Their inability to look out for themselves. They need somebody to help them, to take care of them, to love them."

The Sacred Heart children live in clean, no-frills dormitories, one or two to each room, with a sister's room at each end of the corridor, one sister for each eight children. In the morning, school buses take them to public schools in Laredo. In the early evening, when the children have returned from school and have had their snacks, teachers come to tutor them for ninety minutes each day.

At six P.M., they eat their main meal of the day, then play for a while, or listen to music or finish their homework, then bathe and get ready for school again the next day.

The sisters feed them, clothe them, shelter them, care for their health needs. "We try to give our children as much as we can of a family life style," says Sister Yolanda.

Discipline problems are rare. "When children are small, you can still do a lot of things with them. But sometimes parents bring their children to us when they're twelve or thirteen, complaining that they can't handle them anymore. They no longer know what to do. We have to tell them this is not a correctional house. The children who are here are not here because they misbehave; it's because they have a need.

"Most of the time, if the children stay here for a few years," she says, "the cycle gets broken. They change the way they see life. They get married. They have their homes. They take care of them. They take care of their children. It makes them very proud. It makes us proud, too."

A number of the children who grow up at Sacred Heart go on to college and become teachers, nurses, psychologists. Like Mrs. Vásquez, many stay in touch with Sister Yolanda and the other nuns. They return to Sacred Heart to marry, to attend Mass at Christmas or Easter. They bring their own children with them and show them proudly to the sisters, the only family they remember loving them.

But not all the Sacred Heart stories end happily.

"One time, a young man twenty-seven or twenty-eight years old came back here," Sister Yolanda says. "I was scared. I didn't know what he wanted. We were cleaning the back yard, and he asked if he could help us. I said yes, and he helped us. He stayed for supper, and after supper I told him, 'You have to go now. We're about to close the gate.' He said, 'I'm not going. This is the only place where I was ever happy.' I said, 'You have to go. This is a home for children.'

"We had to call the police. The police wanted us to file a complaint against him, but I said, 'No. He hasn't done anything wrong. He just cannot stay here.'

"He was killed in Corpus. We don't really know how. We understand he was on drugs.

"But he had two sisters and a brother who were here, too, and they are doing great. One of the girls became a high school cheerleader. She became the girlfriend of a border patrolman and married him."

Sister Yolanda smiles sadly and shrugs the shrug that all along the border means, "That's how it goes."

"It has been a very satisfying way to spend my life," she says. "One time a woman came to place her children here. She said, 'Are you married?' I said, 'No, we make a vow not to do that.' She said, 'Oh, poor you. I feel so sorry for you.' She said, 'Where do you live?' I said, 'I live here.' She said, 'Oh, I feel so sorry for you.' She kept on saying that.

"I started taking down the history of her children and why she wanted to put them here. She told me the history of her life. It was terrible. I wanted to laugh, but I didn't.

"Sometimes people don't understand the religious life. Sometimes they have a husband who beats them and is drunk all the time, and they think that's normal and natural.

"Who should feel sorry for whom?"

Boys

Now my boys are grown. Ted, a captain in the air force, recently celebrated his thirty-first birthday. Pat will turn twenty-nine in December. He's a senior research associate on the Human Genome Project and about to embark on a Ph.D. in philosophy. Both live in California.

Another trip to Fort Davis was their idea. When they were children, they spent part of all their summers there, but they hadn't been back in years. Wouldn't it be grand to make a sentimental return to that place where they were so happy being children? We would revisit old haunts, recall old times. We would be together as we were then.

Once our plans were made, I actually counted the days. I was made a little anxious, too, by my memory of the first time we had gone to Fort Davis together—just the three of us—twenty-two years ago.

Ted and Pat were children of divorce. They lived most of the year in another state with their mother. When they were small they came to me for part of the Christmas holidays and during their spring breaks and for their summers. With experience we would learn to make do with this unnatural arrangement, but the boys' first brief visits felt empty and futile. We spent so many hours at the airport, filling out those forms for children who are flying away alone, pinning name tags on them, turning them over to flight attendants. Our times together seemed to consist of awkward hellos and anguished goodbyes.

In the summer of 1978, a year after the divorce, I took a leave from my job. As soon as Ted and Pat arrived, we piled into my old Volkswagen and headed west to my tiny hometown, where my mother and grandmother still lived.

We spent the summer there, playing Frisbee and dominoes, watching Bugs Bunny every afternoon, climbing Sleeping Lion Mountain. I showed Ted and Pat the Cave of the Winds, where I hung out when I was a boy.

I read them fairy tales. One night I took them into the yard and showed them the bright millions of stars, the constellations, the pale streak of the Milky Way. My city sons had never witnessed such splendor. What are they, they asked. How far away?

They caught grasshoppers, built a dam in front of the house when it rained, played with their friend John, got to know their cousins, made paper flags for the Fourth of July, learned table manners from their great-grandmother, a retired teacher who had infinite fellow feeling for children and small animals.

Then the summer ended. Heavy with despair and guilt, I drove my sons back to Dallas and put them on the plane to their mother, not to see them again until Christmas.

It was a sorry way to be a father. Now my boys are grown.

I met them at D/FW airport as I had when they were small. This time we didn't make the trek westward by Volkswagen. We flew to Midland and traveled the last hours by rental car. Since no kin of ours lives in Fort Davis anymore, we took a suite at the old Limpia Hotel. We had a little porch and red rocking chairs.

For the next three days, my boys and I did things we had done that first summer. We strolled about the frontier army post that gave the town its name and drove to McDonald Observatory to look at the scenery and the great telescopes. We examined local relics at the little Overland Trail Museum and browsed the shops and galleries along the main street.

The boys had seen the Marfa Lights on *Unsolved Mysteries,* but they had never seen them in person. "Some nights they don't show up," I said, to prepare them for the disappointment so many feel, sitting in the night for hours and seeing nothing. But the lights were spectacular, zipping across the flat, mysterious and beautiful.

Ted and Pat climbed Sleeping Lion to the Cave of the Winds. This time I waited at the foot of the mountain and watched them scramble confidently over hard places where I used to help them. We walked and drove about every neighborhood, remembering people and their times. Again and again, we passed our old family home, which now belongs to somebody else and doesn't look at all as it used to. We visited the grave of my grandmother, who had taught my boys manners and how to make paper flags.

Standing on the high school football field one night, we marveled at the heavens again and tried to name the constellations. One evening Pat said, "I wish there would be a thunderstorm." On cue, jagged bolts lit the sky over Blue Mountain and thunder boomed through the canyons.

Nothing we did was out of the ordinary. But we were together on common ground that had become hallowed to us.

We ended each day on our porch, rocking in the red chairs late into the night. We talked of kin, living and dead. Of my sons' ambitions and dreams. Of books I wrote and read and things I did. Of Ted's new job at a new air force base, and of Pat's just-completed master's thesis, "Light As a Scientific Model for Eternity." We spoke softly, as men do in the dark.

Pat said it was that night in the yard when he first saw the stars that inspired his present fascination with light and eternity and the universe.

"This trip has been the best yet," Ted said. "One I hope to relive with my children someday."

We parted at the airport, as always. There was no despair or guilt this time. Sometimes things turn out perfect.

Quanah's People

Baldwin Parker Jr. says he was in Palo Duro Canyon only once before. He was just a boy then, five or six years old. "I didn't have no good sense," he says. "I didn't know where I was at."

He's eighty-three now. He and Marguerite, his wife of sixty-two years, are resting in the shade of a grove of cottonwood and juniper on the canyon floor. The day is sunny and hot, but a nice breeze is moving through the cottonwood leaves. Its sound is like a rushing river.

Children and grandchildren, nieces and nephews surround Mr. and Mrs. Parker. There are more than fifty in all. They're gathered in the canyon for a purpose.

"We're here to make Palo Duro a sacred place again," Mr. Parker says. "This was a place of refuge and safety for our people. And today I've got it back. Somewhere here, I've crossed my grandfather's tracks."

The adults are sitting in circles of chairs near three canvas teepees, talking quietly. The children are running, laughing. They're all waiting for a drum and four singers to arrive from Oklahoma. Then the ceremony can begin. There will be drumming and singing and dancing and flute music and speeches and prayer.

The Parkers say they mean to return the spirit of their people to beautiful Palo Duro, where it hasn't been for 127 years.

The Parker family is Comanche. Baldwin Parker's grandfather was the most famous Comanche of all and a major figure in Texas history. He was Quanah, half white, half Indian, last war leader of the Quahadi band of Comanches in their desperate fight to drive white settlers and buffalo hunters from the Great Plains.

When their cause failed, it also was Quanah who led his people to peace and a reservation in Oklahoma and "the white man's way."

His mother was Cynthia Ann Parker, who as a young girl was taken captive during a raid on Parker's Fort in 1836. She grew up in the Comanche way and married Peta Nacona, a noted war leader of the Nocone band. Quanah, her eldest child, was born sometime between 1845 and 1852.

In 1860, Sul Ross led a company of Texas Rangers against the Nocone encampment on the Pease River in the Texas Panhandle. They killed Peta Nacona, captured Cynthia Ann and her little daughter Topasannah (Prairie Flower) and almost wiped out the Nocone band. The orphaned Quanah (Fragrance) took refuge with the Quahadi band on the Llano Estacado.

The Rangers' "rescue" of Cynthia Ann and her daughter proved disastrous for them. Cynthia Ann was unwilling or unable to adjust to life among her unfamiliar white relatives. She grieved for her absent son and tried several times to escape back to the Comanche life. Topasannah died still a child, and her mother quickly followed.

Although half white and gray-eyed, Quanah developed into a superb horseman and respected war leader among the Quahadi, the most independent and warlike of the Comanche bands. The Quahadi were the only band to refuse to enter into the Medicine Lodge Treaty of 1867, which assigned the Comanches—along with Kiowas, Apaches, Cheyennes, and Arapahos—to reservations in Oklahoma.

The U.S. government failed to honor its treaty. The food and supplies it had promised the Indians too often never arrived. Outlaws who stole Indian livestock from the reservation weren't pursued or punished. The army refused to enforce treaty provisions that forbade white encroachment on reservation lands. Organized bands of hunters were entering tribal lands to slaughter thousands of buffalo, leaving their carcasses to rot on the prairie.

"The hunters were killing the buffalo needlessly, all for the hides," Baldwin Parker says. "They were doing away with our source of food. And my grandfather, in the Wichita Mountains, he knew about this. So he and his tribesmen rode into the Panhandle."

In June 1874, Quanah Parker and a Comanche shaman named Isa-tai urged the reservation Indians to join them on a raid through Texas. They recruited a band of 700 warriors and attacked a party of buffalo hunters camped at the ruins of an old trading post called Adobe Walls in the Texas Panhandle.

Baldwin Parker, telling the story, picks up a small drum and beats out a rhythm. "On their way up to Adobe Walls, this is the song they sung," he says. And he sings a song in the Comanche language and ends it with a small cry. "This is Quanah's medicine song," he says. "It makes you strong. It makes you feel mean."

Although hugely outnumbered, the Adobe Walls defenders—twenty-eight men and a woman—were strongly fortified and, with their powerful buffalo rifles and superb marksmanship, held off the attackers for five days.

Only one hunter was killed. About fifteen Indians were killed or wounded. When 100 reinforcements arrived to aid the white hunters, the Indians rode away.

After the disappointment of Adobe Walls, many of the reservation Indians returned to Oklahoma. But the battle touched off a two-year series of raids and battles that historians call the Red River War. Quanah and his warriors rode on bloody raids in Kansas, Oklahoma, and Texas, while the army and Texas Rangers rode in pursuit, determined either to destroy the Indians or force them to accept the reservation.

Whenever the government forces came near striking distance of their prey, however, the Comanches would disappear into Blanco, Tule, Palo Duro, or some other of the canyons along the rugged Caprock at the edge of the Llano Estacado.

Palo Duro had been a hideout and wintering ground for the nomadic plains tribes for many generations. "It's nice down here, and you can't see the canyon from a long way off," says Jacquetta Parker-McClung, one of Baldwin and Marguerite's eleven children. "Our people could roam, and then they could come here to their home and rest. They could feel safe here."

A Kiowa shaman named Maman-ti assured Quanah's hungry and weary followers that they would be safe from the soldiers in Palo Duro. But it was within that canyon's steep walls that Colonel Ranald Mackenzie and the Fourth U.S. Cavalry would break the back of Quanah's resistance.

In late September 1874, hundreds of Comanche, Kiowa, Arapaho, and Southern Cheyenne men, women, and children were camped in Palo

Duro, their teepees strung out along its floor, a thousand feet below the surface of the flat, treeless plains.

At dawn on September 28, Colonel Mackenzie led his men down the steep, narrow trail into the canyon and rode through the encampment.

"As we galloped along, we passed village after village of Indian lodges both on the right and left, totally abandoned," Captain R.G. Carter wrote years later. "The ground was strewn with buffalo robes, blankets, and every imaginable thing, in fact, that the Indians had in the way of property. . . ."

By scrambling up the steep canyon walls on foot, most of the Indians escaped. Only three, and one white man, were killed in the battle. But the soldiers burned the teepees and destroyed the Indians' food and belongings.

In an even more devastating blow, they also captured the Indians' herd of more than 1,500 horses. Colonel Mackenzie presented about 300 of them to the Tonkawa Indian scouts who had led him to Palo Duro, then ordered his soldiers to drive the rest out of the canyon and shoot them.

It took the soldiers a whole day to pile up their dead bodies. The great mound of horse bones amazed passersby for many years, Captain Carter wrote.

Most historians believe Quanah was not in Palo Duro on the day disaster struck. But without the teepees, supplies, and horses destroyed there, he couldn't long hold out against the army and the rangers.

"When our people were attacked here in Palo Duro, they were at the end of their rope," says Dr. Parker-McClung. "It was the end of a beautiful way of life."

Within a year of the Battle of Palo Duro, Quanah and his hungry warriors surrendered to Colonel Mackenzie and moved to the Kiowa-Comanche reservation near Fort Sill in southwestern Oklahoma.

There, for a quarter of a century, he performed perhaps his greatest service as a leader: teaching his people how to survive in the white man's world. He promoted the construction of schools for Indian children and encouraged the Comanches to go into farming and ranching and get along with the whites.

He numbered among his friends President Theodore Roosevelt and

Charles Goodnight, who within two years after Quanah's surrender had established his famous JA Ranch in Palo Duro Canyon.

The ceremony to make Palo Duro sacred again is supposed to begin at one P.M. The drum doesn't arrive from Apache, Oklahoma, until three. "We were late two hours, but we were on time, Indian time," says Kenny Looking Glass, the drummers' leader.

Indian time continues. The dancing doesn't begin until five, after everybody has eaten.

Then, the drummers begin their beat and raise their voices in Comanche song. Baldwin Parker rises from his chair. A son places a red-and-black shawl about his shoulders. Mr. Parker takes his rattle and joins a dozen of his kin—a group ranging in age from his eighty-three to Jessica Waltrip's six—in the Gourd Dance.

After the dance, Brittany Parker, a young girl, says the Lord's Prayer in the Comanche sign language. Then Baldwin's son, Ron Parker, whose idea it was to have this ceremony, rises to speak.

"I've lived out west in Arizona and New Mexico for the last fifteen years. So I've come across this country in all seasons and all times from sunup to sundown. I've seen all kinds of weather. I've dodged tumbleweeds as high as my hood."

His voice begins to break. "Every time I come across this country, I see coyotes and I see rabbits and I see deer. But I don't see the buffalo. I don't see my people.

"I just wanted to come back to where my people sheltered. Some of them died in here. They're probably buried in here."

Ron's brother Don sings a song used in the peyote ceremony of the Native American Church. Quanah was one of the founders of the peyote religion on the reservation, and Don still practices it.

"The American Indian is caught in a conflict between the demands of modern society and his traditional culture," he says. "For some of us, that's hard. I have to put on a tie and a suit. I have to use proper English. And, you know, in the evening time, I want to go to a peyote meeting. I want to be me.

"It's a duality. But life is like that. Quanah understood that. His mother was white. His father was a leader of the Comanches. He had to know both ways."

As the sun is setting, Don sings the ceremony's final song. It's about death and grief and recovery. While he's singing, six deer—five does and a buck—suddenly appear at the top of a peak along the canyon's edge. The buck cocks his head. He stands for minutes, listening.

Patriot

Along the leafy corridors of East Texas, through Jacksonville or Lufkin or any town, Old Glory is everywhere. It waves in front yards and school-yards and hangs in living-room windows. It adorns the tailgates of trucks.

Sonic and Dairy Queen advertise patriotism alongside their burgers and ice cream. "Support Our Troops," their signs urge their customers. "God," they plead, "Bless America."

Patriots are easy to find in East Texas. They're part of the landscape, like trees.

But there's none like Robbie Maxwell.

When the war broke out in Iraq last March, Mrs. Maxwell, like most Americans, was "just glued to that TV." The more she watched, she says, the more agitated she became. She felt a strong need to do something for the young men and women she calls "my troops." Something beyond the flags and yellow ribbons that already were breaking up the monotonous green of the Angelina County countryside. Something more personal.

So Mrs. Maxwell made herself a sign. It's like a picket sign, two sheets of cardboard attached to a slender pole. On one side she wrote, "Proud Of Our Troops." On the other side she wrote, "God Bless Our Troops." She stuck a little flag into one corner of her sign and tied a yellow bow beneath it.

"My troops are fighting for me," she says, "so I figured I would fight for them."

She drove her blue 1991 Buick down to U.S. Highway 69, the main route through Huntington, a town of about 2,000 souls. She asked the owner of the Joc Stop, which sells Exxon gas and Subway sandwiches, if he would mind her standing beside the road in front of his store and hold-ing up her sign for passing drivers to see.

The Joc Stop owner said he didn't mind.

Throughout the war, when the air force and the navy were bombing

Baghdad and the marines and the army were struggling through sand-storms and gunfire, Mrs. Maxwell stood by the highway, holding her sign, five or six hours every day.

"The first day, it was raining," she says. "It was cold. I was wearing a thin black sweater. I thought I would freeze to death. I got sick off of that for about three weeks, but it didn't keep me away from the road."

People honked their horns and waved as they drove by. A few would stop and talk.

"At first, my husband, Earl, and my son, Cameron, wasn't for this," she says. "They thought somebody might haul me off to jail. But the police have been just as friendly . . ."

As weeks passed and the sun grew hotter, Mrs. Maxwell moved across the highway to a big live oak tree in front of Homer Masonic Lodge No. 254 AF&AM, next door to the post office. She set up an aluminum-and-plastic lawn chair in the oak's shade so she could rest her sixty-year-old legs from time to time. "I've got a bad back," she says. "I've got arthritis bad in the hips. My knees is just about gone."

Before the school year ended, Mrs. Maxwell tried to be at her post each morning in time for the children on the school buses to see her. Two teen-age girls used to drive by and honk and wave every day. One day they pulled over and rolled down their car window. One of them said, "I think you're the coolest woman I've ever met."

"That was the first time I've ever been cool," Mrs. Maxwell says.

Others stopped, too. A marine gave her a collar insignia from his uni-form. A sailor gave her a navy neck lanyard. A medic gave her his medic's badge. A marine's mother gave her a marine corps T-shirt. A World War II vet from VFW Post 1836 gave her a sheaf of patriotic poems he had writ-ten. A young family gave her a stuffed bear that sings "God Bless the U.S.A." "To the one lady who sits here daily to support our troops," they wrote on the box. "We love you."

Soldiers just returned from the Middle East gave her Coins of Excellence that commanding officers had presented to them as tokens of jobs they had done well. "Those meant something to the people who gave them to me," Mrs. Maxwell says. "That makes them mean much more to me."

Each coin has its story. "The boy who gave me this one was on leave from the Roosevelt aircraft carrier," Mrs. Maxwell says. She caresses the brass discs like trophies. "The man who gave me this one has been in the service for twenty-eight years. He was on his way to Iraq. He and his wife and granddaughter dropped by. He took a picture with me. And this man here had been in the service twenty-six years. Before we got through talking, me and him and his wife was all crying."

She raises her eyeglasses and brushes at tears with her fingers.

"I met a boy yesterday, his wife has health problems, he's got two little babies. And he had to come back from Kuwait. He hated to. He said he might go back later. I feel like he's done his turn. Let somebody else do his turn now. It done my heart good for him to stop and talk to me. He stayed a long time.

"They're strangers when they're coming down the highway," she says. "But, like I told the boy yesterday, when they stop and talk to me, they're family."

Mrs. Maxwell says she admires President Bush. She voted for him. "I think he has done a fine job," she says. "So far."

But lately, some people have become irritated, seeing her still beside the road. "They drive by and yell, 'The war is over!' They don't yell, 'dummy!' but they mean it."

Mr. Bush is wrong about that, she says. "He told us the war is over, but it isn't. He's not getting shot at, but our boys are dying over there every day.

"A lot of people say, 'Well, how long are you going to stand out there?' and I say, 'As long as it takes.'"

Lately she has shortened her vigil to three days a week—Mondays, Wednesdays, and Fridays—for sometimes the diesel fumes from the eighteen-wheelers roaring by and the exhaust from the cars are so bad she can't breathe. And sometimes the arthritis really hurts.

"If my health gets so bad I can't come that often, well, I'll come just on Fridays," she says. "That's when I figure a lot of the boys are coming through, you know, going home to visit."

But so long as her troops are being killed in Iraq, she says, she will be beside Highway 69, fighting along with them.

"It could be a long war," she says. "I could wind up being out here for two or three years."

Monster Man

Joe Lansdale is sitting on top of his bizarre world. His new novel has already gone into its second printing. His new short story collection is doing well. And one of his Texas Gothic thrillers is being adapted for the screen.

The new novel is *The Bottoms*, a harrowing story of serial murder, racist brutality, and family crisis in the dark, steamy woods of East Texas. People are comparing it to *To Kill a Mockingbird* and *Intruder in the Dust*.

The short story collection is *High Cotton*, a selection of Mr. Lansdale's best tales of horror and the supernatural from the more than 200 he has written.

The may-be-made movie is *Mucho Mojo*, one of his blood-and-guts adventures featuring East Texas buddies Hap Collins (straight, nervous white guy) and Leonard Pine (gay, tough black guy).

New Line Cinema has struck a deal with Hollywood screenwriter Ted Tally to turn the novel into a screenplay. Mr. Tally won an Oscar for his *Silence of the Lambs* script and adapted Cormac McCarthy's *All the Pretty Horses* for the movie starring Matt Damon.

"I've had more than twenty-five movie options over the years," says Mr. Lansdale. "None of them has ever been made. This one's got as good a chance as any. And *Bubba Hotel*, a novella of mine, is in pre-production now, so I assume it will get filmed. Who knows?"

In the twenty years or so since he began writing, Mr. Lansdale has published—besides five Collins/Pine adventures—fourteen novels, twelve short story collections, two nonfiction books, one juvenile book, and a few adult comic books. He has written several screenplays and four scripts for the Batman animated TV series. He has edited five short story anthologies.

His works bear such evocative titles as *The Two-Bear Mambo, Bad Chili, Dead in the West, Freezer Burn, Blood Dance, Electric Gumbo,* and

Weird Business. Some are crime novels, some suspense novels, some horror stories, some fantasy, some Westerns, some mainstream novels. Some are so out of orbit that they defy classification. One of them, *Tarzan's Lost Adventure*, was begun by Edgar Rice Burroughs and finished by Mr. Lansdale many years later.

Bizarre humor suffuses nearly all his work. Some stories, such as the ghoulish one-page short-short called "My Dead Dog Bobby," have become classics of macabre laughter.

"I try to be my own genre," says Mr. Lansdale. "I want people to pick up my books for *me*, because I wrote them. I want them to pick them up because they want to read Joe Lansdale."

Whatever the genre, the constant in his work is violence plain and fancy. The terror and pain inflicted on his characters are heightened by the sheer banality of the evil events befalling them. His villains often are animalistic cretins bumbling their way through murder and mayhem simply as a means of coping with life.

"I think the happily stupid, those people who are that way because they choose to be, or are too lazy or uninspired to be otherwise, are among the scariest people in the world," he writes in the introduction to one of his stories in *High Cotton*. "They are also, if you squint slightly and can deal with a lot of sadness, pretty funny."

Mr. Lansdale was born in Gladewater, Texas, in 1951 to a father who was an auto mechanic and a mother who sold encyclopedias and other products door-to-door and was also "sort of a free-lance florist." They were older parents. Joe's brother John was seventeen years his elder.

"My father never learned to read or write," Mr. Lansdale says. "His mother died when he was eight, and he went to work in the cotton fields. His father was a tyrant. He whipped my dad with a horsewhip. During the Depression, my father left home and rode the rails and fought at fairs, boxing and wrestling."

After he married, Buddy Lansdale decided he wanted to be a mechanic. His wife bought him a Model T Ford and told him, "Take this apart and figure out how to put it back together."

"And that's how he became a mechanic," Mr. Lansdale says. "He was a helluva guy. Very much my hero."

The illiterate mechanic's little son learned to read early and fell in love with anything with print on it. His mother encouraged him, and provided him books and comics. By the time Joe was in high school, he was dreaming of writing. In the real world, he was working in an aluminum chair factory.

"It pops up in my stuff from time to time," he says. "I had a work permit and would get out of school early. I worked from three-thirty till midnight. We were all kids, sixteen and seventeen years old. Bunches of us were doing it."

After graduation, Mr. Lansdale entered Stephen F. Austin State University in Nacogdoches, hoping to learn "something to fall back on," in case his writing career didn't take off. In four years he amassed only sixty credits but won his wife, Karen, whom he met in an anthropology class.

They left school and labored in the East Texas rose fields. "We got sick of roses," he says, "but when we got married, they told us to come out and cut as many roses as we wanted for the wedding. That's the best thing that came out of the job."

For three years, the Lansdales tried to make a go of a truck farm near Gladewater, with Joe plowing behind a mule. In 1976, they gave up and moved back to Nacogdoches. Joe got a job as a janitor. Karen worked at Montgomery Ward, then as a dispatcher for the fire department.

"All that time, I was writing," Mr. Lansdale says. "And I had started selling stuff. One day when we were about to have our first child, Karen said, 'Why don't you go full time? You've got books sold. You've got all these contracts. You can take care of the kid while I'm at the fire department.'"

So that's what they did. "And it snowballed. *Slowly* snowballed," Mr. Lansdale says. "The books have gotten better and better each time out, in terms of sales and popularity. I acquired a group of dedicated fans who bought everything I did. They've kept me in beans."

The child, Keith, now eighteen, will start college next fall. "He wants to be an English professor, bless his heart," says his father. "That's even worse than wanting to be a writer." Keith's sister, Kasey, is fourteen and wants to be a singer. "And she's got the chops for it," Mr. Lansdale says.

He writes for three hours and produces three pages of manuscript daily.

On a great day, he says, he might get five. The important thing is being persistent and finding the rhythm that a story must have to get written.

"I start with just a general idea in my head of what I want to do," he says. "It's more of a feel. I start writing and I get a rhythm. And when I get the rhythm, I know I've got a story. The characters start to do stuff I want them to do, and sometimes stuff I don't want them to do or don't expect them to do."

Many of his creepier ideas—a corpse stashed in a home freezer, a mummified baby wrapped in newspapers—come straight out of the news. "It's hard to get weirder than reality," he says.

Others have a personal origin. Years ago, when Mr. Lansdale was writing a lot of short stories, his wife would make a big batch of popcorn just before bedtime. Mr. Lansdale would overindulge and get a stomachache. "Then I would go to bed and I would dream an entire story," he says. "I would get up and write it. I wrote a whole series of them and sold a bunch."

Nearly everything he writes has gruesome elements in it. That's one of the secrets of his popularity. "People like being scared, because it stimulates us to know that we're living," he says. "On the other hand, horror stories are preparations for death. They're light inoculations against fear of the unknown. These inoculations make it a little easier to accept the inevitable."

A new Lansdale novel appears about once a year, and he usually has a short story collection or a reprint of an old book coming out as well. "It averages out to about a book and a half a year," he says.

Twice a week, he teaches at Lansdale Self-Defense Systems, a martial arts studio he opened in 1994. It employs several instructors and has about fifty students. "My father introduced me to boxing and wrestling, and I went on to judo and hapkido and other martial arts," he says.

He has created his own system, which he calls "shen chuan" ("spirit fist"), and has been inducted into the International Martial Arts Hall of Fame four times.

Those butt-kicking buddies, Hap Collins and Leonard Pine, know a lot about martial arts.

"I would love it if that movie got made. I've always wanted to sell out.

I just don't know how," Mr. Lansdale says, laughing. "I would love for one of my novels to hit the best-seller lists, just for the pure greed of it. I want more people to read my books. That's why I write."

Mother Road

From Chicago through St. Louis, Joplin, and Tulsa, Route 66 falls across the map at a southwesterly slant. But at Oklahoma City it takes a hard turn toward the west, then disappears into the urban sprawl.

You have to fight your way through the city, on past suburban Yukon and Bethany and El Reno. Then, a few miles west of the federal prison, the old road suddenly reveals itself as it used to be: two narrow lanes of pinkish concrete dipping and rising through low hills. Wire fences and trees hugging it close. Horses and longhorns grazing. Farmers plowing so near the highway that you hear their tractors and taste their dust. Dogs trotting down red-clay lanes to bark at you.

Millions of cars and trucks used to hum across this gentle countryside. They rolled through every town and paused at every traffic light along the highway's 2,448 miles between Lake Michigan and the Pacific. In all the little towns, mom-and-pop proprietors of homemade gas stations, cafes, "See Our Rattlesnakes" roadside attractions, motor courts, and curio shops kept their eyes on the traffic, hoping a few of the travelers would stop to grab a bite, buy gas, see the sights, spend the night.

Everybody loved Route 66. The chambers of commerce advertised it as "The Main Street of America."

But on this cool, overcast morning west of El Reno, America's Main Street is empty. Yours is the only car as far as the horizon. The action is a few hundred yards to the south, where semis, pickups, RVs, and automobiles roar along Interstate 40 hellbent for somewhere. They'll skip the little towns and their little businesses, drying them up, killing them.

☆

Route 66 began as a glint in the eye of Cyrus Avery, a Tulsa businessman who early in the 1920s started lobbying Congress for a highway that would connect the crowded East with the still-almost-frontier West. Oh, and it should pass through Oklahoma.

In 1926—seventy-five years ago—Congress gave Mr. Avery his road and designated it U.S. Highway 66. In those early automobile days, major federal highways were given names as well—the Lincoln, the Dixie, the Bankhead. Route 66 was christened the Will Rogers Highway.

But John Steinbeck gave it its best name: "66 is the mother road," he wrote in his great 1939 novel, *The Grapes of Wrath*. He also gave it a darker name: "the road of flight."

In his story, Tom Joad and his family lose their farm to the wind and the bank, load their fragile jalopy with belongings and family and trek out of the Dust Bowl along Route 66 to California, dreaming of a better life. They find only more brutality and pain. Mr. Steinbeck's book opened many eyes to the depth and meaning of the Great Depression. It won the Pulitzer Prize and gave the world "Okie," a word that many Oklahomans still despise.

But times turned better. By 1946 the Depression and World War II were over. Cars, tires, and gasoline were available again. And Bobby Troup wrote America's love song for the open road:

> *If you ever plan to motor west;*
> *Travel my way; take the highway that's best.*
> *Get your kicks on Route 66 . . .*

Bobby made a popular recording of it. So did Nat "King" Cole, Rosemary Clooney, Bing Crosby, Bob Wills, Perry Como, the Four Freshmen, Johnny Mathis, the Rolling Stones, Charles Brown, Paul Anka, Bob Dylan, Chuck Berry, Van Morrison, Mel Torme, Michael Martin Murphey, Asleep at the Wheel, the Lamont Cranston Band, Sammy Davis Jr., Tom Petty and the Heartbreakers, and Buckwheat Zydeco, among others. People still like it.

In the fifties, Jack Kerouac's novel, *On the Road*, has Sal Paradise and Dean Moriarty and their friends cruising 66. It's our modern classic road story. And in a popular sixties TV series called *Route 66*, two buddies named Tod (Martin Milner) and Buz (George Maharis) roam the road in a

Corvette, working odd jobs and helping people in trouble, encountering plenty of adventure and chaste romance along the way.

For six decades, if you wanted to know what America was about, Route 66 was the way to go. It crossed rivers, plains, mountains, deserts, and several Indian nations. It offered all the greasy diner food you could stand, inexpensive motel rooms, and such roadside entertainments as reptile pits and miniature golf courses. It was gaudy and exciting and not at all like home.

But when the last stretch of I-40 opened in 1986, the eight Route 66 states—Illinois, Missouri, Kansas, Oklahoma, Texas, New Mexico, Arizona, California—murdered the mother road. They decommissioned it, removed its shield-shaped "U.S. 66" signs, and erased it from the official road maps. Route 66 was no more.

These days, however, eight state Route 66 volunteer associations and a national one are replacing the official "U.S. 66" shields with unofficial "Historic Route 66" signs. And a new generation of Route 66 boosters is restoring some of the old art deco buildings along small-town Main streets, putting in new businesses and painting the familiar 66 shield on their fronts.

During this seventy-fifth anniversary year, who-knows-how-many adventurers are unfolding unofficial maps and thumbing guidebooks, looking for remnants of the mother road, planning. Packing. Going.

You pull into Hydro, Oklahoma, in search of Lucille Hamons, who styles herself "the mother of the mother road." Her Historic Highway 66 Station is in all the books. She bought the combination station-diner-motel in 1941 and has run it ever since. She loves to tell tales to her customers. She's one of the highway's legendary characters, loved and admired by Route 66 regulars, the books say.

When I-40 shut down the other businesses along her stretch of 66, Lucille found a way to stay. She installed a beer cooler. Her best regulars were the boys at Southwest Oklahoma State University in nearby Weatherford, a dry town. Whenever guys announced they were "making a Hydro run," everybody knew what they meant.

So you want to meet Lucille. You park in front of the North Side Drug on Hydro's Main Street and step in to ask directions. The first thing you see is Lucille's obituary, displayed in a glass case. "She died last August," says Kathy Thomas, the pharmacy technician. "She was eighty-five. We sure do miss her."

Strangers come into the store thinking Hydro is on Route 66. It's not. The highway is a mile away. But the North Side owner, Johna Roof, has hung a Route 66 shield on her building anyway, hoping it will attract customers. It does.

"Many come in here who can't speak English," she says. "When I bought the store, I was really shocked by this. So many foreigners. They get lost and come in here looking for Lucille."

"Most of them are from Germany," says Kathy. "Looking for Lucille and wanting to know how to get back on the road."

Lucille kept her station open until the day she died, August 18, 2000. But her name already is fading from her sign. Weeds grow in the yard of her small house behind the station. Her gas pumps are rusting, their glass broken by hail or vandals.

Route 66 in front of her place is still the thin ribbon of pinkish concrete. But it's the access road on the north side of I-40 now.

At Clinton, Oklahoma, you learn that "Mrs. Route 66" has died, too. Just a few months ago. Gladys Cutberth was the widow of Jack Cutberth, a Clinton barber who so tirelessly promoted the highway that he became "Mr. Route 66."

"He traveled the road and passed out brochures all the way from Chicago to Santa Monica," says Pat Smith, director of the Oklahoma Route 66 Museum. "Gladys would go with him. She was kind of his secretary. The headquarters of the National Route 66 Association was in the basement of their house for many years. People from all over the world would come and visit them." Gladys was in her nineties when she passed away.

Because of the Cutberths, Clinton is a sort of headquarters city for Route 66. Colorful banners mark the various routes that the road took through the town over the years. Its "Historic Route 66" signs are plentiful. The museum, which was created by the Oklahoma Historical Society, has an exhibit room for each of the road's decades from the twenties through the sixties, when I-40 bypassed the town.

On display are automobiles and other vehicles from each decade, including a loaded Okie truck like the Joads' and a psychedelic sixties VW bus. Also relics from along the road: a diner booth, a Wurlitzer jukebox playing period music, old gas pumps, a "See the Rattlesnakes" sign, old curios once sold in the roadside shops, old license plates from the eight Route 66 states, old snapshot cameras.

On a wall, visitors post their Route 66 memories:

"Been wanting to do this for forty years; should have done it then . . ."

"Forty-eight years ago, traveled Route 66. Remember buying water bag, hanging it on the front of the radiator."

And from a newer generation: "My friend and I are on a road trip to see new and cool things. Hey, you have only one life, might as well 'get your kicks.'"

Looking over all this are Kirk and Tina Johnson, a thirty-ish couple from St. Louis, who sold their family business and decided to hit the road.

"Route 66 was a really big thing in St. Louis," says Kirk. "I grew up listening to my father and grandfather telling tales about the good old days of the highway. Easter Sunday, Tina and I had the family over for dinner like we do every year. Then we said, 'We're leaving. We're doing Route 66.' We already had the car packed in the garage. They all were freaking out.

"We drove to Chicago to do it right and start where it starts. We've been stopping wherever we are at twilight and talking to people we meet. However long it takes, it takes."

"We're on our ninth roll of film already," Tina says.

A cherry red-and-white 1956 Thunderbird is parked in the front window. It's the centerpiece of the whole museum. When it was built, you were eighteen. You stand and gaze.

"Oklahoma has more driveable miles of Route 66 than any other state," the museum director is saying. "Kansas has the least—thirteen miles."

You try to listen, but you're in a Thunderbird daydream, driving. The wind is in your ears.

Across Route 66 from the museum, the sign in front of the Best Western Trade Winds Inn reads: "Sleep Where Elvis Slept."

According to the motel's story, which is printed up and available at the registration desk, the King stayed at the Gold Crown—as the place was called in his day—every time he motored through Clinton. He didn't book his own rooms, of course, and his entourage protected him from public view. Until the time a housekeeper delivered the meals to Room 215 and Elvis didn't hide in time. She spread the news all over town.

When Elvis opened his door the next morning, the parking lot was full of fans. He treated them nice. He even played ball with some children for a few minutes. Then he and his people boarded their bus and drove away.

He never came back.

"Is Elvis' room available?" you ask the clerk.

"It sure is. You want it?"

It costs $20 more than a regular room. Never mind.

On down the road in Elk City you look for another Route 66 character mentioned in the guidebooks. Lloy Cook. Lloy owned a famous hubcap shop. But a docent at the National Route 66 Museum (which is owned and run by the city) says Lloy sold out and left town and his building has been torn down.

A recording at the museum tells you how Phillips 66 gasoline got its name. In 1927, when Route 66 was only a year old, a chauffeur named Salty Sawtell was driving a Phillips Petroleum executive named John Cain between Tulsa and Oklahoma City. Phillips had developed a powerful new gasoline, and John was trying to think of a catchy name for it. He noticed that Salty was driving faster than usual, and he asked how fast they were going. "Sixty-six," Salty replied. Just then they passed a Route 66 sign. "Sixty-six on 66!" exclaimed John. "It's going to be Phillips 66!"

That's the way they tell it in Elk City anyway.

Oklahoma ends at Texola, a tiny place turned into a ghost town by I-40. Its few buildings are empty and decaying. At two-thirty P.M., not a person is in sight. A sign on the front of a beer joint reads: "There's no other place like this place anywhere near this place, so this must be the place." The only other business in Texola is another beer joint, next door to this place.

"The newcomer to this region is impressed with the almost limitless emptiness of the countryside," wrote Jack Rittenhouse in the first Route 66 guidebook, published in 1946. In his day, the road between Texola and the Texas line ran between wooden oil derricks owned by Phillips and Magnolia. Now they're gone, too.

But in the center of Shamrock, Texas, at the junction of 66 and U.S. 83, still stands one of the most fabulous buildings along all the road's miles. The books tell of John Nunn picking up a rusty nail and kneeling in the dirt to draw the design of a building that could have stood in Oz. In 1936, J.M. Tindall built it in Shamrock and called it the Tower Conoco and U-Drop Inn Cafe.

It's an extravagant art deco affair, built of brick and concrete, with towers reaching skyward above the station and the cafe next door. When it opened, the local newspaper described the building as "the most up-to-date edifice of its kind on U.S. Highway 66 between Oklahoma City and Amarillo" and the restaurant as "the swankiest of the swank eating places."

The U-Drop Inn's painted window advertises "Home Cooking," "Steaks," and "Daily Special $4.95," and the sign says its open, but it isn't. A few booths hug the walls of the empty room. A broom and a mop bucket stand in a corner.

Orfelio Briones of Slinger, Wisconsin, has pulled into the driveway of the vacant Conoco. On a trailer behind his pickup, he's hauling home a red-and-white 1955 Chevy Bel Air that a guy in Vernon, Texas, has restored for him. He jumps out of his truck with a camera in his hand. He wants a picture of his car at the famous station.

"My wife didn't want me to stop, but I did," he tells you. She's still in the truck, honking the horn.

Ravena Emmert, proprietor of Ravena's Corner, a curio shop down the street, used to work as a waitress at the U-Drop Inn.

"I worked there when it was just a cafe, and I worked there when it was a café and a bus stop, and I worked there when it was just a cafe again," she says. "It really was a busy place.

"But they lost their lease. They was a man and wife, and they got to feuding. The people took it back that owned it. The bank bought it and got nearly $2 million in grants, and they're going to put a tourist center in it."

Ravena's Corner has been in business in another old gas-station building for almost six years, says Ravena, who's sixty-six.

"I started out as a flea market with a bunch of junk and garage sale stuff. Then one day a guy named Buzz stopped in here and I bought a bunch of Route 66 stuff from him. And people started coming in and buying it. So the next year I started buying T-shirts and all kinds of stuff. I have the biggest bunch of T-shirts and postcards in town."

West of Shamrock you notice that the trees are disappearing. The few hills are lower. By the time you get to Groom, you're on the table-flat High Plains of Texas. If you had a cosmic pencil, you could use the horizon as a ruler and draw a perfectly straight line across the bottom of the vast dome of sky.

But the people of the town have done their best to give you something to look at. On the north side of Route 66 and I-40 is the Leaning Water Tower. It's an ordinary small-town water tower, but it leans. Like the Leaning Tower of Pisa. A little High Plains humor, you figure. The Christmas star on top also leans.

On the south side of the highways are the tallest cross in North America and a sign advertising the Blessed Mary Restaurant. The cross is constructed of stainless steel and stands 190 feet high. That's nineteen stories. On a nearby manmade hill—any hill at Groom would have to be manmade—Jesus and the two thieves are being crucified in bronze. The cross was erected by the Cross of Our Lord Jesus Christ Ministries out of Pampa, Texas. The parking lot is full of eighteen-wheelers.

Across the Panhandle, Route 66 runs parallel to I-40, sometimes north of it, sometimes south. Sometimes it's an access road of the bigger, newer road. Sometimes it just disappears.

At Amarillo, it becomes Sixth Street, through the middle of town. You drive past Route 66 Guitar, the 66 Antique Mall, Salon 66 (offering hair designs by Deward and Judy), the J&M Route 66 Cafe, and the Route 66 Roadhouse.

The most famous Route 66 landmark in Amarillo is the Nat, at 2705 W. Sixth. Its real name used to be the Natatorium, because it was an indoor swimming pool. But in 1926 its owner laid maple flooring over the pool area and converted the Nat into a dine-and-dance palace. The great bands of the thirties and forties, traveling 66 from east to west and back, would stop and play the Nat. The Dorsey brothers, Duke Ellington, Jan Garber, Harry James, Bob Wills, Guy Lombardo.

Now the old building is an antique mall, owned by Mike Baker and Pete Elkins. But a couple of times a month it becomes a dance hall again. "We have a crew come in and move everything," says Mike. "We move the antiques into the alcoves and curtain them off. We had 800 people here on New Year's Eve."

Three years ago, a psychic named Bubbles determined that the Nat is haunted. "She wanted to do what she called a ghost hunt," Mike says. "So about forty-five people came in and we spent the night. They filmed it with infrared cameras, and there were a few things. We picked up a drum solo on the stage and a lady singing."

An employee, Phyllis Brown, believes she has seen a ghost. "I was here behind the counter one day and I saw a little girl," she says. "She was standing there by the door. She had on a blue-and-white print dress and had something in her hands. And she was looking down, like her mother had got on her. About thirty minutes later, these two ladies were leaving the store and I said, 'You forgot your little girl.' And they said, 'Oh, we don't have a little girl with us.' Later I heard that a little girl had drowned in the pool, and she had been seen holding a lunch pail."

A few miles beyond Amarillo, two young men are looking at Cadillac Ranch, Stanley Marsh 3's famous monument to the American car culture. Ten Cadillacs from the era of tail fins, stuck nose down into the earth in the middle of a wheat field. A kind of High Plains Stonehenge.

Some travelers pull off Route 66 or I-40 and spend a couple of hours studying the old cars, reading the graffiti that visitors have spray-painted on them. Others trudge out to the monument, take a quick look, shake their heads, and trudge back to their cars.

"This is a dream since I was a child," says Matteo Maletti of Reggio Emilia, Italy. "I remember the song of Bruce Springsteen, 'Cadillac Ranch.' Bruce is my favorite singer above all. And I heard about this...this...*thing*. I don't know how to call it."

Matteo and his companion, Roberto Bizzetti, are thirty-one. They've been buddies since they were fifteen. They've been traveling about Texas and New Mexico for two weeks. Now they're headed back to Houston to catch a plane home.

"Going west is every day discovering things," Matteo says. "Texas is even better than I expected. It's so huge, and so very, very, very interesting. It's a long road, but there's always something to reach.

"Yesterday we drove on old 66. It was hard traveling. But it was an emotion, really an emotion. We were in the past."

Roberto has found a spray can with a little paint left in it. He's adding his graffito to the others.

The "Welcome to Adrian" sign across Route 66 from the Midpoint Cafe and Gift Shop has an arrow pointing both ways: "Los Angeles 1,139 miles; Chicago 1,139 miles." The cafe, whose motto is "When you're here you're halfway there," is owned by Fran Houser, a Massachusetts Yankee who moved to Texas years ago for her daughter's asthma. Fran is also the cook.

"This place has been in business since 1928, when 66 was new," she says. "In those days it had a dirt floor."

She says she started noticing a change in the traffic four or five years ago. "Suddenly there were a lot of Japanese and Germans traveling Route 66. They're very disenchanted with us Americans because we're not preserving the old structures along the road. They don't understand the shambles. They don't understand why we don't have pride in our history."

She keeps a thick scrapbook of all the press she and her cafe have gotten. There are magazine articles from the Netherlands and France. Her collection of business cards in the back of the book includes several from Germany.

"The Americans who travel 66 are looking to escape the bedlam of I-40," she says. "They want to just take their time and do what they want. They want to see a part of Route 66 before it disappears."

A few miles west of Fran's cafe the road leaves the smooth, fertile plains and enters rugged, broken ranch country. Low hills, arroyos, cholla, and juniper. The West.

Glenrio, smack on the Texas-New Mexico line, is a true ghost town: decaying gas stations, a motel, gift shops, all deserted. A faded sign portraying a sombrero and advertising the Little Juarez Diner. An acre of junked cars and trucks, rusting.

The wind is kicking up. Past winds have blown down most of the sign that used to say "First in Texas Motel" or "Last in Texas Motel," depending on which direction you were going.

The "Tucumcari Tonight" signs that you've been seeing along the road are more frequent, now that you're in New Mexico. In the old days, they had a second line reading: "2,000 Motel Rooms."

Mike Callens, owner of The Tee Pee, says Tucumcari's down to about 1,200 motel rooms now. Most of the newer places are out on I-40.

"Last of the Old Rt. 66 Curio Shops," his business card reads. "Damn Fine Stuff."

"People will come in and ask what 'curios' means," he says. "It's a word you don't see much anymore. They're called 'gift shops' now. When my uncle and aunt had the place, they used to sell plaster figurines, water bags, chili ristras."

The Tee Pee, built in 1944, is a Route 66 classic, a still-functioning relic of the old times. You enter it through a white concrete teepee. Its current stock includes turquoise jewelry, moccasins, Indian rugs, postcards, bumper stickers, refrigerator magnets.

"We lived in California when I was a kid, but we came back to Tucumcari every summer to visit my grandparents," Mike says. "Half the fun of traveling 66 was stopping at all the curio shops and the rattlesnake pits and the little museums with their two-headed calves. I lived for that stuff. There's still a few old holdouts. But it's getting harder to make it. Every year, you hear of another one biting the dust.

"It's the Germans that have kept 66 alive. They have a real feel for the history of it. Americans have a short-lived love affair with anything. But I know some Germans who have traveled this road five, six times."

Just down the street from the Tee Pee is another classic, the Blue Swallow Motel. It was built in 1939 and has been in operation ever since. Dale and Hilda Bakke bought it three years ago and are restoring it.

The blue swallow still flutters across its neon sign, which still advertises

"Refrigerated Air." Old-fashioned steel lawn chairs sit outside its cabin doors. Each cabin has its own garage.

"When we first took it over, the foreigners were the only people who would stay with us," Dale says. "People from Japan and Belgium and Germany. The Americans would come and take pictures of the place and then stay somewhere else. That's starting to change, now that we're restoring it. We're doing better every year."

That night in your room, you pick up the heavy Bakelite receiver of the 1939 Western Electric telephone. You stick a finger into the rotary dial and call home.

The best miles of Route 66—the mountains and deserts and canyons of New Mexico and Arizona—still lie ahead. But it's time you went back.

You turn around. You take I-40 this time.

Blues

Clyde Langford's grandmother used to come and stay with his family from time to time in their little white frame house on the edge of Centerville. Her name was Georgia Bladen Price. And she had a beau whose name was Joel "Thunder" Hopkins. He lived not far away.

Thunder was an older brother of Sam "Lightnin'" Hopkins, one of the greats of the East Texas blues men. "And there was another older brother, John Henry," says Mr. Langford. "He's the one that showed Lightnin' how to place his fingers on the guitar and like that."

The Hopkins brothers, says Mr. Langford, were distant cousins of his.

"Joel was sweet on my grandmother," he says, "and teaching me the guitar gave him an excuse to come see her, to be around her, you know. That's how I got started."

On a sunny morning, Mr. Langford is sitting in the living room of that same white house, which has been his home for fifty-three of his sixty-six years. He's dressed for company in blue and purple and an open nylon shirt of many colors. He's wearing a derby and a ponytail and picking a beat-up flattop guitar. A piece of silver duct tape covers a hole that his fingers have worn in the top. He's singing:

> *She's a long, leany mama, and she's real sweet to me.*
> *She's a long, leany mama, and she's real sweet to me.*
> *She's a long, leany mama, and she don't know when to stop.*

His voice is rough and nasal. The accompanying notes from the old guitar are twangy, metallic, wild. So blue.

When his song is over, Mr. Langford says, "Joel succeeded with my grandmother. She loved him. He was a good clown, a good dancer, a good guitar-picker. My mama didn't think much of him because he didn't go for working. He was a big gambler."

It has been said that the blues arrived in Texas with the first slaves. And, except for the Mississippi Delta, more country blues musicians have come out of the cotton fields and steamy forests of East and Central Texas than any other place. Huddie "Leadbelly" Ledbetter was born near Caddo Lake. Mance Lipscomb came from Navasota. And Lightnin' Hopkins grew up in Centerville, on the edge of the East Texas forest. Blind Lemon Jefferson was from Wortham, a little to the west. They were the best of many who left the countryside and migrated to Dallas' Deep Ellum or Houston's Third Ward and farther into the world beyond the trees.

Blues is about love, sex, drinking, prison, poverty, and death, and there was plenty of all that in East Texas when Thunder Hopkins was showing young Clyde his way around a guitar. Black people there lived according to certain "rules and regulations," as Mr. Langford calls Jim Crow law and racist custom.

Before the Langfords moved to the little house in Centerville, they lived in a tiny rural community called Nubbin Ridge. At the Nubbin Ridge general store, Mr. Langford says, black people weren't allowed to buy Coca-Cola. "That was the rules and regulations," he says. "If nobody was in the store except a good white friend of yours, he might buy you a Coca-Cola and hand it around his back and say, 'Drink this quick, now, before somebody sees you.' The main drink for blacks was what was called a Juneteenth, a strawberry. And the strongest drink we could buy was RC.

"They would ask, 'What's for you, boy?' Even if you was 100 years old, they always called you 'boy.' You asked for a pound of bacon, and they gave you sowbelly, the meat from the hog's stomach. It still had the tits on it."

One morning at the breakfast table, his father complained about having to eat sowbelly all the time. Later, Clyde's mother sent him to the store to buy bacon, expecting him to return home with more sowbelly.

"I can remember it as clear as yesterday," he says. "I said to the store-keeper, 'We're sick of eating that old sowbelly. Why can't you sell us (and I used that n-word, you know) the same bacon you sell to the whites?'

Everybody in the store laughed and laughed. But, bless my soul, the man went back and got some of that beautiful bacon, the kind from the side of the hog. He wrapped it and gave it to me.

"I carried it back to the house. Mama unwrapped it. She hollered, 'Fred! Come here!' Daddy looked at it and said, 'I don't know what I'm going to do with that boy. I can't teach him nothing.' I told Daddy what I had said to the storekeeper, and he said to me, 'You ain't got no sense. You've got white-folks bacon here. You get on that horse and take this back.'

"There were so-called 'special' blacks. Everywhere you went, there was blacks that the whites was extremely partial to. My dad was one of them. White people would slip my daddy something and maybe ignore the other blacks. But what I done had scared the devil out of him. That story spread like wildfire. All the blacks in the world was talking it up.

"That appears to offend my kids when I mention it to them. But that's the way it was. They say, 'I wouldn't have put up with that.' And I say, 'Yeah, you would have put up with it or you would have got your neck broke.' That was the rules and regulations.

"All of that is nothing but the blues. All of that is the blues."

He bends over the guitar again.

> *Well, I bought me a knife, one that I could afford.*
> *Well, I bought me a knife, one that I could afford.*
> *It was too long to be a knife and too short to be a sword.*

"The blacks and whites here did not go to school, did not go to church with each other," he says. "But we visited each other. On a weekend, a white family that lived three or four miles from us would come visit us and come to our table and eat. But if another black family would come, they would leave. Just like when we went over to their house. If we saw some more white friends coming, we automatically would leave. That was the rules and regulations."

Mr. Langford's father made his family's living by digging water wells by hand. When Clyde was thirteen, the Langfords moved to Centerville, current population 812, the seat of Leon County. Clyde helped his father with the digging, hauling the mud out of the holes. In his spare time, he mowed white people's lawns and chopped weeds out of their flower beds to earn money to buy a guitar.

"It took me a long time to get ahold of about $15," he says. "Mama had a big, thick Sears and Roebuck catalogue, and in there was a little old standard guitar, flat top, round hole, for $8.95 or $8.98. So I ordered it. I was so proud that morning when Daddy went to the post office and came back and said, 'Boy, your guitar came.'

"Joel tuned it up and hit some numbers on it and showed me how to play some things. I got this one little old sound going: *TUNG-tung, TUNG-tung, TUNG-tung.* Daddy said, 'You know, I'm sorry that boy got that thing.'"

Mr. Langford laughs at the memory. "The Hopkinses never learned to read no music," he says. "Just like me. I don't know how to read no music. It's all by what they call 'ear.' Once I hear something I like, it pictures on my brain system. And once I picture it, it's there. I picture it in my head first, and then I learn how to play it."

When he was fifteen or sixteen, Clyde got a gig playing the blues every Sunday morning on KIBY, the radio station in Crockett, thirty-three miles east of Centerville. He had a manager named Bob Green. "He gave me my musical name, Spike Langford," Mr. Langford says. "He gave me gas money and half a gallon of wine and two or three dollars to put in my pocket over there every Sunday."

Clyde graduated from high school in 1953. His father, he says, was "heckbent" that the boy was going to college and make something of himself. Clyde was just as "heckbent" that he wasn't. He ran off to Fort Worth, worked a bit, and played in the little honky-tonk joints. In 1954, he joined the air force. After basic training at Lackland Air Force Base in San Antonio, he was assigned to Edwards Air Force Base in the Mojave Desert, where the B52 bomber was being tested.

"There was a little town near the base, but blacks were not allowed in there at all," Mr. Langford says. "So I played my guitar around there on the base, in the little theater and what-have-you." Then he was shipped to a base in Japan.

"I had precious little money," he says. "The biggest portion of my pay, I was sending it home to help my dad buy a new pickup. I didn't have much chance to go downtown, so I spent many an hour hanging around the base, picking my guitar. A lot of people would gather around and listen. Mainly big wheels. Those lieutenants and those colonels."

From time to time, though, he would get to leave the base. "I played in a lot of cities in Japan, in little old honky-tonks they had there," he says. "The Japanese loved my music. I used to have some pictures of me with some Japanese girls in my lap, but my wife got hold of them and ripped them up."

When he had been in the air force for "two years, five months and nine days," he was discharged and returned to Centerville. He helped his father with the digging and started playing and singing in joints in Mexia and Huntsville and other towns in the area. Two guys and a girl sang with him, and there was another guitar player named Joe Lee Lacy, who was known around town as Joe Boy.

"Joe Boy played with me just about everywhere I went," says Mr. Langford. "But sometimes he would be down the street drinking a gallon of wine. About forty-five minutes before closing time, he would show up so he could get his portion of the money."

> I know you're in love with another man, baby, and that's all right.
> I know you're in love with another man, baby, and that's all right.
> Every now and then I wonder what other man you're gonna love tonight.

"The blues came out of nowhere," Mr. Langford says. "It just got picked up. It's solid and it's not solid. It kind of created itself. It kind of accumulated. Blues has no end. It has a meaning if you can figure out what the meaning is. Once you figure out the meaning, it's something you can't explain. It's like trying to reach out and catch air. It's there. We know it's there. But where is it? We can't catch and hold it."

After World War II, Lightnin' Hopkins had moved to Houston, where he was making a name for himself. So Mr. Langford went to Houston, too, to see if Mr. Hopkins would introduce him around and give his career a boost.

"He would not," says Mr. Langford. "He would permit me to play two or three numbers with him at a dance or something. That was all. I got me a little place to stay. I stayed down there a week. I would see him every morning. I was over to his house, begging him to let me play with him. I tried to get him to teach me one particular chord. He never would. And anytime he would get ready to make that chord, he would always look at me to see if I was noticing. And if I was noticing, he would turn his back to make the chord. He didn't want me to learn it."

So it was back to Centerville and water wells. He played at dances and picnics and house parties. He played in "little old honky-tonk places" out in the countryside, where drunkenness, lust, and jealousy often led to violence. "I wouldn't play them places for big bucks now," he says. "I can't run and dodge like I used to."

He married a twelve-year-old named Annie Louise, who tore up his pictures of the Japanese girls. She bore him four children. "My wife, she never went for my music," Mr. Langford says. "All the years we were together, she didn't go for it. I think where I made a mistake is that I carried her with me one night to a dance, and she seen all those girls all over me, and it just melted her mind. She said, 'You've got to make up your mind: Your music has got to go or I'm going. So the music got gone."

Twelve years ago, after being married to Clyde for twenty-three years, Annie Louise died. She was thirty-five.

So over the past few years, Mr. Langford has been performing in public again, a little bit. On Juneteenth in 1999, he took his guitar and sat in the gazebo on the Leon County Courthouse lawn and played the blues. "I was extremely happy and thrilled to be there," he says. "You see, blacks weren't allowed to participate on the street. Not with no music. Not even on Juneteenth. The only way a black was permitted to participate on the street in Centerville, you had to be a rassler or a boxer.

"But I did last year, and also this year. I played in the gazebo. Even lots of whites came out to hear me. Some of them came up to me afterwards and said, 'Oh, we always loved the blues, but we didn't want nobody to know it.'"

Mr. Langford leans forward in his chair. His voice drops to a whisper. "And they said to me, 'Clyde Langford, if I or any other whites had recognized the blues, it would have caused the blacks to try to equalize.' And I said, 'Equalize? What's that?'"

He laughs. "I had a lot of fun with that."

He closes his eyes and touches the guitar again.

I love you in the morning time, I love you late at night.
Please, pretty baby, why can't you treat me right?
Let's talk it over, baby, let's talk about a thing or two.
Let's talk it over easy; we might even talk about me and you.

He sings verse after verse after verse after verse. The song lasts almost thirty minutes. When it ends, he opens his eyes and says, "Have mercy! Have mercy!"

Then he says: "The blues is something blacks got out of the sky somewhere. And we own it."

Fair

When Big Tex learned to talk, I was there. Well, I wasn't there the first time he opened his mouth, maybe not even the first day. But I definitely was there the first year Big Tex said, "HOWDY, FOLKS!"

1953. It was his second year at the State Fair of Texas, and my first.

I don't know who had the idea that the entire student body of Fort Davis High School should get on the bus and ride 450 miles to the fair, but it was one of the best ideas that anybody in Fort Davis ever had.

We were very isolated back then, a village of maybe 800 people in rugged mountains surrounded by rugged deserts. We were almost 200 miles from the nearest city, El Paso, where we went once or twice a year on shopping trips. The road was narrow and full of slow-moving trucks, many of them hauling cattle. We could get stuck behind a string of them forever, creeping along at their speed. Going to El Paso was a job.

We had no TV because the signals couldn't get over the mountains and cable hadn't been invented yet. At night we could pick up the clear channel radio stations like WFAA in Dallas and WOAI in San Antonio, but in the daytime we could hear only one. KVLF in Alpine, "Voice of the Last Frontier." (Sometimes Gene Hendrix, the station's owner and announcer, would goof and say, "Last Voice of the Frontier." We always laughed.) The movies we saw at the Palace in Marfa and the Granada in Alpine were at least a year old, usually older.

So going to Dallas for the State Fair was as big a thing as we could imagine. And all of us were going: all the forty or so students of FDHS, nearly all our teachers, and several of our parents as chaperones. My mother was one of them. (I was a sixteen-year-old junior, but in those days it wasn't uncool to have your mother along. I was proud she had been asked.)

We all—with our suitcases and bedrolls—could fit into our only school bus and two or three cars.

Everybody wanted to ride in the cars because they were so much more comfortable. It was decided that we would take turns. Whenever we stopped to eat or buy gas, all the car-riders had to switch with somebody on the bus.

I got to ride in Sheriff Tom Gray's police car, the best one. When we were rolling through the wide open spaces with no towns or traffic in sight, he let us blow the siren for a few seconds. Every time we entered a new county, he called the local sheriff on his radio—they all were buddies of his—and let us talk to him.

We were to sleep in the Mesquite High School gym, girls at one end of the basketball court, boys at the other. We arrived late at night. The Mesquite principal was there to unlock the door for us. Everybody was excited. There was a lot of horseplay in the dark. We couldn't sleep.

Next morning, the drive from Mesquite to Dallas—down a narrow country highway between cotton fields—seemed long and monotonous. People who lived near Fair Park were renting out their yards as parking spaces, and Coach Diddle Young parked our bus in one. Our teachers and chaperones made us stay together until we were inside the park. Just as we walked through the gate, Big Tex bellowed, "HOWDY, FOLKS!"

Like thousands of teachers and chaperones since then, ours decided Big Tex would be the place to reconvene when it was time to return to Mesquite. "Be here at ten o'clock on the dot or be left behind!" they warned. Then we scattered. The first of three days of freedom and wonder!

My memory of those days is kaleidoscopic. The animals didn't impress me much. We had plenty of those at home. I was so disappointed with the prizes I actually won on the midway, compared with those on such prominent display in the booths, that I stopped playing games. A lesson.

I saw the Car of the Future. Its speedometer went up to 140 m.p.h. It was a swank red-and-white convertible with a huge V-8 engine and a clear plastic bubble for a top. A Texan driving such a thing would fry like bacon. Ethel Merman was performing at the Music Hall, but I couldn't afford a ticket. I rode my first roller coaster, that creaky old wooden one that used to stand at the back of Fair Park.

A couple of buddies and I were admitted unchallenged into the tent with the hootchy-kootchy dancers. We felt devilish and manly. The dancers were awful and didn't take off much of anything. One had a big bruise on her left thigh. I bought some overpriced taffy because every box had a prize in it. One of the prizes was a wristwatch, the hawker said. The prize I got was one of those little Halloween clickers. There were only four pieces of candy in the box.

One day we all got on the bus and rode downtown to watch a movie at the Palace Theater, the most luxurious place I had ever seen. A mighty Wurlitzer rose up out of the floor with the organist already sitting on his bench and playing! The movie was a brand new one called *The Robe*.

One morning on the midway, I noticed that my buddies and I were the only white fairgoers in sight. A concessionaire told us it was Negro Day. That odd information reduced our fun not at all. Did I realize what it really meant? No.

And Big Tex kept saying, "HOWDY, FOLKS!" Just like now.

Stars at Night

In the early evening Christopher Johns-Krull can see the Conchos Mountains, 120 miles away in Mexico. They're the palest blue line. Closer in are Mount Chinati, fifty-five miles away, and Goat Mountain, forty miles, and Cathedral Mountain, thirty-seven miles. The closer the mountains are, the darker blue they seem. Blue Mountain, looming huge before him, is deep purple.

To the east, great piles of pearly cumulus move across the sunny sky. Their shadows slide across the hills. To the west, the air is black. Jagged lightning flashes, then flashes again. Thunder rumbles through the canyons. Wind carries the heady scents of pine and ozone. Rain descends as a delicate veil over the faraway peaks.

Dr. Johns-Krull is an astronomer. He's standing on top of Mount Locke in the heart of the Davis Mountains of the Trans-Pecos, near one of the five white domes of McDonald Observatory. Hundreds of scientists like him have come to this remote mountaintop over the years to study the heavens. The night sky here is reliably dark and clear.

But sometimes nature sends them away disappointed. Dr. Johns-Krull is watching the rain fall on the slopes and canyons, watching it move eastward toward him.

He knows that the ranchers who own the pastures below are rejoicing. The region has suffered five years of severe drought. But lately the rains have returned. Throughout the afternoons, clouds gather over the mountains, darken into thunderheads, then hurl their rains upon the just and the unjust. Not sufficient yet to declare the drought over, but enough to dress the slopes in new green and bring hope to the heart.

"While I'm hoping it'll clear up, the people down there probably are praying for more rain," Dr. Johns-Krull says. "If it would rain during the day and clear at night, that would be fine for all of us."

Dr. Johns-Krull and a colleague, Dr. Jay Anderson, have come from California to be on Mount Locke during a certain phase of the moon. McDonald Observatory has awarded them three precious nights of stellar observation at one of its smaller telescopes, the thirty-incher.

Dr. Johns-Krull is a 1985 graduate of Skyline High School in Dallas. When he was nine years old, he went to a slumber party at a friend's house. His friend had a telescope, and they looked at stars. "I was smitten," he says. That Christmas, his father gave him his own small telescope. "I've known I wanted to be an astronomer since I was really young," he says. "My whole life has been planned around that."

He joined the Dallas Astronomical Society, an amateur group that then owned an observing site near Kaufman, somewhat away from the metropolitan lights, and spent many nights there with his telescope.

He majored in math and physics at the University of Texas at Austin and earned a Ph.D. in astronomy from the University of California at Berkeley. Now he's a research scientist at Berkeley's Space Sciences Laboratory.

"We're here to measure the parallax of the Pleiades," he says. "We're trying to measure the motion back and forth on the sky of the Pleiades stars with respect to the background stars as Earth orbits the sun. We're trying to measure the distance to the Pleiades from Earth."

In Greek mythology, the Pleiades, who were the seven sisters of Atlas, fled the advances of the hunter Orion and sought help from the gods. They were turned into doves and flew into the heavens, where they were transformed into a constellation of seven stars. To the naked eye, only six of the sisters are visible. They appear like a circle of jewels in the constellation Taurus.

But to Dr. Johns-Krull the Pleiades are simply "a young cluster of stars, all about the same distance from Earth, that have settled down into their regular lives."

McDonald's thirty-inch telescope has an unusually wide field of view that will allow him to observe a large swatch of the heavens at a time. It's the closest telescope to Berkeley that's suitable for his work.

Measuring the distance to the Pleiades is "just doing trigonometry," he says. "We know Earth's distance from the sun. So that's one side of the triangle. By measuring the wobble of Earth, we're measuring the angle of that right triangle. The sine of that angle is equal to Earth's distance from the sun divided by the distance to the star. It's really the only direct way we can measure the distances to stars other than the sun."

Until recently, scientists thought they knew how far away the Pleiades are. Then the Europeans sent out a satellite named Hipparchos, which reported that the Pleiades are closer to Earth than the astronomers had thought.

"They were thought to be 132 parsecs from us," Dr. Johns-Krull says. "But Hipparchos said they're 116 parsecs away. One parsec is about 3.2 light years."

The distance to the Pleiades doesn't matter at all to the cowboys in the canyons below, or to the oil field hands in the flat desert that surrounds this sky island of green mountains, or to the immigrants trying to cross the Rio Grande somewhere to the south, or to the border patrol officers chasing them.

But in Dr. Johns-Krull's universe, it matters. "The distance from Earth to those stars is important to the whole theory of stellar structure that has been known for the past century," he says. "It's generally regarded as a very successful theory. But if the Pleiades are really where Hipparchos says they are, there's a problem."

The sky over Mount Locke usually is perfect for such a job. Two-thirds of the nights every year are clear enough to do astronomy. One-third are so pure that millions of stars and planets seem close enough to pluck like fruit from an overburdened tree. On those nights the Milky Way looms over the horizon as dramatically as the thunderheads now.

"This is one of the darkest skies in the world," Dr. Johns-Krull says. "I've done a lot of observing at Lick Observatory, twenty-six miles from San Jose. The lights of the city and the whole San Francisco Bay area are in the sky there. I've used the National Observatory at Kitt Peak, Arizona. It's close enough to Tucson that the sky can be pretty bright. I've observed on Mauna Kea on the big island of Hawaii. It's very dark, but it's also 14,000 feet high. There isn't enough oxygen. When you go outside and look up, you don't see as many stars as you do here because your brain is suffering a lack of oxygen. You can't see as faint a star as you can see here."

The immense darkness, coupled with Mount Locke's altitude of almost 7,000 feet and long stretches of bone-dry weather, has made McDonald one of the world's important observatories.

This is Dr. Johns-Krull's second visit to work on his Pleiades project. Ideally, his observations will be six months apart over two-and-a-half years, to view the constellation from the farthest sides of Earth's orbit around the sun. He must work at a time of the month when the moon isn't too bright.

The moon will be right tonight. But the black cloud and the veil of rain are rushing toward him from the west.

"My object doesn't come up until three A.M.," he says. "A lot of times the clouds will dissipate. By morning it will be OK. That's what I'm hoping for, anyway."

In 1926 a bachelor banker from Paris, Texas, named W.J. McDonald, died and left $850,000 to the University of Texas to build an observatory. The first site considered was Cat Mountain, just outside Austin. If the observatory had been built there, it would be surrounded by the city now. "My house is farther out from the center of Austin than Cat Mountain is," says Ed Barker, a UT-Austin research scientist and an assistant director of McDonald Observatory. Besides, Austin skies are cloudy too often to be good for astronomy. So scientists and engineers scouted the peaks of the Davis Mountains wilderness for a better place to build their dome.

"They put it on Mount Locke mainly because they could get a road up here in the 1930s," Dr. Barker says. "They couldn't build a road to the top of Blue Mountain, where they really wanted to put it."

The nearest cities—El Paso and Odessa-Midland—are almost 200 miles away. The closest town—tiny Fort Davis—is sixteen miles down a winding mountain road, almost 2,000 feet below the observatory. Other towns—Marfa, Alpine, Balmorhea—are scattered about, but they're small, too.

"The townspeople and the ranchers give us terrific cooperation, shielding their lights," Dr. Barker says. "Fort Davis has been a model city for years. You can look down Main Street and not be blinded by glare. Parts of Marfa are in that state, too. And Alpine has a new lighting ordinance going into effect, requiring shields. I wish all cities would do that. Their people could see some stars then. They don't realize that a third of the light from their street lights goes straight up and never comes back down."

Black skies are critical when scientists are looking at very faint galaxies outside our own solar system, Dr. Barker says. "You have to see them in contrast against the sky. And the skies here are the darkest in the continental U.S. and probably in the entire world."

Dr. Barker first came to the mountain in 1965 as a graduate student. Except for two stints with NASA, he has been associated with the observatory ever since. He served twice as its superintendent and lived on the mountain. Through McDonald's telescopes, he has been monitoring water vapor on Mars for thirty-five years. He hasn't found much. "If you collected all the water on the whole planet, you might fill up a couple of football stadiums," he says.

But this time he has come to observe Iapetus, an outer satellite of Saturn, for someone at the University of Hawaii. "Iapetus revolves around Saturn once every eighty-two days," he says. "It's a leftover building block of the outer solar system. It's covered with water ice, and then it's covered with some sooty, carbon-type material on one side."

The scientist in Hawaii is trying to figure out what that sooty stuff is. So Dr. Barker hopes to collect data from Iapetus for three nights and ship it to him.

He's at McDonald's eighty-two-inch telescope, the original instrument built with the banker's money. When the observatory opened in 1939, it was the second-largest telescope in the world. Now it's dwarfed even on its own mountain by a 107-inch instrument that UT and NASA built in 1969 and the new state-of-the-art 432-inch Hobby-Eberly Telescope on nearby Mount Fowlkes. Beside these huge instruments the old telescope seems a dignified grandmother. "But it still produces good science," Dr. Barker says.

Dr. Barker hopes the rain clouds will be gone by four A.M., when Iapetus is to appear. If they are, he and Dr. Michael Kelley, a NASA scientist who has come along to learn how to use the telescope, will open the dome, train the great telescope on Saturn's companion and gather data into their computer until six-thirty A.M., when sunrise will force them to shut down and go to bed.

But right now it's raining. Dr. Barker and Dr. Kelley sit in their dome and wait.

☆

About 200 astronomers come to watch McDonald's skies every year. Dr. Mark Adams, the observatory's superintendent, is looking over the telescopes' schedules for the next few weeks, naming the universities from which the observers will come: "Case Western Reserve University, the University of New Mexico, the University of Montreal, the University of Tokyo, the University of Chicago, Boston University. That's typical," he says. "About fifteen percent of the time, the observatory is being used by non-Texas people."

Most of the Texas people are faculty, graduate students, and scientists from the UT-Austin astronomy department. Others—from the University of Texas at El Paso, Texas Christian University, the Southwest Research Institute—use it, too. They come to the mountain for three or five nights, observe the heavens, and go away again.

On the mountain, they live in a dormitory-like building called the "TQ" (transient quarters) just down the slope from the 107-inch telescope's dome.

Hallway signs warn visitors not to talk or make noise during the day. Astronomers are sleeping. Thick black shades block sunlight from their windows. Thick doors shield their rooms from the cook's clatter in the kitchen and the drone of CNN and the click of billiard balls in the lounge.

The astronomers set their alarm clocks to conform to their targets in the heavens. If their stars will rise early in the night, they may get up in time for TQ lunch at noon. Those whose targets won't appear until the wee hours may sleep until three P.M. "It's hard to keep awake at four in the morning when you're switching from a day schedule to a night schedule," says Dr. Barker.

But in a few days he will be back home in Austin, Dr. Johns-Krull will be back in California, and other astronomers will be at work in the domes. Jane Wiant, the observatory librarian, has watched them come and go since 1969, when her husband, Jerry, came to Mount Locke to fire lasers at reflectors that Apollo 11 astronauts left on the moon. Like Dr. Johns-Krull, he's measuring distances.

The Wiants are one of about twenty families who live on the mountain. Their daughter, who was eight months old when they moved here, is thirty-one years old now. Their son is twenty-seven. "It's a great place to raise kids," Mrs. Wiant says. "There's no trouble to get into. It's like living in a fish bowl. Everybody knows your business or thinks they do. There aren't any secrets."

For Mrs. Wiant, grocery shopping means an eighty-six-mile round trip to the Furr's supermarket in Alpine. Just buying gasoline requires a thirty-two-mile round trip to Fort Davis. The malls where she buys her clothing are 200 miles away in Midland and Las Cruces, New Mexico, where her parents live. "I find it cumbersome to have to plan so much," she says. "Sometimes we get cabin fever. Sometimes I can't wait to get to a big city. For about that long." She snaps her fingers.

"Then I can't wait to get back. Living up here so long, I sort of take the sky for granted. But when I go away and come back, it hits me in the eye every time, 'Oh, yeah! I knew I was missing something!' It's so gorgeous. It gets under your skin. It puts you back in your place."

Dr. Johns-Krull is in his dome waiting for his part of the sky to clear. David Doss, an observatory employee, drops by to chat. "What if you're clouded out?" Mr. Doss asks.

"I'll be back next month," Dr. Johns-Krull replies.

During his first night he never sees the Pleiades at all. On his second, he sees them only an hour. Walking to his dome for his final attempt, he says, "Even if we have a perfect night, we won't get all the data we need. We'll have to come back next month."

But the seven sisters surprise him. "We actually got some good data," he says later. "It wasn't a wasted trip after all." He'll come back in February to measure his Pleiades parallax from the other end of Earth's orbit.

The sky is even kinder to Dr. Barker. The clouds lift during all three of his nights to reveal Iapetus in the dark morning.

Audie

A prayer has been said. The speeches have been made. "A police officer never knows when a life-threatening moment might come," the master of ceremonies has said. Candles—thousands of them—have been lit and lifted toward the night sky in remembrance. A trumpeter has played "Taps."

The roll call begins at 9:15 with Alabama, then continues alphabetically through the states. Three hundred thirteen names are to be read. They have been carved into the marble walls of the National Law Enforcement Officers Memorial. They join more than 15,000 already there.

At 9:50 comes the name I'm listening for, "Audie Lee Gibson, December 16, 1932." My grandfather. I never knew him.

"We were getting worried because he hadn't come back," my mother is saying. We're sitting in a Dallas cafeteria, having lunch. "We heard somebody coming up the front walk, and we thought it was him," she says. "We opened the door, and it was these people coming to tell us he had been killed. Dr. Kennedy and his wife and Mr. Waldrop and another person I don't remember."

It was the early morning hours of December 16, 1932, just nine days till Christmas. She was sixteen. The man who didn't come home was her father, Audie Lee Gibson, a farmer who also served as deputy sheriff for the tiny community of Carlton in Hamilton County, Texas.

"Nothing ever happened in Carlton," my mother says.

Around midnight the phone had rung. The caller was G.L. Griffin's sister. Mr. Griffin was co-owner of the Griffin & Pierce Drug Store. He also owned the local telephone office and lived in the building. He had rigged an alarm that would sound at the telephone switchboard if someone broke into his store. It had sounded. While Mr. Griffin went to investigate, his sister called Audie and Sheriff Mack Morgan in Hamilton, eighteen miles away.

It was cold. Snow was falling. Audie had drained his car radiator to keep the block from freezing. He said he would walk to the drug store. It was about four blocks away, just down the hill. He got his gun and left. His wife, Clora, and his daughter, Beatrice, wouldn't see him alive again.

When Mr. Griffin arrived at his store, he saw a man sitting in a car. Mr. Griffin spoke to him, but the man didn't respond. Mr. Griffin reached inside the car and jerked out the keys. The man got out and ran. Mr. Griffin heard a commotion inside the store and shouted for the burglars to come out.

Two men dashed out the back door and fled. Near the railroad depot they encountered Audie. He struggled with them. They wrestled his gun from him and shot him with it.

Apparently nobody heard. Falling snow soon covered the body. When Sheriff Morgan arrived, he organized a small posse and found footprints in the snow along the road toward Dublin. The posse followed them.

A few miles outside Carlton, Jim Pierce, Mr. Griffin's partner in the drug store and a member of the posse, noticed footprints toward a stand of timber. He went to investigate and saw two men crouching in dead weeds. Mr. Pierce was unarmed, but he held his flashlight like a gun in his coat pocket and accosted them. They surrendered. Following more tracks, the posse found the driver of the car. He had sought shelter at a farmhouse.

Nobody knew the burglars had killed Audie. As the hours passed, his wife and daughter were more and more frantic. When Sheriff Morgan returned to Carlton with his prisoners, Clora was able to reach him by telephone. "Where is Audie?" she asked. "Where is my husband?"

The sheriff organized another search. Because of the snow, it took awhile. The searchers at first thought he was a junk car fender.

When Clora opened her door and saw the four callers, she knew why they had come. "Mother and I nearly went out of our heads," her daughter says.

☆

Almost sixty-nine years have passed since that terrible night. Audie was forty-one when he died. His widow, Clora, never married again. She lived to be ninety-one and wore his gold wedding band always. Nearly everybody who knew Audie is gone. The little town he died defending has almost disappeared. The drug store is a roofless ruin. His daughter Beatrice soon will turn eighty-five. His five grandchildren and thirteen great-grandchildren have seen a few pictures of him and have heard the story of his death. It's all we ever had of him.

At the memorial during the roll call, there are more than 3,000 people like us. "Survivors," the speakers kept calling us. Wives, husbands, mothers, fathers, sisters, brothers, children, grandchildren of men and women who died defending the law, protecting the community.

Many survivors are weeping. Their grief is still new and raw. Of the 313 men and women whose names are being read, 150 were killed in 2000. Many left young widows, children, even infants. Thirteen were Texans. One of them, "Aubrey Wright Hawkins, December 24, 2000," of the Irving police, died like my grandfather, shot by burglars just before Christmas.

The other 163 officers added to the memorial walls have been dead for a long time, some for a century or more. Until now, their service and sacrifice, the master of ceremonies said, "had somehow slipped through the cracks of history."

Who were the survivors of "Robert Goode, July 28, 1868," or "Alpheus D. Neill, February 6, 1877," or "Dallas Hodges, May 5, 1881," or "Hatch York, January 22, 1896," or "Ben J. Hill, October 19, 1902," or "Peter Howard, August 16, 1915?" Does anybody still say their names?

Forty-eight Texans are added to the wall this year, more than twice the number of any other state. Many, like my grandfather, died in other centuries in out-of-the-way places where record-keepers were few and news coverage was scant. Many of their names are etched in marble in the nation's capital now because Terry Baker, a retired Dallas County deputy, spends his days searching out their stories.

Balloonist

Every morning as soon as he gets up, Coy Foster turns on his computer and checks the long-range weather forecast that a meteorologist friend has sent him during the night. For sixteen months now, he has been looking.

"I need seventy-two hours of predictable, stable wind and weather," he says. "I haven't had it yet. The normal weather patterns have been out of whack since 1992."

When the right forecast comes along—and Dr. Foster has faith that it eventually will—he and his crew will race to the place where his balloon is stored and lay it out and fill it with helium until it resembles a thirty-foot beach ball. Then he will climb into a small basket hung underneath it and float into the blue yonder.

The balloon, he hopes, will rise to an altitude of 2,000 to 3,000 feet and glide across the landscape of North Texas into Oklahoma and Kansas or into Arkansas or northern Louisiana and Mississippi, depending on which way the wind is blowing. "Anywhere but the Gulf or the swamps of Louisiana," he says.

Then, after twenty-four to thirty-six hours in the sky, Dr. Foster will slowly deflate his balloon and land it 350 to 400 miles from where he started. If the flight has gone as he has planned it, he will have broken eight to ten world records for manned flights in super-pressure balloons. That would boost to fifty-seven or fifty-nine the number of world records that he has accumulated in several types of balloons and airships. As for his national records, "I have no idea how many," he says. "I've lost count."

The forty-nine world records he already has set are for altitude, distance, duration, and speed. They have made him one of the more famous balloonists in the world. But they happened long ago, during the 1980s, in the part of his life that Dr. Foster now calls "Before the Accident." Before

August 15, 1992, the day he crashed a hot-air balloon into an electrical power line during a Tyler, Texas, balloon festival and burst into flame.

He suffered third-degree burns over eighty percent of his body. Physicians have a way of calculating a patient's chances of surviving such injuries: They take the victim's age and the percentage of his body that has been burned and add them together. If the sum is less than 100, the victim may have a chance. The smaller the sum, the better the chance. Eighty percent plus fifty-two years—Dr. Foster's age at the time—gave him a score of 131. He wasn't supposed to live.

The first doctors who saw him at Parkland Memorial Hospital in Dallas told his family and friends, "If he lives, there's no way to know what he'll turn out to be."

But, after lying two months in a coma and three months in the intensive care burn unit, and after enduring years of surgeries, skin grafts, and physical therapy, Dr. Foster has beat the odds and is well into the part of his life that he calls "After the Accident."

"The way I see it, Before the Accident was the first half of my life," he says. "After the Accident is the second half. I can remember things that happened before the accident, but After the Accident is much clearer to me. I kind of started fresh in '92. The accident led me to reflect on life and what I really want out of it. The most important things now are health and the lovely wife that I have and a few friends. That's really all that life's about."

After the Accident has become an enormously happy era. He's married to Caroline Street, the fiancée who stuck with him and helped him through the long, painful months of recovery. Childless himself, he enjoys being with her grandchildren. They have become his own. He's practicing medicine again, part-time as a family physician and part-time in his old specialty, plastic surgery. But it doesn't add up to a full-time practice. "I do only as much as I want to and when I want to," he says.

And he's doing the thing he once declared he would never do again. "I can say right now, officially, that I'm retired from world records," he said about six months after his accident. "I've done enough. I don't need to do any more."

He never intended to give up ballooning entirely, he says, and he didn't stay away from it long. Less than a year after his accident, Dr. Foster ran into an old friend, Per Lindstrand, at a balloon festival in Greenwood, Mississippi. Mr. Lindstrand, a world-class balloonist himself, owns Lindstrand Balloons Ltd., the company in Great Britain where all of Dr. Foster's record-setting balloons were built. During the festival, Mr. Lindstrand invited Dr. Foster to accompany him on a flight.

"I was very nervous," Dr. Foster says. "They had to forklift me into the basket because I wasn't flexible enough to climb in. And I could hear the power lines humming. They were talking to me."

Soon after that ride he went to Britain and had Mr. Lindstrand modify a hot-air balloon so that he could handle it with his disabilities. "Then I took it to Albuquerque and worked with some friends out there, developing the skills to fly again," he says. "It has been a long road."

Eventually he recovered so much of his old confidence that he told Mr. Lindstrand to make him a super-pressure balloon, only the third of its type ever built. Besides Dr. Foster, only three living persons — Tom Heinsheimer in the 1970s and Julian Nott and Roger Barker in the 1980s — have ever made flights in super-pressure balloons. In 1991, a fourth pilot, Fumio Niwa of Japan, took off in one and tried to fly it across the Pacific. He died in the ocean.

Unmanned super-pressure balloons are commonly used in scientific experiments. They come in sizes, like shoes. Size 1 is the smallest, size 14 the largest. Dr. Foster's balloon, which he calls Super2 after its size, is smaller than the balloons used in earlier manned flights.

A super-pressure balloon is a grown-up, sophisticated version of the toy helium-filled balloon that a child buys at the zoo. If the child's balloon is released into the air, it rises to a certain altitude and stays there until the gas leaks out of it through the pores in the rubber. But if something punctures it and the gas rushes out of it suddenly, it pops.

The Super2 is made of a very strong fabric called Kevlar®, the material used in bulletproof vests. "My balloon doesn't leak," Dr. Foster says. "I could climb to a certain altitude and stay there until I run out of candy bars."

But in the unlikely event that something were to puncture its skin, it would pop like the child's balloon. Its basket, with its instruments and its passenger, would plummet like a stone. "There is no margin of error," Dr. Foster says.

He has flown the Super2 only once. Last July, he took off from a Plano parking lot and floated almost to Oklahoma City. "It was a very successful test flight," he says, "but it was 115 degrees in the basket. I was slow-roasting for fourteen hours. With my skin, that isn't good."

Despite the risks, Dr. Foster, at age sixty, with another Texas summer coming on and with all those power lines still out there, is eager to fly. All he needs is a few hours notice that the right winds and no lightning are headed his way.

"It isn't the records that are important to me," he says. "Some of the people in my crew have been with me for twenty years, since the beginning. They're like family. I want one more chance at getting them back together and sharing this.

"I believe that if you don't have things to do with your life besides going to work and coming home, you've got a fairly shallow life."

Columbus

In the pre-dawn dark of March 9, 1916, several hundred Mexican revolutionary soldiers under the command of General Pancho Villa crossed the border and attacked the tiny village of Columbus in the desert of southern New Mexico, west of El Paso.

The residents of the town and the soldiers at Camp Furlong, the U.S. Army base at its edge, were asleep. The attack took them by surprise. The invaders burned buildings, looted stores, and, as the alarm spread and people began running into the streets, shot eighteen Americans.

As soon as the few army officers on the scene were able to organize their men, the Americans returned a deadly fire. At 6:15 A.M., as the sun was rising, the Mexican bugler blew retreat. The raiders fled back across the border with a troop of the U.S. Cavalry in pursuit. Villa lost about 200 men in the two-hour fight.

A week later, President Woodrow Wilson sent General John "Black Jack" Pershing and 5,000 U.S. troops into the mountains of northern Mexico to find Villa, "with the single object of capturing him and putting a stop to his forays."

So it was odd, says Columbus historian Richard Dean, that the TV news anchors and commentators kept telling us that the terrorist murders at the World Trade Center and the Pentagon on September 11 were the first attack on the continental United States by a foreign enemy.

It took them a long time to remember that the British invaded Washington in 1814 and burned the Capitol and the White House. And they had forgotten—or never knew about—little Columbus.

"Our claim to fame has always been that we were the *last* place in the continental United States to be attacked by a foreign enemy," says Mr. Dean. "I guess we'll have to stop saying that now."

He's standing in Valley Heights Cemetery on the edge of Columbus, beside the grave of James T. Dean, his great-grandfather. "He was killed in the raid," he says. "He was on his way down Main Street to help fight the fires when they shot him.

"The civilians who got killed were the ones who got caught in harm's way by not staying inside. Except for the guests at the Commercial Hotel. The Villistas went into the hotel and dragged them out and murdered them. We have to use the word 'murder,' because when you have an undeclared war, and they come in and kill people, that's murder."

A dazed populace emerged from their houses in the early light to see the havoc the attackers had wrought.

"According to my family, the town was a real mess," Mr. Dean says. "Buildings were in ashes. There were more than ninety dead Villistas in the streets, and an awful lot of dead horses around. There was a real sanitation problem. So they did the logical thing. They loaded the bodies on wagons and took them out east of town and burned them.

"My great-uncle Edwin Dean helped with that. It was while he was helping the army load the Villista bodies on wagons that he found the body of his dad in a pile of dead men at the corner of Broadway and Main. Can you imagine that? He went home and told his mother that he had found Papa killed. They got the car out and went down and removed his body and took it home."

James T. Dean was a merchant. His was one of the stores that the invaders looted. Buried next to him is Bessie James, the only woman killed in the raid. She was pregnant.

"A lot of people left town because of the stench," says Richard Dean. "And all the Mexicans left town because of the threat to them by the Gringos. Even Juan Favela, who had given the warning. He left. He didn't feel safe. Just like the Muslims now."

Columbus is an isolated village sixty-five miles west of El Paso. Its population is about 300, roughly the same as in 1916. The Mexican border—a fence stretched across the desert—is three miles to the south. A two-lane highway leads to a two-lane port of entry where U.S. Border Patrol and customs officers monitor the sparse traffic between the countries. South of the fence is the small, equally isolated town of Las Palomas, Chihuahua.

In 1916, Juan Favela was foreman of an American-owned ranch in Mexico, near Las Palomas. He saw Villa's troops—between 600 and 1,000 of them—moving toward the border. Mr. Favela rode pell-mell to Columbus and told Colonel Herbert Slocum, commander of the 13th Cavalry units stationed at Camp Furlong, what he had seen.

"Juan Favela was an American citizen," says Mr. Dean. "He was a very truthful, very upstanding man. He was not prone to telling stories or lying. Everybody respected him. His warning should have been heeded."

But Colonel Slocum ignored him. The border was always buzzing with rumors, especially about Pancho Villa. The revolution had kept Mexico in turmoil for six years already, and wouldn't end for four more. From time to time, Mexican bandits—some affiliated with Villa, some not—would cross the border and raid ranches on the American side. President Wilson had stationed troops all along the border to try to prevent such incursions.

In January 1916, rumor had it that Villa's army was about to attack Presidio, Texas, across the Rio Grande from Ojinaga, Chihuahua. But it hadn't. There were always rumors. Nothing serious had happened.

The power of Villa—who only a couple of years earlier had been the most popular and adored of the revolutionary generals—seemed on the wane. His civil war against the current Mexican president, Venustiano Carranza, was going badly. Recruits had once flocked to Villa's banner, but now he was resorting to force to add new soldiers to his army. The desertion rate was high. Supplies and ammunition were low.

The American government, which once had favored Villa, had turned against him. In October 1915, the U.S. recognized Carranza as the legitimate president of Mexico. President Wilson even allowed Carranza's troops to use American railroads and move through American territory to gain faster access to Agua Prieta, Sonora, on the border near Douglas, Arizona, and defend it from Villa's attack. Carranza's army soundly defeated Villa. He was furious at President Wilson.

Some historians think the Columbus raid was revenge against the U.S. for its pro-Carranza policy. Some think it was a simple looting expedition. Others think it was to punish Sam Ravel, a Columbus merchant whom

Villa had accused of cheating him. Still others think Villa was deliberately goading President Wilson into sending American troops into Mexico. The divided Mexican nation then would unite behind Villa, the theory went, and throw out the Americans and topple Carranza, their lackey. A few think Germany paid Villa to make the raid, hoping to start a war between the U.S. and Mexico and thus keep the Americans out of the world war in Europe.

Historians also disagree whether Pancho Villa personally led his soldiers into Columbus. Several eyewitnesses said they saw him there. Mr. Dean, the unofficial local authority on the matter, agrees with them.

But Angel Borunda, who's minding the museum down at the old railroad depot, says Villa remained on the Mexican side of the border during the attack.

Mr. Borunda's father, David Borunda, worked for Sam Ravel's mercantile firm, which had been selling ammunition and rifles to the Villistas. His father, says Mr. Borunda, knew Villa personally. Two of his father's brothers, he says, were generals in Villa's army.

Mr. Borunda points to a small brass telescope in a museum showcase. "General Rodolfo Fierro gave that to my father," he says. "Fierro was the one they called 'The Butcher.' He was Villa's executioner.

"My dad said Villa never crossed the border on the day his men attacked Columbus. He stayed on the other side on a hill called Cerro del Gato with fifty soldiers and horses. There were four generals that came in here, but Villa didn't.

"My father said Pancho Villa could have been one of the best men for president of Mexico. But he made a boo-boo when he came here."

Of course, the country was outraged. Patriot fever ran high. Editors and politicians blasted President Wilson for treating Villa too leniently in the past, and called for swift and severe punishment. They wanted Villa's head.

Some accused the president of cowardice. "We are too proud to fight," complained William Randolph Hearst's *Los Angeles Examiner*. "Why, even a little, despicable, contemptible bandit nation like Mexico murders our citizens, drags our flag in the dirt and spits, and defies this nation of ours with truculent insolence."

President Wilson emphasized that Pershing's mission would not be to make war on Mexicans, but solely to capture Villa. "This," the president said, "can and will be done in entirely friendly aid to the constituted authorities in Mexico and with scrupulous respect for the sovereignty of that republic."

Carranza gave permission for the Americans to enter and promised to help them get rid of Villa. But he was nervous.

Finding the "Tiger of the North," as Villa was called, wouldn't be easy. The mountains of Chihuahua and Sonora were his home. He knew every cave, crevice, and arroyo. It was among their torrid and barren peaks that he had destroyed the forces of the dictator Porfirio Diaz and the usurper Victoriano Huerta in the earlier days of the revolution.

But Pershing would have at his disposal the latest in American military technology. In addition to 5,000 cavalrymen, the army sent most of its fifty-four trucks and eight of its eighteen airplanes to Columbus, where Captain Benjamin Foulois, commanding the 1st Aero Squadron, set up the first operational air base in U.S. history.

"They were biplanes," says Mr. Dean. "The army used them for reconnaissance, and for delivering and picking up messages. They were with Pershing for five months, but they lasted only thirty-eight days in Mexico. Their engines were too weak for flying over the mountains and through the canyons."

Fuel for the trucks had to be hauled into the mountains on mules.

General Pershing and his men stayed in Mexico for eleven months, but never found Villa. The longer the Americans remained and the farther they rode into the interior, the stronger the anti-American feeling grew among the people.

On February 9, 1917, President Wilson ordered Pershing to withdraw. In a few months, the general and most of his men would be fighting in France.

"The army went into Mexico looking for only one person," says Angel Borunda. "When you're trying to find only one guy, there's only one place you can go to find him. That's hard."

Wyman

Wyman Meinzer once read an account by an Indian about what it was like to be shot at with a buffalo gun. The Indian said the sound of the bullet passing was like the sound of a hummingbird. Mr. Meinzer then persuaded a friend to fire a Sharps .50-caliber rifle at him while he lay behind a hummock, so he could hear the bullet's hum as it whizzed over his head.

"Another time, Wyman was reading about nineteenth-century dentistry in Texas," says Andy Sansom, a friend. "He got a local dentist to fill his tooth using the techniques that he had read about. It was horrible! Hearing him tell about it, you say, 'Oh, my God!' But he just wanted to know what it would have been like to live back then."

Mr. Meinzer, who by living much of his life in the wild has become the most authoritative photographer of Texas wildlife and the rougher regions of the state's landscape, knows he was born into the wrong century. He acknowledges that he's only awkwardly at home in the twentieth and seriously out of synch with the upcoming twenty-first. But that doesn't bother him at all.

He finds his bliss far from the madding crowd, hunkering in the mesquite to capture on film the private moments of coyotes and roadrunners, and chasing tornadoes across the badlands in a pickup truck, and rearing his sons in the tiny town of Benjamin where he grew up, within sight of the middle of nowhere, and communing with ghosts of old-time Texas.

"Ever since I was a small child," he says, "I've had a fascination with the Native Americans, the people who were here long before us. And the people who were here before them. The Clovis people. The Folsom people. They were not pampered folks. Only the strongest survived. If you lived to be thirty, you were a tough son of a gun.

"The white people who came to this part of Texas in the 1850s and

'60s were a breed different from us, too. The buffalo hunters, the soldiers, the early ranchers, the cowboys. Some of them were good people and some were bad people, but they all were strong-willed and very healthy people. And they were wise to the ways of the wilderness. It's a wisdom that we've lost."

In 1979, David Baxter, then editor of *Texas Parks and Wildlife* magazine, published the first Wyman Meinzer nature photographs. They were of coyotes. Since then, Mr. Meinzer's pictures have appeared in more than sixty state, national, and foreign magazines and in almost a dozen books. Nearly all his work celebrates the unforgiving beauty of the Texas landscape and the often violent power of its weather and the savage grace of its animals.

Many of his images, like the photographer who shot them, seem throwbacks to a place and time before cities and electronics and noise, when Texas was almost empty of people, when the prehistoric Clovis and Folsom people tracked woolly mammoths across the Rolling Plains, and the later Comanche and Kiowa followed the buffalo.

"My sense of Wyman is that he's kind of a reincarnation of a buffalo hunter," says Mr. Baxter. "He knows too much about that country, too much about its wildlife and its history, to have learned it in one lifetime."

The Meinzers live in the jail. The homely brown sandstone structure, erected in 1887, stands amidst the mesquite in the middle of Benjamin, population 224, the seat of Knox County, Texas. Black iron bars still cover its windows. Some have saw marks where long-ago prisoners tried to escape.

Inside, a braided Indian bridle hangs from a pillar, and steel wolf traps dangle by their chains from the mantel. A wood-burning iron stove provides the only heat. It burns eight cords or more of firewood every winter, Mr. Meinzer says, but the house remains cold. The ceiling of unfinished oak, some of the furniture crafted from weathered barn wood, and a bleached cow skull on a bookshelf all imply their owner's stern frontier values.

"I think about the people who built this jail, how many tons of rock they hauled in here with wagons and mules," says Mr. Meinzer.

He's sitting on a couch near the stove, his long legs stretched before him, crossed at the ankles. He's dressed as he always dresses, dark cotton shirt and jacket, faded jeans tucked neatly into calf-high, laced-up hunting boots. If he were outdoors, a brown slouch hat or a knit cap would cover his dark, graying hair. He wears glasses now. He's forty-eight years old, but a good forty-eight, slender and flat-bellied. He's smoking a fine cigar, sipping a glass of cabernet.

"They used primitive tools," he says. "But you look at the edges of this building, and they're absolutely perfectly straight."

It was his ex-wife, Sarah, who really wanted the jail, he says. "All I could see was just a horrible amount of work. But I went along with it, and now I'm glad I did, because of its historical significance to this community."

They married in 1978, bought the abandoned jail, full of rats and cockroaches, in the early eighties, worked three or four years on it and moved in. "We put so much work into it, I thought, 'Well, my God, I'm not leaving here,'" he says.

But Sarah did. Their divorce was final in early 1999. "That's probably a result of my being so focused on my work," Mr. Meinzer says. "I let too many things slide. Sarah is a good woman." Sarah now lives in Lubbock, where she works as a therapist.

Their relationship is still an amiable one, he says, and Sarah remains close to their sons, sixteen-year-old Hunter and fourteen-year-old Pate, who now "bach" it with their father. When Mr. Meinzer is away on a shooting trip—a frequent thing, often for three or four days out of the week—the boys go it alone.

"I worry about them," Mr. Meinzer says. "They're at the point when they need their pop around. They're solid boys. They're real independent. They take care of themselves quite well. And they have two grandparents here. But hell, kids will be kids. If they need to ask me a question, I need to be here. Kids at that age can make decisions that aren't exactly good."

Hunter and Pate are deeply involved with animals, too, of the more domestic sort. They buy horses and break them and trade them. They raise chickens and sell eggs.

"It teaches them the meaning of what it's like to make a dollar," their father says. "They buy a lot of their own stuff. They go float their own loans to buy a horse. I think too few kids are raised in that way today. It's too easy to give to them. I want my boys to realize that money doesn't come floating down from the sky, that you have to earn it."

It's one of the lessons he learned himself growing up on the League Ranch, eleven miles out of Benjamin. A year and a half after Wyman was born in Knox City, the Meinzers moved to the League, a 27,000-acre spread established in the 1800s. Wyman's father was its foreman for thirty years.

"I hunted all the time and was trained as a youth to be a cowboy," Mr. Meinzer says. But as soon as he finished Benjamin High School, where his sons now go, he was off to Texas Tech. In 1974, he got a degree in range and wildlife management. While in school, he did a two-and-a-half-year research project on the feeding habits of the coyote.

He took up photography as a research tool with a camera he borrowed from the university. He enjoyed it. When he graduated, he bought some photography equipment of his own, but didn't yet dream of making his living with a camera.

"After Tech, I came back to the Rolling Plains because I thought I was going to be a government trapper in Reagan County," he says. "That fell through. I didn't get the job. So I decided to hang out here anyway and do some hunting on my own."

For three winters, he lived in a half-dugout on a ranch and trapped and shot coyotes and sold their pelts. On his living room wall today is a blow-up of a black-and-white picture he took of himself then. He's seated in front of the dugout, Winchester in hand, with a long string of coyote pelts hanging like a fur curtain. The photograph could have been taken 150 years ago almost anywhere on the western frontier.

"I became a virtual vagabond," he says. "I just kind of bounced around. But I like this country. I like to have lots of elbowroom. Once you're raised in a big country like this, where within three minutes you can be in almost a wilderness situation, surrounded by thousands of square miles of space, it's almost impossible to live anywhere else."

In 1978, while he was eking out his meager livelihood as a hunter, Mr. Meinzer discovered a roadrunner's nest near his father's house. He began photographing the bird's life. In 1982, he found another nest and photographed it, too. In 1984, he found a third. "About that time," he says, "an editor saw some of my pictures and suggested I do a book." He laughs. "Then six years passed before I found another roadrunner's nest."

He practically moved in with the birds, recording them courting, mating, nesting, hunting and killing lizards and snakes, and rearing their young. He became such good friends with them that a nesting female accepted food from his hand and allowed him to touch her.

John Graves, author of the classic *Goodbye to a River* and other books about Texas nature and history, met Mr. Meinzer during that period. It was on one of the annual fishing trips that Mr. Graves and a group of friends took on the James River. One of the friends had brought Mr. Meinzer along.

"He's no fisherman," Mr. Graves remembers. "He spent most of his time trapping mice and lizards to take home for his roadrunners."

In 1993, Texas Tech University Press published *Roadrunner*, Mr. Meinzer's first book.

Meanwhile, his regular presence in *Texas Parks and Wildlife*—Mr. Baxter estimates that he used thousands of Meinzer photographs during his two decades as editor—had attracted attention at other hunting and nature publications. His work began showing up in *National Wildlife*, *Texas Highways*, *American Hunter*, *Audubon*, and magazines in Europe and Japan.

"At some point he made a pilgrimage to New York to call on the editors of such national magazines as *Sports Afield* and *Field & Stream*," says Mr. Baxter. "It must have been kind of a Crocodile Dundee thing. I'd love to have been there to see him walk in the door in his old felt hat and his jeans tucked into his hunting boots.

"Of course, they love that in New York. The guy from the wild frontier. They probably ate it up."

"I pretty well owned the cover of *Outdoor Life*, *Field & Stream*, and *Sports Afield* for three or four years," Mr. Meinzer says. "Once I had six covers there in the course of a single year. Then by the late eighties I realized that focusing my interest on just wildlife was a dead end. I felt I had more to offer. So I started expanding my photography into people and landscape."

He also has devoted more and more of his effort to books. "I love shooting books, because you know you're doing the whole story," he says. "You're not after just one image that will be used on a magazine cover."

A couple of years after *Roadrunner*, he published *Coyote*, about the life of the animal that got him interested in capturing wildlife on film in the first place, and still his favorite animal to photograph. He has published *Playas: Jewels of the Plains* with writer Jim Steiert; *Texas Lost: Vanishing Heritage* and *Texas Past: Enduring Legacy* with Texas Parks and Wildlife Department executive director Andy Sansom; *Texas Quail* and *Texas Whitetail* and *Texas Seasons* with *Dallas Morning News* outdoor writer Ray Sasser.

His most ambitious book to date, which took many years to complete, was *Texas Sky*, published in 1998 by the University of Texas Press. It's a slick coffee table volume, full of astonishing images of the sky in every part of Texas in all its various beauty and power. There's little text except a brief introduction by John Graves, and that's all it needs. Words would only detract from the strength of the pictures.

"West Texans are peculiarly fascinated with the weather because our lives and our livelihoods are tied so closely to it," Mr. Meinzer says. "Everybody out here is a student of the atmosphere. If I didn't do what I do, I would like to be a meteorologist. I love northers and what they do. And there's something fascinating about the structure and formation of thunderstorms."

On the Rolling Plains, a storm can be seen building from 100 miles away. Whenever Mr. Meinzer spotted one, he would jump into his pickup and track it across the rugged landscape.

"I've driven every back road in this part of the state," he says. "I know where the great locations are for viewing the approach of big storms. The best photographs occur in the storm's final moments, at sunset, when it's dying. That's when you get the drama. At the storm's death."

Mr. Sansom says the photographer is "singing" in *Texas Sky*. "It's like he's performing. Wyman's inspired by what he does. Some of his photographs are like Beethoven."

Now Mr. Meinzer is collaborating with John Graves on Texas rivers. Together they're exploring the Pecos, the Neches, the Llano, the Clear Fork of the Brazos, the Canadian, and the Sabinal. Their work is being published as a series in *Texas Parks & Wildlife* and then will be expanded into a book.

"This is a large project," Mr. Meinzer says. "This is tremendous. I don't want to go and just spend three days on a river and shoot the water and maybe a bridge or two and go home. I want to spend two or three weeks on each river and get it in the best light I can. And John wants to do the definitive story on each river."

"Wyman is a delightful man, but he'll wear you out," says Mr. Graves, who's seventy-nine. "When he's out shooting, he doesn't walk from point to point, he runs. He works and works on individual shots. He takes them from all different angles at different times of day until he's got what he thinks is right. I've gotten to where I just go with him where I can, and where I can't, I don't. Two days with Wyman is about all I can go."

Wyman Meinzer's work is his identity, says Mr. Sansom, and his identity is his work. He loves the country and the animals he photographs and immerses himself totally in them.

That, says Mr. Meinzer, is what makes him a fortunate man. "Just in the process of trying to live a life that makes me happy, wonderful things have happened."

In 1997, the legislature named him Texas State Photographer, the first and only person to receive such an honor. He has won awards and considerable fame. He's a popular public speaker. Almost everyone he meets considers him a friend. In 1999, Texas Tech named him a distinguished alumnus and invited him to deliver its summer commencement address. "That," he says, "was a defining moment of my life."

His eyes widen at the memory.

"I walk into the coliseum, and the orchestra is playing "Pomp and Circumstance," and I'm thinking, 'The last time I was on this floor, I was registering for school, searching frantically for a nine o'clock Thursday class or something.' I was living from one semester to the next. I didn't have the money to plan beyond one semester. And I went from that to standing up in front of 6,000 people and giving the commencement address at Texas Tech University!

"That really hit home. It made me realize that maybe I do have something significant to say."

He takes a pull on his wine, a puff of his cigar, and smiles.

"I've not made a lot of money by any stretch of the imagination," he says. "But the recognition that has been bestowed on me has been awesome. I think it's the result of just being different and saying, 'I'll not forsake what I believe is right, and I'm going to live in Benjamin, Texas, regardless of the consequences.'"

Kingdom

There are no tombstones, Rodolfo Silguero says. The wooden crosses that used to mark the graves have long since rotted away. There's no sign a cemetery ever was in the little grove of trees.

This morning is humid, following days of rain. Haze hugs the ground. Mosquitoes swarm. Grass and weeds stand high in the pasture between the grove and the stable where Mr. Silguero is working.

"My great-grandmother is buried over there," he says. "She was born here on Santa Gertrudis in 1888. Her father and mother were working here already."

He's moving a brush over the broad, red back of a young bull, one of several he has tied to the stable fence. He's trying to gentle them to be led by a halter. "When they know nobody is going to hurt them, they settle down," he says. He croons as he brushes, calling them "sweet thing" and "baby" and "son."

Mr. Silguero, seventy-four, has come out of retirement temporarily to train the bulls, which are to be sold at an auction. He's the eldest of the ten Silguero children of their generation. His youngest brother, Emiterio, sixty-one, works with the bulls, too.

Their great-grandmother's name was Maria Susana Rodeo. When she was still very young, she married a cowboy named Macario Alegura, who also worked on Santa Gertrudis.

"On my other side, my grandfather and my father came to the King Ranch in 1909 from Mexico," Rodolfo says. "My grandfather's name was Hipolito Silguero. My father was Emiterio Silguero. He was nine years old at the time. He started working for the ranch when he was ten. He worked here until he was seventy-three. Their graves are over on the Laureles division."

☆

Santa Gertrudis and Laureles are the northern divisions of the King Ranch, oldest and most famous of the great Texas cattle baronies. All through this autumn the ranch has been sponsoring events commemorating the 150th anniversary of its founding. One of them was the cattle sale for which the Silguero brothers were training the bulls.

Santa Gertrudis, established by a steamboat captain named Richard King in 1853, is the oldest part of the ranch and is where the great castle-like main house stands. Santa Gertrudis and Laureles lie south of Corpus Christi and almost surround the town of Kingsville (population about 26,000) that the ranch founded in 1904. Farther south, about halfway between Corpus Christi and Brownsville, are the Encino and Norias divisions.

The four divisions total about 825,000 acres of brushy flatlands spread over four counties. The King is the third-largest ranch in the United States. It supports about 57,000 head of cattle and about 1,000 horses. Over the years, vast amounts of oil and gas have been extracted from its earth.

Beginning in the early 1950s, the King Ranch expanded into Argentina, Australia, Brazil, Cuba, Morocco, Spain, Venezuela, and several of the United States. It used to raise thoroughbred racehorses, and in 1946 a King Ranch horse, Assault, won the Triple Crown. It still raises fine quarter horses.

During the early twentieth century, the ranch developed the first American breed of beef cattle, the Santa Gertrudis, by crossing Brahman cattle from India with English shorthorns. Since the 1980s it has developed the Santa Cruz breed, a cross of Santa Gertrudis with red Angus.

All the foreign holdings are gone now, and the King Ranch no longer raises racehorses. But, along with cattle, it's big into sugar, citrus, cotton, and other crops in Florida and Texas.

In 1885 Captain King's widow, Henrietta, named her husband's lawyer, Robert J. Kleberg, as her business manager. He later married Alice, the youngest of the King daughters. In 1934 the King Ranch became a corporation, which is now headquartered in a Houston skyscraper. Until a few years ago, the head of the corporation was always a member of the Kleberg family.

Generation after generation, families such as the Silgueros have done most of the work on the ranch. Early in their history they acquired a name: *Kineños*. It means "King's men" or "King's people."

There's a story about how the first *Kineños* came to the ranch:

In 1854, Captain King, who with a partner had bought the first tract of the land that would become the great ranch, rode into Mexico to buy cattle with which to stock it. In the state of Tamaulipas, in a desert at the foot of the Sierra Madre, he came to a village called Cruillas. Its 100 or so inhabitants, poor even in good times, were suffering terribly from a drought.

Captain King bought their cattle and told them that if they would come with him to Texas, he would give them jobs. The villagers held a meeting and accepted the offer. They packed their belongings onto burros and carts and trekked several hundred miles to Santa Gertrudis. Many of their descendants have lived and worked on the King Ranch ever since.

Rodolfo Silguero doesn't know whether his great-grandmother's forebears were among those villagers or not. But he knows his family have been *Kineños* for a long time. "My great-grandmother's father, my great-grandfather, my grandfather, my father and myself, and my sons," he says. "And my grandson will be seven. Seven generations."

Next morning, Robert Silguero and his cousin, Dave Gerragauch, ride into a pasture to gather a small herd of bulls and drive it to the corrals where a veterinarian will test them for tuberculosis and brucellosis. The sun is out now, but only a single day of the last ten has passed without rain. Some of the pastures resemble lakes. As the bulls trudge along, water seeps into every hoof print.

The cowboys whistle and yell, urging the bulls. In the trees along the lane, birds are whistling, too, as if trying to help. Cows beyond the fence, surrounded by snowy cattle egrets, gaze incuriously at the procession.

Robert is one of Rodolfo Silguero's three sons. He's thirty-nine years old, a stocky, strong-looking man, every inch a cowboy. Like his father, he has lived on the King Ranch all his life. So have his children, thirteen-year-old Randy and twelve-year-old Roxanne. Robert's wife, Rhonda—not a native *Kineña*—is the administrative assistant to Paul Genho, vice president of ranch operations, whose office is at Santa Gertrudis. Robert's brother, Rudy, is a heavy-machinery operator on the ranch. He clears brush, works on roads, ditches, and fences. The third brother left the ranch years ago.

Robert is a unit manager, a job with plenty of responsibility. For three years he has overseen about 4,500 acres of the Santa Gertrudis division, plus 1,000 purebred cows and their calves and 300 bulls. Like his father and all the *Kineño* generations before them, Robert and his family live in a house provided by the ranch.

He loves his life and his work. "Since I was a kid, I've always liked being around horses and cattle," he says. "My toy was a rope. Everything scattered when they saw me coming. Chickens, dogs, cats. When I was eight or nine years old, I told my dad I was going to go to college so I could study to be a cowboy. But you don't need college for that. Just the school of hard knocks."

His father taught him how to be a cowboy, as his father's father had taught him. Robert began working on the ranch when he was eleven, helping out after school and on weekends with whatever needed to be done. The ranch has been his fulltime job for twenty years.

Now he's teaching Randy the skills he learned from Rodolfo. The boy, with the reticence typical of teenagers around strangers, outlines his own ambitions:

"You like working around animals?" he's asked.

"Yeah."

"You want to be a cowboy like your dad?"

"Yeah."

"You want to work here on the ranch when you get through school?"

"Yeah."

In the afternoon, after the vet has finished with the bulls, Robert and Dave Gerragauch are to drive them back to pasture. But first, Robert goes to Randy's school in Kingsville and gets him out of class for a little on-the-job training.

"He's been riding since he was seven," Robert says as he helps his son saddle his horse. "Now the length of his stirrups is the same as mine."

Robert takes pride in the fact that his son wants to be like him.

"Working with Randy is totally rewarding," he says. "Teaching him to do things, watching him learn. I know what his limits are. I know what he can do and can't do. So I can push him, but yet take care of him so he doesn't get hurt."

If Randy wants to follow him into the *Kineño* life, that's OK, Robert says. "My reward is just being here, getting up in the morning and knowing that I'll be working with the horses and the cattle. Knowing that I've been here for generations."

But there aren't so many *Kineños* on the great ranch now as in the old days. The cow camps where crews of cowboys used to live, scattered over the vast range, are empty. So are most of the houses where the married *Kineños* raised their families. When too old for work, they continued to live out their old age in those houses, and eventually were carried from them to the little cemeteries in the little groves of trees.

Now, with modern vehicles and ranch machinery, Robert and Dave can take care of their unit's 4,500 acres and 1,300 cattle all by themselves.

Rodolfo Siguero retired in 1991. The ranch gave him a choice: He and his wife could remain in their house on the ranch and begin paying rent, or the ranch would give them $20,000 to leave. They took the money and now live in Kingsville.

"A lot of guys, as soon as they got married, their wives tried to talk them into leaving the ranch," he says. "They didn't see much money coming in. They didn't see the benefits. My wife tried to talk me into leaving, but now she's glad I never listened."

The ranch pays him a pension to augment his Social Security. It pays all medical expenses for him and his wife—including prescriptions—that aren't covered by Medicare. It provides him a life insurance policy. "The ranch has taken care of me," he says. "In the long run, it paid off. I'm glad I stayed."

But Santa Gertrudis is different now.

"It used to be, the *corrida* had about twenty cowboys," he says. "Another five were at headquarters. Now they have four unit managers like Robert and one cowboy to work with each. Eight people.

"They used to have a fence crew and a windmill crew who did their work by hand. Each crew had its camp and its own cook. Now they have tractors and machines to dig the postholes. The wells have electric pumps now. They're serviced by outside workers. Machinery has taken over everybody's job.

"But people don't want to go back and do that hard labor the way we used to. When I was young, some of the people here on Santa Gertrudis had never been out. They had no experience of the outside world. Now everybody wants to go out and make big wages.

"I wanted my boys to go to college, but they didn't want to. And they're happy where they are. To me, that's the important thing. If you're not happy where you are … Well, you're only here once."

He gives the young bull another swipe with his brush.

Cold Drink

Seven people are in the black 1939 Chevrolet. They are a grandmother, a mother, and five children. The eldest child is eight. He's riding in the front seat, between the grandmother and the mother, who is driving. The youngest—a toddler—and the three others are lined up along the back seat. The two brothers are picking at each other as small brothers do, pinching, hitting. The older sister is whining, "Mother, make them stop!" The younger sister, the toddler, is crying. They have been on the highway since early morning. They are sweating and miserable.

The mother stares grimly through the windshield at the tail end of the truck lumbering slowly before her on the narrow two-lane highway. The Chevrolet has been behind the truck for miles, kept there by oncoming traffic. It is August. The temperature is 101. The mid-afternoon sun is blazing. All the car windows are open, but the breeze generated by the car's movement is hot and smelly from the truck's exhaust. In the mesquite beside the road, locusts whir.

The grandmother tries to comfort the children. "When we stop for gas, we'll get a cold drink," she says.

A cold drink. We don't call them soda water or pop or soft drinks in the un-air-conditioned West Texas of the forties and fifties. They are cold drinks. All of them. Coca-Cola, Dr Pepper, 7-Up, Pepsi-Cola, Royal Crown Cola, Squirt, NuGrape, Delaware Punch, Big Red, Grapette, Nehi Orange. Cold.

In the 1940s, they are to be found in the big metal box that sits in the driveway, against the front wall of every gas station. The box is full of ice that has been brought from the local icehouse and chipped by hand with an ice pick. The drinks in their thick-glass bottles stand in ranks like soldiers. Ice and icy water surround them to their necks. To tell them apart, the child has to read the names on their metal caps. The child then must give the gas station man a nickel, choose a cold, wet bottle, and pry off the cap with the bottle opener that is attached to the front of the box.

Often the box is bright red, with "Coca-Cola" emblazoned across the front in white. Sometimes the box is pale green and displays the familiar Dr Pepper clock with hands pointing to 10, 2, and 4, the hours at which we are supposed to slake our thirst.

The women and the children in the Chevrolet do not get cold drinks anywhere near that often. For them, a cold drink is a semi-rare treat, to be savored and appreciated. On a torrid afternoon beside an endless highway, the first swig is a foretaste of heaven.

When small, the children favor the Nehi Orange, the NuGrape, and the Big Red. As they grow older, they move on to Pepsi-Cola and Royal Crown Cola (also called RC) because they are in bigger bottles than Dr Pepper and Coke and 7-Up, which are the choices of nearly all grownups.

While the station man fills the gas tank and washes the windshield and checks the oil, the radiator, the battery, and the tire pressure, the mother and the grandmother and the children stand in the driveway watching him. And they drink their cold drinks, wanting to guzzle, but sipping to make them last.

When the car has been made ready to go, some of the children are still sipping. So the mother pays the station man a deposit of three cents for each bottle and hustles the children into the car. Farther down the highway, another station man will take the bottles and repay the deposit, or take them in partial exchange for full ones.

In time, a black 1950 Plymouth replaces the black 1939 Chevrolet. Sometime in the fifties, the roadside cold-drink ritual changes, too. The drinks are still in their thick-glass bottles. The deposit is still three cents. But the box of ice near the gas-station door disappears. A tall electric, refrigerated machine stands in its place. The price of a cold drink rises to a dime, which is paid not to the station man but to the machine itself.

But the highways of Texas are still long, the summertime still blazes, mirages still quiver in the distance, and most of the cars and trucks are not yet air-conditioned. The smart ones among the gas-station men set the thermostats on their electric cold-drink machines to a low, low temperature. So low that when a tired and sweaty traveler shoves his dime into the slot, opens the door of the machine, receives his cold drink, and pries off the cap, crystals of ice form inside the bottle!

What traveler would not stop again at that station next time down that hot highway, and buy his gas, and shove another dime into that machine?

The gods of Olympus would weep for such a treat. And there is nothing like it in our air-conditioned, aluminum-canned, plastic-bottled world.

Bronze

The bronze knight standing near one of the entrances to the Lubbock Civic Center doesn't look like a conquering hero. He isn't on horseback. His sword isn't drawn. His face isn't brave or proud.

"He's tired," says Eddie Dixon. "He hasn't found anything and he has no hope of finding anything. All he wants to do is go home."

The statue is called "Knight of the Llano Estacado." Mr. Dixon made it. He says it portrays "a generic conquistador" representing the men who accompanied Francisco Vázquez de Coronado across the Texas Panhandle in 1541. They wandered over the tabletop-flat Llano Estacado (Staked Plains) in search of the golden cities of Quivira, which, the local Indians always told them, were just beyond the horizon.

The Spaniards found no gold, of course. Just lots of grass and buffalo, a few Indians living in tepees and miles and miles of treeless, featureless land under a vast dome of often-dangerous sky.

"These plains were as alien to them as the moon," Mr. Dixon says.

Although he calls his knight "generic," the sculptor made up a life for him while he was creating his image. "His helmet is decorated with a fish's head because he came from a village on the Spanish coast," Mr. Dixon says. "The flowers on his armor symbolize the beautiful rolling hills he knew. He has brought a piece of his home out here to the Plains. The expression on his face is forlorn. He's exhausted. He's homesick. He wonders if he will ever see his home and family again."

The City of Lubbock commissioned the twelve-foot-tall statue—fourteen feet if you include its base. It's the latest of the major statues Mr. Dixon has created on historical figures. The Spanish knight is something of a departure for him. Most of his subjects are black people, African-American heroes who have been left out of the standard histories of America.

"Black people of my generation had no heroic role models," says Mr. Dixon, who is fifty-three. "We would go to the movies and see John Wayne, and he was our hero. But when we came home, we were still black. And black people were not accomplishing anything that we were aware of. They didn't tell us about black heroes in the history books. The only black people we were told about were Booker T. Washington and George Washington Carver. All we could relate to was slavery.

"I want my sculptures to show coming generations that we do have heroes, that black people have contributed as much to the development of America as anyone. We're part of the American family. We're not guests here."

In 1992 the U.S. Army unveiled Mr. Dixon's most famous work, a large bronze statue of a black frontier cavalryman, at Fort Leavenworth, Kansas. It's a tribute to the men of the 9th and 10th Cavalry regiments. The units, which were organized and trained at Fort Leavenworth after the Civil War, were made up of former slaves. During the Indian Wars their foes nicknamed them "Buffalo Soldiers," a sobriquet that black American soldiers wore proudly until President Harry Truman desegregated the armed forces in the 1950s.

Since the unveiling, the army has created Patriots Park around the Buffalo Soldier memorial, and Mr. Dixon has added two more statues honoring black heroes: Risco Roberson, who became a four-star general, and Lieutenant Henry Flipper, the first black officer to graduate from West Point.

The Fort Leavenworth statue is the third Flipper bronze that Mr. Dixon has done. Another stands at Fort Davis National Historic Site, the frontier West Texas post where the lieutenant was court-martialed on racially motivated charges of "conduct unbecoming an officer" and drummed out of the army. Congress didn't clear his name until the 1970s.

Mr. Dixon also made a statue of Flipper for Thomasville, Georgia, his hometown, where he's buried.

Still another soldier statue by Mr. Dixon stands at the Fort Leavenworth gate. It represents Sergeant Major William Moses, the first Medal of Honor winner in the 10th Cavalry. "They tell me he gets as much attention as the Buffalo Soldier monument," Mr. Dixon says. "Everybody who enters the fort sees him."

And Mr. Dixon's statue of Eugene Bullard, a black American pilot who flew for the French during World War I, is in the Smithsonian Air and Space Museum in Washington.

"Bullard flew with the French escadrille before the Americans got involved in the war," Mr. Dixon says. "When the Americans came into the war, they recruited all the American volunteers who had been fighting for the French. But they wouldn't take Bullard because he was black. So he stayed with the French. He fought with the French underground during World War II as well.

"Then he came home and died in a cold-water flat in Harlem. When the French learned that he had died, they took his body to France and gave him a hero's burial."

One of Mr. Dixon's military pieces has yet to find a home. It's a statue of Cathy Williams, a black woman who changed her name to William Cathy, disguised herself as a man, and joined the army in 1867.

"She served for two-and-a-half years, until she became ill and a doctor examined her," Mr. Dixon says. "The statue was supposed to go in a park in Kansas, but it proved too controversial. She's still in limbo. I don't know where her final resting place will be."

Mr. Dixon's interest in military figures comes naturally. His father was a career air force man. "I was raised all over the world," he says. "We lived in Japan, in the Philippines. We traveled all over. But there's a disadvantage to that. You have no camaraderie. You have so very few attachments. You don't develop lasting friendships. It's almost like having no history."

Growing up, he never intended to become an artist. His undergraduate degree was in zoology and chemistry. Then he became a futures broker on the Chicago Board of Trade. "Futures can make you or break you overnight," he says. "You've got to be very careful." So he moved to Lubbock and earned a master's degree in medical entomology at Texas Tech.

One night he tried to carve a fancy candle using a stick and a butter knife. The candle turned into a warrior of the Punic Wars era. "I had been reading about Hannibal fighting the Romans," Mr. Dixon says. "I showed it to a lady named Verta Mae Todd, a teacher. She thought it had potential and told me I should have it cast. I didn't know anything about that, but Jerry House at House Bronze here in Lubbock cast the first pieces for me free. That's how I got started.

"I sold quite a few copies of my warrior. I don't think the people who bought him ever realized that he had six fingers on each hand. I thought a hand balanced out better that way. He had no eyes, either, because I hadn't discovered how to make them yet. He had heavy eyelids."

In 2000, the Texas Emancipation Juneteenth Historical and Cultural Commission, which was created by the legislature a few years ago, commissioned Mr. Dixon to make a memorial to be installed on the Capitol grounds. He competed for the job with sculptors from across the nation.

State Representative Al Edwards, Democrat of Houston, who wrote the 1979 law that made Juneteenth an official state holiday, is leading the effort to raise $1.5 million in state and private funds for a sculpture commemorating the emancipation of Texas slaves. ("Juneteenth" is the name the freed slaves gave to June 19, the day in 1865 that a Union general proclaimed their freedom.)

"As far as I know, this will be the first statue anywhere in the world depicting the freeing of the slaves," Mr. Edwards says.

Although it will be a memorial to liberation, Mr. Dixon sees it as a solemn piece.

"A lot of people think the slaves were happy and danced in the streets with tambourines when they heard the news," he says. "But I don't think so. In my design, a man is sitting on a cotton bale, showing other slaves a paper that says they're free. Some of his listeners are pensive. Others just don't believe it. And some are looking fearful. *Where will I go? Where will I work? Where will I live? How will I eat?* People don't dance in the street over such questions. One of the women is holding a child. The child is crying. She's symbolic of the future.

"I think we owe a historical legacy to the generations coming up," he says. "We need to tell them the story of what has gone before. I hope my sculptures do that."

Barrett World

When Neal Barrett, Jr., wrote his Tom Swift books, he was Victor Appleton. When he wrote his Hardy Boys mysteries, he was Franklin W. Dixon. When he was writing his sex-in-the-sagebrush adult westerns, he was Wesley Ellis, Terence Duncan, or Clay Dawson. Other times, he was J.D. Hardin, Chad Calhoun, Steve Atley, or Rebecca Drury.

As Neal Barrett, Jr., he wrote "novelizations" of Sylvester Stallone's dreadful movie *Judge Dredd* and the role-playing game *Dungeons and Dragons* and a novel about Spiderman. He wrote novel-length comic book scripts with such titles as *Bigfoot in Manhattan, Shootout at Ice Flats,* and *Jurassic Park: Death Lizard,* and one about Batman.

"I just kept writing," he says. "I've had good years and bad years, some dips and depressions. I just about burned out my brain on the westerns, writing so many of them so fast."

During one three-year period—1982-85—Mr. Barrett wrote ten westerns, two Hardy Boys, two Tom Swifts, three soft porn books for Playboy Press, and several science fiction novels.

Since he sold his first science fiction story to *Amazing* magazine in 1960, Mr. Barrett has published fifty-seven short stories and novelettes, fifty-one novels, two nonfiction books (histories of the YO Ranch and Texas A&M University), and twenty comic strip adaptations and original scripts.

"Hey," he says. "It's a check."

Despite his non-stop output and his willingness to take on almost any hack project when times were lean, Mr. Barrett has hard-won a reputation among critics and fellow authors as one of the keener practitioners of the writing craft, one of those guys who get called "a writer's writer." In almost every genre—science fiction, fantasy, western, mystery, even literary fiction—he has at least one book or story that's considered a classic. The thing they have in common is that they're all (pick your adjective here) weird, gonzo, off-the-wall, over-the-top, bizarre, oddball, outrageous. And utterly original.

"It's either genius or some form of insanity," says Joe R. Lansdale, another prolific Texas author whose fiction often is as bizarre and over-the-top as his friend's. "Neal has the ability to take small things and look at them in such a unique and odd way, a way that you've never seen before. He has the ability to look around corners imaginatively. He's one of the most creative writers I've ever read."

Let's take a tour through the Barrett *oeuvre*. Not the all-day Grey Lines trip, just a short walk, glancing at a few landmarks:

In a short story called "Sally C.," Orville and Wilbur Wright, Billy the Kid, Pat Garrett, and a young lad named Erwin Rommel, the future Nazi "desert fox," encounter each other at an isolated hotel in New Mexico. Garrett is trying to woo young Rommel's mother.

In a story called "Winter on the Belle Fourche," a mountain man rescues a New England prude named Emily Dickinson from lethal cold and marauding Indians in the Big Horn Mountains. She rewards him by stealing a sheaf of poems he has written. She takes them back to Massachusetts and uses them to launch her own poetic career.

Both stories are in *Perpetuity Blues and Other Stories*, the best of Mr. Barrett's several short-fiction collections.

In a novel called *Interstate Dreams*, a metal plate in the head of a damaged helicopter pilot called Dreamer inexplicably disarms any burglar alarm, security system, or fire alarm he happens to be around. This gets Dreamer—who now sells aquarium fish for his living—into trouble with competing gangs of bad guys, the cops, and several women.

Mr. Barrett's latest novel is *Piggs,* which is also the name of a strip joint where dancers Gloria Mundi, Whoopie LaCrane, and Minnie Mouth take it all off in the employ of Cecil R. Dupree, a redneck mobster. Gloria lives in a German bomber high up in a tree. A simple ex-con, who washes dishes in the world's worst Chinese restaurant, plots against the murderous Dupree and others for her love. Mr. Barrett advances bizarreness to new frontiers.

In 1991, after establishing himself during the eighties as a distinctive science fiction writer, Mr. Barrett published a literary novel called *The*

Hereafter Gang. It's about Doug Hoover, a Texas man in his fifties with a job in advertising and a bad marriage. He's a decadent Peter Pan who has no desire to grow up. Luckily, he doesn't have to. He dies.

Doug's journey to heaven is a road trip over torrid Texas highways in a Cadillac convertible with a sexy honey named Sue Jean. Heaven, it turns out, is in Oklahoma. It's very like the small town where Doug grew up. All his dead pets and girlfriends and heroes are there, healthy and happy. Everything—sports cars, candy bars, you name it—costs a nickel, and Doug can get all the nickels he needs from the barrels of them that are arranged along the sidewalks. He can be young forever, have all the model airplanes he wants, hang out with Jesse James, dogfight with the Red Baron in a World War I plane, and play basketball with Jesus.

"My heaven is a place where anybody would want to go," says Mr. Barrett. In a sense, he already has been there. The heaven in *The Hereafter Gang,* he says, is based on his memories of 1930s Ferris, Texas, where Neal the boy used to visit his grandmother.

Critic John Clute, reviewing *The Hereafter Gang* in *The Washington Post* called it "one of the great American novels." Then he added, "Find it if you can."

It was published by Ziesing, a small press in California with almost no resources for publicity or marketing. So the work that might have made Mr. Barrett a best-selling author if it had been published by a large commercial house became, instead, a cult classic.

It's a fate he has become used to. "When they call you a 'writer's writer,' that means the critics love you and the publishers *say* they love you, but they don't want to publish you because they don't want your weird stories on their record. They don't want to have to explain you to their bosses."

Also, some New York editors have told him, his work is too "regional." That might seem a strange thing to say about a science fiction writer. But the weirdness in a Barrett tale nearly always takes place in Texas, Oklahoma, or New Mexico. His science fiction, he says, is "county-wide, not galaxy-wide."

He likes to tell of a conference he had with a New York editor when he was trying to get *The Hereafter Gang* published:

"He says to me, 'Well, this is entirely too Southern. If you could set

Doug and Sue Jean in some place like Vermont, I might be interested.' In other words, he lives up there in New York and probably goes to Vermont from time to time. He never saw Texas or Oklahoma in his life, so he has no interest in it. Can you see Doug and Sue Jean up there with all that maple syrup? Can you see them any place in the world except Texas? That's the sort of thing that just gives you the shakes."

Mr. Barrett suspects the weirdness of his mind—or "genius," as Mr. Lansdale calls it—may have been the result of a number of unsettling experiences with celebrities when he was a little boy.

"My dad managed a radio station in Oklahoma City," he says. "It was pre-TV, so all the celebrities who came to town would come to the radio station. My dad would pick me up at school, and we'd go to their hotel room to meet them.

"They were always changing clothes when we arrived. Gene Autry would be wearing his shorts and his shirt and socks with those garters that men wore back then. I was just crushed. It did something to a little boy's dreams to see Gene and Roy in their underwear."

Furthermore, when he bragged to his friends that he had met Gene or Roy or Bob or Bing, they never believed him. "I'd say, 'I met Gene Autry.' And they'd say, 'You sure as hell didn't.' And they would beat me up."

Despite its shaky beginning, Mr. Barrett's life seemed normal for years. He graduated from high school in 1948, got a degree from the University of Oklahoma, and worked in Dallas from the mid-fifties to the mid-seventies as a public relations man. While cranking out press releases and in-house newsletters for Southwestern Life, Braniff Airlines, LTV, and other big corporations, he also was writing books on the sly.

"I wrote them on company time," he says, "on their typewriters. And copied them on their Xerox machines."

The real Neal Barrett, Jr., began to blossom. In 1960, *Amazing* accepted a short story called "Made in Archerius," the first of many he would sell to science fiction magazines. Ten years later, he sold three sci-fi novels—*Kelwin, The Gates of Time*, and *Highwood*—to mass paperback houses. "*Kelwin* is about a post-apocalypse antique dealer," he says. "He sells hubcaps and stuff." In 1975, Mr. Barrett quit his PR job and never looked back.

Several years ago, he sold the film rights to one of his crime novels, *Pink Vodka Blues,* to Paramount in "a mid-six-figures deal." But Hollywood has proved as puzzling to him as New York. "To this day, I don't know why they bought it," he says. "They've never done anything with it. Why would they want to own it and not make a movie of it?"

So he sits at his desk in his comfortable little room in his purple house in a modest South Austin neighborhood and writes. Constantly. "A lot of people do good work and don't get to the top," he says. "And a lot of people do bad work and do get there. I'm doing my best work for small publishers because the big publishers won't touch it. They don't know how to categorize it. They don't know what genre to print on the spine."

He says he's working on "kind of a semi-Victorian novel that's not a fantasy, not science fiction. It's kind of an altered-history Victorian. Some peculiar things take place."

The bookshelves in his room are full of old historical novels—*Captain from Castile, Prince of Foxes*, the works of C.S. Forester and Patrick O'Brien—and model airplanes and Big Little Books and the works of Neal Barrett, Jr.

His twelve-year-old squirrel-colored cat, Sue Jean, is curled on a chair, sleeping. His wife, Ruth, is in the next room, talking quietly on the phone.

It could be heaven.

Hotel

For decades, the Hotel Limpia on the Fort Davis courthouse square was a Duncan family heartache. It was such a heartache that when Joe Duncan tried to buy the hotel from his brother Jim twelve years ago, he was turned down flat.

"No." Jim said. "I'll sell it to anybody but you. I won't do that to my little brother."

Jim Duncan, an electrical engineer, was running his own company in Dallas. He had bought the old stone hotel from his widowed mother just to take it off her hands. "She was aging and unable to run the business," Joe says.

After trying for a while to operate the hotel from Dallas, Jim found a buyer and was about to unload it cheap. "It was a worry on his mind," Joe says.

Joe also lived in Dallas. He was in real estate, managing commercial properties for Henry S. Miller. "I had kissed Fort Davis goodbye more than ten years before and thought I would never come back," he says.

"We were enjoying the city life in Dallas," says Lanna, his wife. She was a counselor in the Highland Park schools in those days. "We were having a ball."

But there they were, begging Jim to sell them a hotel built in 1912-13 and badly in need of renovation. It had been a failure since World War II, and hadn't amounted to much before that.

"The more determined Jim became not to sell it to us," Joe says, "the more determined we became to buy it."

At last, Jim gave in. On New Year's Eve 1990, Joe and Lanna signed the papers. Then they drove the eight hours from Dallas to Fort Davis to have a look at their new—but old and familiar—property.

Their first night in the Limpia, Lanna says, "We just lay there on the bed, staring at the ceiling, and thinking, 'What have we done?'"

Today Joe and Lanna Duncan are proprietors of a small far West Texas tourist business empire. During the twelve years they've owned the Limpia, their town has become a major tourist destination. "There's very little we can take credit for," Lanna says. "We hit Fort Davis when it was ripe and ready." The hotel is a big success. So are its associated restaurant and gift-and-book shop and its bar, the only watering hole in Jeff Davis County.

Meanwhile, the Duncans have bought and renovated the adobe hotel annex—built in the 1920s for summer-long residents—and have converted it into comfortable suites. They've bought the stone Dumas Building across the street from the Limpia and have turned it into a second gift shop with guestrooms upstairs. They've bought five residences in the town—most of them more than 100 years old—and turned them into guesthouses. In all, the Duncans now have thirty-nine rooms to rent in Fort Davis.

"Buying the old homes has been our way of expanding our business, rather than building units onto the hotel," Mr. Duncan says. "That way, if hard times come again, we could sell the houses as residences."

In 2001, the Duncans expanded beyond Fort Davis into neighboring Marfa, twenty-one miles to the south, where they bought the historic Hotel Paisano at an auction on the Presidio County courthouse steps. The move surprised even them.

The Paisano was the elegant showplace of the Big Bend in the 1930s and 40s. It had housed director George Stevens' crew when he was filming *Giant* on a nearby ranch in 1955. Briefly, before they moved into private homes in the town, even the film's stars—Elizabeth Taylor, Rock Hudson, and James Dean—lived at the hotel.

But the Paisano had fallen on hard times and had been made victim of a number of half-baked business schemes. Most recently it had been an unsuccessful time-share condominium with more than 800 small shareholders. When it was announced that the famous hotel was going on the auction block to recover delinquent property taxes, people all over Texas were interested. It was rumored that a very wealthy man from Dallas was going to buy it and fix it up again.

Joe and Lanna drove over to Marfa to watch the auction. "It was a big social event," Joe says. "There were luncheon tables with white tablecloths on the courthouse lawn. Two hundred people were there. But they were all locals. They had come just to see who bought the hotel."

Lanna persuaded a reluctant Joe that they should sign up to bid, just for the heck of it. Then things started to happen. The Dallas rich man changed his mind and scratched his name from the bidders' list. The only remaining potential buyer was an architect from Florida.

So Lanna opened the bidding at just $158,500. "Nobody said anything," Joe says. "Nobody was prepared to bid." Finally, the Florida man placed his bid. Lanna countered with a bid of $185,000.

And that was it. The Duncans had bought themselves another hotel.

"The whole thing took about thirty seconds," Joe says. "It's not something you casually do on a Tuesday morning—go buy a hotel. We hadn't even looked at the Paisano. We hadn't been inside the building."

A TV reporter from Midland asked Lanna, "What are your plans?"

She replied: "I'm picking up Malcolm [their son] at three-thirty, and we're having tacos for dinner."

The Paisano was in such bad shape that daylight was shining through the roof. But the Duncans already have renovated more than half of its forty rooms and are open for business. Their plans include a restaurant with patio dining, a bar, and a *Giant* museum. They also are going to reopen the swimming pool.

And their luck is holding. After years of decline as a ranch town, Marfa is beginning to flourish as an international art tourism destination, thanks to the modern sculptures that the great minimalist artist Donald Judd installed in many of the town's empty buildings more than twenty years ago. Art mavens from around the world are showing up by the busload to see the works of Judd, Claes Oldenburg, Dan Flavin, and others whose names are far more familiar in Europe than in Texas.

"The clientele at the Paisano is not your West Texas crowd," Joe says. "They're from New York, from Switzerland. They come to Marfa for the art."

Lanna and Joe are children of old West Texas ranch families. Lanna's ancestors, the Tweedys, came from Knickerbocker, New York, in 1878 and founded the village of Knickerbocker in Tom Green County. The Tweedy Ranch is still there. But Lanna's father, Malcolm Tweedy, was a school-teacher, and she grew up in Pennsylvania, where he taught.

Both sides of Joe's family, the Duncans and the McCutcheons, arrived in the Trans-Pecos in 1883 and established huge ranch holdings north of the Davis Mountains that stretched clear to Fort Stockton.

Joe's parents, J.C. and Isabelle Duncan, followed in the family tradition through the early 1950s. Then a devastating seven-year drought hit the region.

"It was terrible times for ranching," Joe says. "When my brother Jim started to school, they moved from the ranch into town. My father liked being in town. He could see that he didn't really want to ranch." J.C. and Isabelle became teachers in the Fort Davis schools.

Early on an August evening in 1953, the Hotel Limpia caught fire. The entire town turned out to watch it burn. By the time the Fort Davis and Marfa volunteer fire departments extinguished the blaze, the upper floor of the old building was damaged badly.

The hotel had been declining for a long time. It was built to cater to wealthy Houstonians who, in the early twentieth century, came to the mountain village of Fort Davis—which advertised itself as "Air-Conditioned by Nature"—to escape the summer heat. But when urban Texas installed its own air-conditioning after World War II, the Houston crowd stopped coming. There was little demand for hotel rooms in Fort Davis.

"Daddy bought it that fall, after it burned," Joe says. "He thought there would be a future here, and someday there would be a need for the hotel again."

While he waited, J.C. converted the hotel's first floor into offices and built several apartments on the second floor. Then in 1959, the year Joe was born, J.C. and Isabelle sold out and moved to Austin for graduate work at the University of Texas. "He thought he wanted to get a Ph.D.," Joe says. "But after a year, he saw that wasn't for him, so we moved back to Fort Davis."

In 1972 J.C. and Isabelle bought the hotel again. It wasn't in shape to receive visitors, but they opened a gift shop on the property. "Everybody in town thought they were crazy," Joe says. "They were saying, 'Why are you messing with that hotel? Why do you think tourism is the future here?' Even my grandmother asked, 'Why are you wasting your time with this?'"

Three years later, J.C. opened the restaurant, and by 1978 he had renovated the hotel.

Joe, who was majoring in business at the University of North Texas, came home in the summers to help out. "My father thought we needed a drinking establishment in Fort Davis," he says. "A lot of people thought we didn't. But he thought if you're going to run a historic hotel, you've got to have a restaurant and you've got to have a bar."

So he sent Joe to bartender school in Dallas. When the bar opened in 1979, Joe was mixing the drinks and Lanna, who had graduated from Penn State and was teaching in Odessa, was the barmaid. She was spending the summer with her parents, who had retired to Fort Davis and had bought a motel.

"Lanna and I got well acquainted that summer," Joe says, "and she came back the next summer. Business was quiet in those days. At eight or nine o'clock we would declare last call so we could go to a street dance in Valentine or Marfa or Alpine."

In the late seventies, just as he finally had got his hotel going, J.C. was diagnosed with Lou Gehrig's disease. He died in the fall of 1982, when Joe was about to graduate from North Texas.

Joe and Lanna married the following summer. Their wedding was in front of the ruins of the old military chapel at the Fort Davis National Historic Site. "It was the first wedding at the fort since 1895," Lanna says. The newlyweds settled in Dallas and meant to stay there.

In 1984 the Duncan family sold the Limpia and its auxiliary businesses. "Then the oil bust was happening," Joe says. "Things were getting even worse out here. Things were sliding." The family eventually had to foreclose. Soon thereafter, big brother Jim bought the property from his mother and prepared to unload it for a song.

At first, that was fine with Joe. "I didn't want to be out here in Fort Davis," he says. "I had always had to wash dishes, wait tables, flip eggs.

I wanted to be a businessman in the big city. I wanted to be in downtown Dallas."

In August 1990, Jim was negotiating the sale of the hotel with his prospective buyer. Joe and Lanna made their annual pilgrimage back home for the Bloys Camp Meeting, a weeklong encampment for religious services and socializing that West Texas ranch families have been doing for more than 100 years. They brought some Dallas friends with them.

"Our friends wanted to see the old hotel," Joe says. "So on the way back to Dallas, we showed it to them. They couldn't understand how we could give up the place. They couldn't understand why we didn't want to live in Fort Davis. They were convinced that we should buy it. All the way back to Dallas they tried to persuade us." By the time they hit the Big D city limits, Joe and Lanna had decided to go back to the tiny village in the mountains.

☆

"We worked hard," Joe says. "We did everything ourselves. The odds were against us. We cooked at night in the restaurant and painted rooms during the day. We had only four employees, which we had inherited."

"Sometimes," Lanna says, "Joe would be painting and would have to stop and go cook a chicken-fried steak for a customer."

They were having to tell their infrequent guests, "Don't fall over the bucket that's catching the leak in the hallway. Don't trip over the hole in the carpet." They were very tired.

In the summer of 1993 their son Malcolm was born. "Lanna and I were on the edge of burnout," Joe says. "But Malcolm's arrival forced us to step back a little and establish a home life."

They hired managers for the hotel and the dining room. They hired people to do the painting and cooking and cleaning. Now they have a staff of fifty or more.

"People always say to us, 'Oh, running your own business is the American dream,'" Lanna says. "And I always say, 'Well, we'll let you know when it becomes that.'"

"But it's no longer a nightmare," Joe says.

Digger

The view from the bluff above Garcitas Creek is unremarkable. Just the dark water below, a stretch of flat coastal prairie on the other side, and a line of scrubby trees along the horizon. On this winter morning, the landscape is gloomy and gray under a cold and gloomy sky, but Jim Bruseth is gazing at it in awe.

"Almost nothing has changed," he says. "It's the same as it was when La Salle was here."

Dr. Bruseth, forty-eight years old, slender as a reed, studious looking in an outdoors way, is director of the Archaeology Division of the Texas Historical Commission. A few yards from where he's standing, several field archaeologists are scraping at the dense, black soil. They're painstakingly unearthing the pitiful remains of Fort St. Louis, the colony established by French explorer Robert Cavelier, Sieur de La Salle.

The site is in Victoria County, a few miles up Garcitas from Matagorda Bay. The explorer and 280 followers stepped ashore on the Texas Gulf Coast in 1685 thinking they were at the mouth of the Mississippi River. Thus began one of the saddest tales in Texas history, made more vivid every day by the artifacts that Dr. Bruseth and his colleagues are uncovering.

A few years before his arrival in Texas, La Salle had floated down the Mississippi and claimed its vast watershed for France. Then he persuaded King Louis XIV to finance an expedition to approach the river's mouth from the sea and build a French colony there to challenge Spain's dominance of the wild shore lands of the Gulf. But La Salle's maps were faulty. He overshot his intended destination by 400 miles. It was the first of many miscalculations and disasters that eventually would doom the great explorer and his enterprise.

For two years, La Salle and his men tramped the Texas countryside looking for his river. Tempers grew short and shorter until finally some of his disgruntled followers murdered him. Meanwhile back at the fort, La Salle's colonists were dying of diseases and snakebites, being eaten by alligators or killed by Indians or murdering one another in drunken brawls. In January 1688 the Karankawas attacked and finished off the remnant of the colony. The handful of settlers who survived all this walked out of Texas to a French outpost in Illinois.

"Because he failed, people don't realize how important La Salle was," says Dr. Bruseth. "But his effort to build a colony here forced the Spanish to send missionaries and soldiers to Texas to hold onto the northern frontier of their empire. Otherwise, the French might come back and try to colonize Texas again."

The diggers, under Dr. Bruseth's supervision, uncovered more than 1,000 French artifacts that had lain hidden in the ground for more than 300 years—bits of glass, china, and pottery, musket balls, gun flints, religious medallions, pieces of copper pots, and the like. They've also found more than 18,000 similar Spanish artifacts from the large presidio that Spain built on the spot to discourage the French from trying again.

They discovered the jumbled bones of two or three people, almost certainly victims of the Karankawa massacre. Dr. Bruseth believes that Spanish soldiers under the command of General Alonso de León buried the remains. The Spaniards had been searching for La Salle's settlement for two years. They found it five months after the Indians had wiped it out and wild animals had scattered the bones of its dead.

"I've worked on a lot of archaeological sites, but it's really wonderful to have one that has such an incredible history surrounding it," Dr. Bruseth says. "The great French explorer La Salle walked on this ground. And the Spanish General Alonso de León and other major figures in Texas history. Events unfolded at this site that changed Texas history and U.S. history. The rivalry between France and Spain was big-time world politics, like the rivalry between the U.S. and the Soviet Union used to be. And the controversy between those two world powers centered on this spot."

He speaks of La Salle and de León and the settlers with the energy of a boy describing an adventure tale he's reading. He's steeped in the ancient journals and letters and reports in which the fate of the colony is told, and can recite passages from memory.

"When you get into the historical documents, you see why Fort St. Louis was so important," he says. "At the time the French landed here, Spain was dependent on its wealth from the New World, which was coming back to Europe on its treasure ships. About sixty percent of Spain's wealth was from silver mines in northern Mexico. Spain was desperately afraid the French would take over some of those mines and the Spanish crown would lose a huge source of revenue.

"So you see why Spain launched some eleven expeditions to try to find the French fort, and why Spain came back later and built an elaborate presidio on the same spot. They wanted to make sure that the wealth from the New World that was propping up the Spanish crown would continue. They weren't going to allow France or any other country to stop it."

Dr. Bruseth's fascination with archaeology dates from his boyhood in Slidell, Louisiana, where he liked to walk around the countryside with his head down, looking for arrowheads. He found a lot of them. He read books about Indians and what archaeologists had found out about them.

"I joined the local archaeological society," he says. "I began to realize there was more to archaeology than just picking up artifacts as curiosity pieces. I quit collecting that stuff and began looking at archaeological techniques and learning how to interpret the things that were found. That got me interested in the Indian cultures of Louisiana and East Texas and Mississippi, who did wonderful things with pottery and stonework."

When he graduated from Slidell High School, his parents told him they would pay his way through college.

"Great!" he said. "I want to be an archaeologist!"

"No, no," his parents said. "We're not going to pay for that."

"They wanted me to get some practical degree," Dr. Bruseth says. "I guess they were worried that they had a kid they would have to support for the rest of their lives." So his undergraduate degree from the University of New Orleans was in business management.

But he filled up his electives with every anthropology course he could cram into his schedule. And as soon as he got his diploma, in 1974, he made a beeline for Southern Methodist University and enrolled as a graduate student in archaeology.

Because he was paying his own way this time and working part-time on archaeological field projects, it took him twelve years to earn his Ph.D. Then he worked for a year in the university administration, helping professors write grant proposals for their research projects.

"I really, really missed archaeology," he says. "So when a job opened up with the Texas Historical Commission, I applied for it. And I got it." He went to work there in 1987, mostly excavating Indian sites in East Texas, which was his specialty.

Then in the summer of 1995, Barto Arnold, the Texas Historical Commission's marine archaeologist, found the wreck of one of La Salle's ships, *La Belle*, on the floor of murky Matagorda Bay.

The commission built a cofferdam around the ship, drained the water out of the enclosure, and excavated *La Belle* as if it were on dry land. Dr. Bruseth directed the work. While the excavation of *La Belle* was still underway, a ranch hand discovered eight French cannons that de León's soldiers were known to have buried. The discovery confirmed the site of Fort St. Louis. Dr. Bruseth's life has been inextricably entwined with La Salle's ever since.

His crew recovered a large piece of the hull of *La Belle*. Inside was a trove of artifacts that Dr. Bruseth describes as a New World "colony kit." Still packed in their barrels and crates were the colonists' supplies for building their settlement, goods to trade with the Indians, hundreds of personal items, and even the skeleton of a man who died on the ship, probably of thirst.

Archaeologists now consider *La Belle* one of the major shipwreck discoveries and excavations in the world.

"I keep saying that I hope my work on the *Belle* wasn't the highlight of my career, but it may have been," says Dr. Bruseth. "For eight months, that was one of the most exciting archaeological projects going on anywhere in the world. And I had the absolute pleasure of directing it. Sometimes I would have to pinch myself and say, 'I'm really here. This is really it. Look at what I'm doing here.'"

Almost immediately after the excavation of *La Belle* was complete, the excavation of Fort St. Louis began. So for five years now, Dr. Bruseth has spent his days on Matagorda Bay and on the bluff above Garcitas Creek, studying La Salle and his doomed followers. He drives back to Austin and his home and his wife, Toni, only on weekends.

"Toni is an extremely understanding woman," he says. "She was an archaeologist, too, until we realized that one of us had to get a real job to make ends meet. She tolerates a lot from me."

But when the Fort St. Louis excavation ends, probably sometime this year, Dr. Bruseth hopes to stay put for a while and write his scholarly reports and maybe a book about all he has found.

"Beyond that, I don't know what circumstances will bring me my next site," he says. "Seven or eight years ago, I never thought in my wildest dreams that I would be doing what I'm doing now."

Columbia

It was the kind of crystal day that, when you saw it, you were glad to be in the world. The sun already was warming, a blessing for the first day of February. The sky spread, from rim to rim, that deep, cloudless blue that makes the heart ache when you look up at it.

Then at eight o'clock, the muffled boom, and windows rattled. The white plume arced across the blue. Columbia was falling, raining its remnants upon Texas.

Death had come again in the bright shiny morning. Quickly our crystal day began to resemble that other bright morning that hurts so much to remember: September 11, 2001, when death flew from the sky into New York City and Washington and the Pennsylvania countryside. And (it seems ancient history now) January 28, 1986, when Challenger exploded before the eyes of the nation's schoolchildren, who were rejoicing because a teacher was voyaging into space.

Numbing images on the TV screen. Repeating, repeating: the white streak across flawless heavens, breaking up, separating, falling. TV voices droning, droning, although they have pitifully little yet to tell. The phone ringing. Family and friends, calling to tell you of the woe in case you haven't heard, their voices full of grief, beckoning you into our latest national sorrow. The president at the microphones again, grim, praising the dead, calling us yet another time to courage.

Such days are becoming too familiar. We begin to worry that they may define our time, these shining mornings of joy and hope that suddenly plunge us into horror and disaster beyond understanding. We seem voyagers through a time of anguish in which our response to recurring national tragedy is, "Oh, no. Not again," and accident is the second or third possibility that enters our minds as the cause of our every injury.

But eventually we shall love looking at the sky again, and we shall hug this sorrow to ourselves as we have so many others in our near and distant past. It will scar over and become part of our national soul. The morning of Columbia, February 1, 2003, will be another of those events that will move us to say, years down our history, "Do you remember where you were when . . ."

And the reply will always be, "Yes, I was . . ."

In Texas, it was one of those crystal days that, when you saw it, you were glad to be in the world.

Road Trip

U.S. Highway 80 crosses from Louisiana into Texas on the eastern out-skirts of Waskom. An old concrete marker shaped like Texas stands in tall grass beside the pavement. Markers like it were set up in the old days beside all the highway entrances to the state, to let travelers know they were entering a special place.

In its glory days, Highway 80 crossed the whole continent, all 2,671 miles from Savannah to San Diego. Through Georgia, Alabama, Mississippi, Louisiana, and about half of Texas, it threaded through miles and miles of pine forests and cotton fields.

Depending on the time of year, motorists could watch poor white and black sharecroppers trudging behind their mules, planting or cultivating their crops, or hoeing or picking them. In winter, the cotton stalks stood dead in the fields and smoke curled from the chimneys of the farmers' gray shanties.

West of Fort Worth, the landscape changed, and the road plunged into cowboy country.

Across the Deep South and East Texas, Highway 80 now shares the lush landscape with newer, bigger, faster Interstate 20, though as a crip-pled and threadbare cousin. In the West, the old road has given up its place entirely to the interstates. Officially, there's no longer any Highway 80 west of Mesquite. But its ghost is still out there, haunting the little towns where it used to go. You just have to get off the interstates to find it.

The East Texas Tourism Association and other boosters in Texas and Louisiana have begun a campaign to have Highway 80 designated a his-toric highway, similar to famous Route 66, which carried travelers from Chicago to Los Angeles and became known as the Main Street of America. The remnants of 66 attract off-the-interstate tourists and adventurers from around the world who want to feel the romance and freedom of an old-fashioned American road trip. They spend a lot of money along the way.

Couldn't a cross-country drive across the South and Southwest be just as exciting and romantic? Or a waltz across 800 miles of Texas?

JONESVILLE

A little west of Waskom and a couple of miles north of 80 stands a relic of those long-gone King Cotton days. The sign says: "T.C. Lindsey Company, Jonesville, Texas. Continuous Operation since 1847." When you step up to the porch of the big white frame building, you feel you're entering an emporium that Faulkner's conniving Snopes family owned, or the store that Paul Newman ran in the movie version of *The Long, Hot Summer*. But the Lindsey family has always owned this one.

"The original Lindseys were Tom, Dick, and Harry," says the eighty-year-old clerk, Sybel Elliott. "Dick had a store across the street, and Harry had a store over in Louisiana. Mr. Dick closed his store the week I came to work over here. That was 1957. Mrs. Tom Lindsey was a Vaughn, and she and Mr. Tom didn't have any children. So when they died, the two nephews, Mr. Sam and Mr. Tom Vaughn, took over the store. The present owners are Mr. Tom and his three daughters and Patsy Vaughn from Dallas. She's Mr. Sam's daughter."

The T.C. Lindsey Company's merchandise is vast and various. It fills glass cases and counters and racks and shelves and hangs from the walls. Kerosene lanterns and lamps, patent medicines, pocketknives, ice hooks, straw hats, shirts, books, CDs, iron skillets, halters and hackamores, ropes, tires, insect spray, Dutch ovens, washtubs, coal scuttles, pocket watches, belt buckles, honey, Campbell's soup, Crisco, pantyhose, first-aid kits, bandanas, suspenders, clocks, thermometers, sun bonnets, walking canes, chewing tobacco, rocking chairs, bib overalls, porch swings, hand-cranked ice cream freezers.

Old Texas auto license plates and a poster of Waskom's own Miss Texas 1962, Penny Lee Rudd, adorn a wall. There are saddles, blacksmith tools, a birdcage, a coffee grinder, meat grinders, old telephones and radios, paint, crockery, motor oil, a weathervane, Longhorn cattle horns, farm tools of every description, the stuffed heads of a deer and a javelina, a whole stuffed bear, a collection of brass knuckles.

"Mr. Sam collected those," says Mrs. Elliott. "He collected everything."

The antiques aren't for sale. But over the years, Mr. Sam's collections have become kind of jumbled in with the merchandise. To know what's for sale and what isn't, you have to ask Mrs. Elliott. She has been sorting it out for forty-five years.

"The last bale of cotton ginned in Jonesville was in 1973," says Mrs. Elliott. The abandoned gin still looms across the street, next to Mr. Dick's abandoned store. "We don't have no cotton around here now," Mrs. Elliott says. "What we have is busloads coming in. Last Tuesday morning we had a bus coming from the Marshall Manor. Senior citizens that came in."

MARSHALL

Marshall, in a quirk of a chaotic time, was the Confederate capital of Missouri. You hear how it happened from the volunteer who shows visitors around the Harrison County Historical Museum in the old Ginocchio Hotel beside the railroad tracks in the town.

Marshall is proud of its Old South past. Relics of plantation days fill glass cases in the museum. A portrait of Edward Clark, a Marshall man who served as the first Confederate governor of Texas, hangs on a wall.

Other cases hold relics of famous Harrison County people from more recent times: civil rights leader James Farmer, boxing champion George Foreman, TV wise man Bill Moyers, Y.A. Tittle, who played seventeen years for the 49ers and the Giants, Dallas Cowboys fullback Robert Newhouse, Captain Mack Henry Hopkins, a Tuskegee airman.

But for those in the know, the real attraction for the back-roads pilgrim in Marshall is Neely's: Home of the Brown Pig, founded in 1927 by James and Frances Neely.

The Brown Pig is a barbecue sandwich. Thousands who have entered the unpretentious diner and ordered a Brown Pig have returned to their cars raving of it in terms usually reserved for French truffles or Russian caviar.

"The secret is in the sauce," says Sue Lazaro, who with her sister Sally Cobb owns the place now. And that's all she will reveal about the Brown Pig.

LONGVIEW

Howard Rosser is the director of the East Texas Tourism Association and Highway 80's most tireless promoter. He lives in Longview. When he talks about Highway 80, he gets excited and emphatic. "We want to be able to erect signs and publicize what there is to see along this road!" he says. "We want to preserve the road itself! We want to get people to cruising Highway 80 the way they do on Route 66! Route 66 didn't even go coast to coast!"

The Vicksburg battlefield, where in 1863 the South lost one of the most important battles of the Civil War, is on Highway 80 over in Mississippi. Dr. Martin Luther King, Jr., led the voting-rights marchers along Highway 80 from Selma to Montgomery in 1965. The first automobile trip in Texas—from Terrell to Dallas in 1899—was along the route that later became Highway 80.

When the government paved Highway 80 through the town in 1932, the road was only sixteen feet wide. Mr. Rosser knows where a stretch of the original highway and an old iron bridge still survive, just east of Hallsville.

It's a forlorn place. Bushes and trees have reclaimed the right-of-way. Just a few small patches of asphalt are visible. The rusty little bridge stands like an archaeological ruin with jungle encroaching. Piles of trash rot in the steamy heat under the trees and vines.

But Mr. Rosser is a visionary. "You can see how this place could be preserved as a place where people could come and walk or ride bicycles," he says.

EAST TEXAS

The highway through East Texas is a journey through green. Forests of pine and broad-leaf species crowd the narrow road, sometimes making it an open-topped tunnel. Meadows and pastures are lush, their grasses long after summer rains. The rails of the Texas & Pacific Railroad (now Union Pacific, after all the railway mergers) are the highway's constant companion. Long, multi-engined freight trains roar through the timber.

BIG SANDY

There's a dance at Family World in Big Sandy every Monday, Thursday, and Saturday nights. Nearly all the people filing through the door and handing over $3.50 each to Alice Nolan are at least sixty years old. Most are older. On this night, the eldest is ninety-four.

"They really enjoy dancing," says Ms. Nolan. She owns Family World with her husband Dick. "They make friends. They have lots of fun. They need something to do. I've had people tell me, 'All day Sunday and all day Monday, I'm waiting for this thing to open.' A lot of them come all three nights every week."

Family World is a rambling frame building beside Highway 80 on the shore of a small lake. Built in the 1930s, it was a skating rink by day and a dancehall by night. When the Nolans bought it two years ago, they decided to stick strictly with the dancing.

"This used to be such a big place," Ms. Nolan says. "They had paddleboats, they had a picnic area, they had a bathhouse, they had a concession stand. A lot of years ago, it was a nice place to be. I'd love to get it back to the way it was."

More than 200 people have come tonight to kick up their heels as best they can. For every man who shows up, there are five or six women. "A lot of the ladies were paying to come in, but they didn't get to dance," Ms. Nolan says. "So the guys in the band started up the chair dance."

A chair dance—designed to get everybody out of their chairs—works like this: Half the ladies line up at one end of the long dance floor and half at the other. When the music starts, each gentleman grabs up the first lady standing in one of the lines and dances her the length of the floor to the other end. There she takes her place at the end of the line to wait her turn again. The man then takes a new partner from the head of the line and dances away. As he drops off each partner, he gives her a polite little bow.

Mr. Nolan and his band Starlight play the songs the dancers knew when they were young and limber: "Waltz Across Texas," "Beer Barrel Polka," "Milk Cow Blues." Everybody literally has a ball.

"I love this place," Ms. Nolan says. "My only problem is that I get so attached to the people who come here. I've lost several this year. We lost one last week. That's hard for me."

GLADEWATER

An old oil derrick and pump jack stand beside the Texas & Pacific tracks in Gladewater, but the town isn't about petroleum anymore. The brick and stone buildings where East Texas oil field workers used to buy their clothes and food and hardware are crammed now with antique furniture and china and knickknacks.

The cloying sweetness of bayberry and the cute signs on the storefronts would draw derision and curses from the roughnecks and roustabouts of yesteryear. Coach House Antique Mall, B&B Antiques, Gladewater Antique Mall, Country Girl Collection, Fuller's Antiques and Goodies, Good Old Stuff, Wayside Shop, Antiques II, The Loft, The Blue Geranium, Peg's Place, Yesterday's Treasures. And that's just one street.

MINEOLA

In Mineola, Jimmy Rushing is sitting in the shoeshine chair at his Broadway Barbershop, awaiting the first customer of his day. His shop harks back to an earlier time, but not because of any effort on his part to be quaint. He's just an old-fashioned kind of barber.

"I'm not a stylist and this shop is not a salon," he says. "I don't do no fancy cutting."

The shop is on Broad Street, downtown Mineola's main thoroughfare, which is also Highway 80. Mr. Rushing has been cutting hair there since 1961.

"We're about halfway between Dallas and Shreveport," Mr. Rushing says. "Before Interstate 20, people would stop here to eat and rest. They would come in off the highway, and I would cut their hair. Several restaurants made their living off the road. People liked to get out of their cars and walk around town a little bit. But as soon as Interstate 20 opened, Mineola started going down. Several years ago, this town was nearly dead."

But business has picked up, he says. "They got some grants to redo the sidewalks and the streetlights and kind of spruce things up. They gave the businesses some money to paint their fronts. Now things are going good."

The shoeshine stand is just inside the door, near the plate glass window. "My shine man passed away five or six years ago back in the back room," Mr. Rushing says. "Heart attack. Tennis shoes busted that business wide open. Nobody can make a living shining shoes anymore."

So nobody works at the stand now. Mr. Rushing sits there during idle time and watches the world pass by.

"It's the same haircut I've been doing for forty years," he says. "If they want something else, there are four hair salons in town."

"What's the difference between a barbershop and a hair salon?" you ask. "About twenty bucks," he replies.

GRAND SALINE

Inside the Salt Palace at Grand Saline, you find out everything you ever wanted to know about sodium chloride: salt through the ages, rock salt production, experiments you can do in your school or home with salt. You hear the history of the Salt Palace itself.

"This is the fourth Salt Palace that has stood in Grand Saline," says Lynn Kitchens, who handles tourist information for the city. "The first three were built of solid salt, about 10 feet square. They were just block on block of salt. So when they began to deteriorate, a wall would fall off. The last Salt Palace lasted eighteen years, which isn't bad for a solid salt building. When it finally came down, it looked like an igloo."

The present Salt Palace—a small square building that serves as the town's visitor center—was built in 1993. Its outside walls are blocks of salt, too, but that's just a veneer. Inside, the walls are of more usual material. "So, with some maintenance, we can repair and replace the exterior salt," Ms. Kitchens says. "This Salt Palace should last indefinitely."

Salt is the reason Grand Saline exists, she explains. Morton, the "When It Rains It Pours" people, have been mining there for seventy-two years.

"There's enough salt left in the mine for about 20,000 years," Ms. Kitchens says. "Then we're going to be in trouble." She laughs.

TERRELL

As Highway 80 nears Dallas, the trees thin out. The road runs through open prairie, under a widening sky. Just east of Terrell, cars and trucks crowd the parking lot at the Ham Orchard. Peach lovers have come for the final glorious days of the summer harvest, and to gorge on Dale and Judy Ham's homemade peach ice cream.

Mr. Ham was a firefighter in Richardson for thirty-two years, and a captain in the University Park Police Department before that. "I finally got burned out," he says. "I never thought I would, but I did."

In 1978, he bought this farm beside Highway 80 and began planting peach trees. He planted 500 at first, then kept adding to them. "The peach business got so big that I couldn't handle it and be a fireman at the same time," he says. "So I retired." Now the Hams have between 3,000 and 4,000 trees.

Mr. Ham loves his land and his trees and his work, and loves to talk about them. "We're just finishing up our three main summer varieties," he says. "Loring, Bounty, and Majestic. They're three of the best that we grow, and they all come off the trees at the same time. Right after they finish, we start on Dixieland, and it's also an awful good peach. We've been picking Dixieland, Cresthaven, and Glory. Then we finish up with Quachita Gold.

"So far, we've just had an unbelievably good season. On Friday, Saturday, and Sunday, it's almost too confusing to try to handle. It's wild. It's just a zoo down here."

MESQUITE

At the edge of Mesquite, Highway 80 melds into Interstate 30. The roadside "U.S. 80" shields disappear. The old road ceases to be an official highway. But if you have an old, old map and want to follow it through the vast metropolitan area, you can.

Just take Samuell Boulevard, Commerce Street (oops, that's one way the wrong way now), and Davis Avenue through Dallas. Then Main Street through Grand Prairie, Division Street through Arlington, and Lancaster Avenue and Camp Bowie Boulevard through Fort Worth.

Now you've arrived in an entirely different country, where the West begins.

Road Trip II

When Highway 80 was the main road across Texas, you couldn't get through Weatherford without driving around the Parker County courthouse. It stood smack in the middle of the highway. Now 80 is gone, and Weatherford is just another ramp off Interstate 20.

Beyond the courthouse, the road that used to be Highway 80 is called Ranger Highway. The tip-off that it once was more than a back road is the Coronado Motel, a small collection of 1930ish white frame cabins with red tile roofs and a neon cactus in front.

Past the motel, the prairie rises into low, wooded hills. Trees suddenly are shorter. Green begins to fade. The first mesquite and juniper appear. You've reached the beginning of the West.

Fort Worth brags that it's where the West begins, but it's too green. The eminent Texan historian Walter Prescott Webb wrote in his classic *The Great Plains* that the West begins at the ninety-eighth meridian, halfway between Weatherford and Santo.

Beyond the ninety-eighth meridian less than twenty inches of rain falls in a year. That thirst defines the West. Out in the brown wilderness, people had to find new ways to cope.

RANGER

The Ranger Hill Motel is falling down. Weeds and brush grow in the drive-in theater. Abandoned gas stations and cafes line old Highway 80 into town.

For a place with fewer than 3,000 people, Ranger has many large buildings. They're empty and decaying, relics of Ranger's brief oil boom. Maybe 30,000 people lived here then.

It had been just another drought-ridden farm town. Then in 1919 an oil well called McClesky No. 1 blew in and precipitated a rush. Derricks sprouted. Wildcatters, speculators, laborers, merchants, grifters, whores, gamblers, and thieves rushed to "Roaring Ranger." Within a few years the wells had petered out and the oil crowd moved on.

The Roaring Ranger Museum door is locked. A hand-lettered sign in the window tells you to "Pick Up the Key at Greenwood's Auto Parts or Call D.W. Boone."

Waymond Greenwood, at his store across the street, takes the key from a nail. "This is an old historical town," he says. You think he's about to tell you about the boom days. "We have a big football heritage here," he says. "We used to be real strong through the years. The Ranger Bulldogs. They won state in '53. They're not so strong now, sir. Nothing like they used to be. These days, people don't want to work hard to succeed, don't seem like."

EASTLAND

Sandy Cagle, Eastland County's tax assessor-collector, is explaining why Old Rip is missing. "He's down at Six Flags, visiting," she says. "They took him away in a hearse with a police escort."

Old Rip is—or was—a horny toad. His embalmed body usually lies in a tiny red-velvet-lined casket in a window at the Eastland County courthouse. On this summer day the window is empty except for a sign: "Old Rip is proudly representing the people of Eastland County at the Best of Texas Festival, Six Flags Over Texas."

"When the news broke that I let him go to Six Flags, it got a little tense around here," says County Judge Brad Stephenson. "A couple of tour buses came by the other day and I squinched completely up. People get upset when they come to see him and he's not here."

Here's Old Rip's story as the judge tells it:

"When they built the courthouse in 1897, they placed a Bible and a few other items in the cornerstone, and they put in a live horny toad. In 1928, they tore that courthouse down to build the present one. A crowd of about 3,000 was present when the cornerstone was opened. They pulled out the Bible and pulled out the horny toad and held him up by one leg.

"The legend goes that he actually started twitching right then and there. After thirty-one years in that cornerstone, he was still alive. There was a lot of press coverage. Old Rip achieved a lot of notoriety. They took him on a railroad tour all around the United States and up to Washington, D.C. President Coolidge saw him. Old Rip died a little over a year later, in January 1929. He was embalmed and put on display in the lobby."

In 1962, Governor John Connally came campaigning to Eastland. The local newspaper editor took Old Rip to meet him. "Governor Connally raised him up by his hind leg to show him to the crowd," says Judge Stephenson, "and the leg fell off. To this day, Rip has only three legs."

When newly elected Eastland County officials take the oath required by the Texas Constitution, they also must take a second oath not required in the state's other counties: "I do solemnly swear (or affirm) that I will faithfully execute the Office of Old Rip Promoter, and will to the best of my ability promote, preserve, protect, and defend the Truth of the Story of Old Rip. . . ."

CISCO

In 1919, young Conrad Hilton arrived in Cisco and took a room at the Mobley Hotel. Cisco, like Ranger, was booming. It had three or four whorehouses and about the same number of banks. Mr. Hilton had come to buy one of the banks. The owner had agreed on a price, but by the time Mr. Hilton arrived, he had upped the price.

"He made me mad," Mr. Hilton said to Art Linkletter in a 1950s TV interview.

The Mobley was renting its rooms in three-hour shifts to the oil field hands. Its proprietor told Mr. Hilton he was making a lot of money. "So I says, 'I'd like to buy your hotel,'" Mr. Hilton said. "Here's where I don't become a banker and I become a hotel man."

The little Mobley was the beginning of Mr. Hilton's hotel empire. It's a museum now.

The most famous thing that ever happened in Cisco was the Santa Claus Bank Robbery. Two days before Christmas in 1927, four men—one of them dressed as the jolly old elf—held up the First National Bank. In the ensuing gun battle, three people were killed, seven were wounded, and two little girls were kidnapped. One of the robbers eventually died of gunshot wounds, one served a prison sentence, one died in the electric chair, and one was lynched from a telephone pole in Cisco after he shot a jailer while trying to escape.

ROSCOE

Sue McClure lives in the Roscoe Trading Post with five cats, four turtles, and a dog named Lucky. The turtles crawl around in terrariums. The cats lurk among the chaos of Ms. McClure's junk and knickknacks. Lucky is in a wire-fenced pen in a corner. He's barking.

"This place is just a total mess," Ms. McClure says. "I used to keep it real clean, but people didn't like it like that. They said it was too perfect."

She says she hates living in Roscoe.

"I lived in Roswell, New Mexico, for twenty-three years. My brother lived in California, but he had lived in Roscoe before, and he moved back here. *Hush up, Lucky! I'm going to pour water on you!* And he wanted me to come to this hellish place. Your little brother, you know. And he wasn't well. So I said OK. I didn't want to come down here, but I did.

"He died three months after I got here and just left me in this hole. *If you don't hush up, Lucky, I'm going to throw you in the river, if I can find one!* The people here have never shopped here. They never came in here. They never even said good morning.

"A year went by, and I thought, 'Well, I didn't die or nothing.' I teach the little kids at Sunday school. Three to five years old. They like me. When they see me somewhere, they hug me and love me. So I feel like I've done good. I've stayed mainly for them.

"My son—my only child—I hadn't seen him for fifteen years, but he finally came to see me, and he wants me to go back to New Mexico. He said he would take me back up there. *Lucky, I'm going to spray you with something!* If he had come for me right after my brother died, I would have gone. But I never saw him, so I'm just here.

"For four years this place made a lot of money for me. Since that 9/11 deal, nobody hardly ever comes through town. You can stay open from sunup to sundown and there's no cars going down the road anymore. *Lucky, I swear!* They used to come from every state in the Union and foreign countries and every place else.

"I'm totally alone. I'm used to it. I've been by myself for many moons. But I know I'm going back to New Mexico sooner or later. I'm saving the money."

SWEETWATER

"How do you milk a rattlesnake?" you ask David Sager.

"Carefully," he says.

Picking up a rattlesnake is a lot like picking up a puppy, he says. "You grab him by the back of the neck."

Mr. Sager is chairman of the milking pit every year at the Sweetwater Rattlesnake Roundup. The milkers extract venom from the snakes to be used in medical research.

The roundup is always the second weekend in March, when rattlesnakes are coming out of hibernation. The Sweetwater Jaycees run it. This year snake hunters captured 3,500 pounds of live rattlers, a little below average.

In dry years, Mr. Sager says, rattlesnakes come into town to find water. That's why the first roundup was held back in the fifties. "It was the middle of a big drought. The town was overrun with rattlesnakes. They were in the streets. You could hardly step out on your front porch."

Mr. Sager is holding a rattlesnake he borrowed from a friend. He sets it gently on the ground, like a kitten. It's whirring. "A snake can't hear," Mr. Sager says. "He locates a moving animal by vibrations in the ground. The secret is to remain still."

You remain still.

THE PERMIAN BASIN

Even the mesquite is scrawny. Across the brown, flat landscape, pump jacks nod. The cenizo is in bloom. The yucca is about to bloom. Paint-and-body shops, radiator shops, rusting drilling equipment stand along old Highway 80 between Midland and Odessa. On the Odessa College campus is a full-scale replica of Shakespeare's Globe Theatre in Elizabethan London. A poster portrays the Bard on a bucking bronc. "Alive and Kicking," it says.

Lawrence of Arabia could have been filmed among the dunes of the Monahans Sandhills. Dwarf shin oak trees grow only three feet tall, but their roots are eighty feet deep. The Sandhills are twenty miles wide and 200 miles long. They extend into New Mexico.

The address over the door of Aunt Jackie's Bar outside Pyote is still 111 Highway 80 East. Pyote was the home of the Rattlesnake Bomber Base during World War II. Its real name was the Pyote Army Air Base, but the fliers gave it the name that stuck. B17 and B29 crews trained there.

After the war, the base was a storage facility, housing as many as 2,000 aircraft, line after line of them, gleaming in the sun. One of them was the Enola Gay, which dropped the first atomic bomb.

FAR WEST TEXAS

A few miles east of Pecos, the pale blue silhouette of the Davis Mountains appears on the southern horizon. The northern horizon is straight and flat as a ruler. The road begins to have a distinctive western feel. The horizon, the wide sky, a change in the light. No more pump jacks.

The brick two-story bank building in Toyah was once a grand building for a little town. Four Corinthian columns stand across its front. It's rotting now. Mesquite grows among its columns.

Carved over the door of another brick two-story building: "High School 1912." Toyah used to be something. Boards cover the windows. Tumbleweeds grow in the schoolyard and on the football field. The goalpost uprights and the ruins of the scoreboard are still standing.

Then suddenly you're in the mountains. I-20 disappears into I-10. Highway 80 used to run by the door of the Kent Mercantile, established 1905. The store has always been owned by the Long X Ranch. It and the post office are all there has ever been of Kent.

It sells groceries, gas, hardware, toys, T-shirts, toothpaste, and Pepto-Bismol to ranchers, tourists, and truckers. Horseshoes are weighed on an antique scale and sell for $2.75 a pound.

Alice Escobedo has worked here for more than twenty years. Her husband, Frank, cowboys for the Long X. He started when he was fourteen. He has worked there for forty-eight years. "He doesn't want to retire," Mrs. Escobedo says. "He says, 'What am I going to do? Just sit back and relax?'"

Dust devils are dancing in the distance. The speed limit is seventy-five out here, seventy for trucks.

VAN HORN

"He was a big guy, wearing a baseball cap, tennis shoes untied. I said to my wife, 'Mary Lou, that's John Madden!' She said, 'Who's he?' I said, 'Mary Lou, I'll explain later.'"

Mr. Madden ordered the machaca, No. 17 on the Chuy's Restaurant menu. Chuy Uranga remembers it so clearly, that first night Mr. Madden ate at his place.

Mr. Madden, the NFL sportscaster, refuses to fly. He travels from game to game on his private bus.

"He has been stopping here at least once a year since 1987," says Mr. Uranga.

Mr. Uranga reserves a table permanently for Mr. Madden. His name is painted on a chair.

A few blocks down from Chuy's, Ran Horn of Van Horn celebrates another famous man. He has the Vincent Gallery, which offers Van Gogh art and second-hand books. A sign on the porch says: "Let's face it. Artist will paint for beer."

The art that Ran Horn of Van Horn sells isn't really by Vincent Van Gogh, and he doesn't pretend that it is. It's copies of Van Gogh masterpieces that Mr. Horn paints himself. If you don't look too closely at the canvases, you could think you've walked into a Van Gogh exhibit.

"I just find a lot of similarities between Vincent and me, and his art resonates with me," says Mr. Horn. "He started out as a missionary, and I was a missionary at the time I started this. He read the Bible and he thought, 'You know, what's there is there, and that's the way you're supposed to take it.' That's what I think, too.

"I'm a Christian, but I'm at odds with the vast majority of Christianity, because whenever I say, 'Hey, Jesus said *this*,' the Christians say, 'Well, he didn't mean it. He's the Lord, but he doesn't mean what he says! You've got it wrong, and I've got it right, and I'm the only one that's got it right!' That's just craziness to me."

He says his real name is Randell Lee Horn, but his mama called him Ran. "And it has a nice ring to it: Ran Horn of Van Horn."

He settled in Van Horn because he loves the solitude of it. Only 3,000 people in a county bigger than Delaware. "On a good day, I might have maybe ten people come in," he says. "If I had people constantly coming in, I'd be running the shop and there would be no time to paint. Every person is given just so much time and energy, and when it's gone it's gone."

Mr. Horn has seen only a few real Van Gogh paintings. He copies them from art books. He says he has sold at least 100 copies of Vincent's work, most of them for $200 to $300. He sold one for $1,000 and one for $2,000. He reproduces most of the paintings smaller than the originals to economize on UPS shipping charges.

His biggest seller is "Starry Night." He has sold about ten copies of that one.

EL PASO VALLEY

West of Sierra Blanca, mesquite yields place to creosote and cholla and yucca. The mountains of Mexico are on the southern horizon. Fields along the left side of the road are green with cotton. Great cottonwoods spread along the ditches that bring precious water from the Rio Grande. A lone worker in a striped shirt is chopping with a hoe among plants as high as his waist, a scene that Van Gogh might have done something with. The right roadside is sand and tumbleweeds. The border patrol is everywhere.

Old Highway 80 through the El Paso Valley of the Rio Grande is called Texas 20 West. Mobile homes have replaced the little two- or three-room adobe houses that families used to build for themselves. Business signs are in Spanish, which always has been the first language here.

The museum across the plaza from the San Elizario chapel is called Los Portales. It was a residence of Gregorio Garcia, a rancher, built in 1855. The chapel was built in 1789. It was part of a Spanish presidio.

Gus Lujan is taking care of the museum. He's telling about the conquistador Juan de Oñate, who led 400 settlers and 2,000 Indians through here in 1598 on his way to founding Santa Fe. Gus says he's a descendant of the only Lujan among those settlers.

"A few days before the expedition reached El Rio del Norte—the Rio Grande—it was out of food and water," he says. "Everybody was in really bad shape. When they reached the river, they held a thanksgiving feast, twenty-three years before the thanksgiving of the Plymouth Colony. El Paso and Ysleta also claim that they had the first thanksgiving, but it was here."

Old Highway 80, only a few hundred yards north of the river, is the main street of all the Lower Valley towns. It's a line of salvage yards, radiator shops, tire repair shops, taco stands, hair salons. It passes the Mission of Ysleta and the Tigua pueblo's Speaking Rock Casino, where the state no longer permits gambling. Our Lady of Guadalupe is peeling off a wall next to a Chevron station.

It enters El Paso on Alameda Avenue, passes used car lots, pawnshops, bars, and shops selling discount mufflers. Near downtown, it becomes Texas Avenue, then Mesa Street. It passes San Jacinto Plaza and the University of Texas at El Paso. Beyond the city it becomes Doniphan Drive and enters the Upper El Paso Valley, passes through Canutillo and used-car land again. To the east, resembling a Spanish mission, La Tuna federal prison gleams white in the hot sun.

ANTHONY

In the farming town of Anthony, an inconspicuous vertical sign on the main street separates El Paso County, Texas, from Doña Ana County, New Mexico, Fernando's El Dorado Saloon is the last business on the Texas side. Rosa's Ropa de Calidad is the first business in New Mexico. They're in the same building. Both are padlocked and barred.

Beyond the state line, old Highway 80 continues to La Mesilla, then turns westward with I-10. You could follow it all the way to the Pacific.

But you stop at the end of Texas and find a table at the Red Rooster Café and order red cheese enchiladas the way God intended them: stacked like pancakes with a fried egg on top.

Painter

In the painting that Barnaby Fitzgerald is working on, two almost nude female figures are flying through a pale sky, their long hair and diaphanous robes flowing behind. One figure is holding a tray of hors d'oeuvres, and one a tray with a fish on it. The left hand of the figure with the hors d'oeuvres is reaching downward. The tip of her finger is touching a third, bare tray, held aloft by an unseen figure. "She's stealing from an empty tray," Mr. Fitzgerald says. "I guess you could call it a kind of angelic dishonesty."

The big canvas hangs on the far wall of Mr. Fitzgerald's studio behind his home in old East Dallas. He has been working on it for a year. He doesn't know when it will be finished. Something about the flow of those robes doesn't satisfy him yet.

Even in its unfinished state, the painting engages the eye and the mind, raising questions and suggestions. Who are these flying figures? Greek goddesses? Renaissance angels? Mortal women in a dream? Where did they get that food? Where are they taking it? Whose fingers are those at the bottom of the painting, holding aloft that empty tray?

Mr. Fitzgerald is telling a convoluted story about the genesis of the idea for the painting. It originated, he says, during his years as a single parent, having to wake every morning to get his children washed and fed and off to school, and wishing that someone would bring him breakfast in bed. The idea has traveled a long, tortuous way since then. No viewer of the painting will detect even a hint of Mr. Fitzgerald's original longing for pancakes and butter and syrup.

He lights his pipe and waves the burnt match toward the canvas. "I wasn't paying attention to common sense things like wind," he says. "Those hors d'oeuvres, if they were flying at any speed, would fly off the tray. In a painting, your mind is not offended by impossible things."

☆

Since 1984, Barnaby John Francis Fitzgerald has taught painting, drawing, and sometimes sculpture at Southern Methodist University. He loves his job. Watching students grow as artists gives him joy. "Teaching is very exciting to me," he says. "Sometimes it's also very humiliating."

The job allows Mr. Fitzgerald a luxury that many artists don't have—the freedom to pursue his own artistic vision in his own way and own time, to experiment with unfashionable images and ideas, to invent such impossibilities as flying hors d'oeuvres trays without worrying about what the public might think of them.

"I light a candle every week for my job," he says. "It makes me independent of the marketplace. I can spend three or four days a week in my studio and don't have to sell my work until I'm satisfied with it. That's such a blessing. If I could, I would buy back a lot of my earlier work so I could either fix it or get rid of it."

Mary Leavenworth, a Dallas painter who studied with Mr. Fitzgerald for six years, describes him as a "great" teacher whose methods are more traditional than most these days. "Barnaby doesn't just tell you to go paint and find yourself," she says. "He actually teaches you about color, about mixing, about stretching canvases. He's also very demanding. He puts pressure on you to be the best that you can be. He doesn't accept laziness. I used to think of his instruction as physical therapy. It hurt like crazy, but I knew it was doing me a lot of good."

Mr. Fitzgerald's slow, painstaking drive for perfection has been a way of life in his family. His father, the late Robert Fitzgerald, was a poet and a classics scholar. He taught at Harvard and spent many years translating Homer, Sophocles, and Virgil. His verse renderings of *The Iliad* and *The Odyssey* are among the most beautiful and most read in English.

Barnaby's mother, Sally, is writing a biography of the great American short-story writer Flannery O'Conner, who in her youth was a Fitzgerald family babysitter. Mrs. Fitzgerald, now eighty-two, has been working on the book for fifty years. "We all presume that she's pretty much finished it," Barnaby says, "But she doesn't want to talk about it."

Barnaby, born in New York City in 1953, is the fifth of Robert and Sally's six children. One of his brothers, Benedict, is a Hollywood film writer. A sister, Maria Juliana, has published two novels and a volume of short stories. She writes under the name M.J. Fitzgerald. "So," says Barnaby, "I really understand revision and editing and all the waiting and all the action that goes into something before it makes sense."

He was still a baby when the Fitzgeralds moved to Italy, where they lived during the sixteen years Robert worked on his translations of Homer.

When Barnaby was still a child, his parents noticed that he did nothing but draw pictures. He would come home from school and sit down and draw all afternoon. "I drew violence," he says. "I drew anything that had swords and arrows."

His choices of subject probably were inspired by his father, who was upstairs in his study, recounting the bloody deeds of the great Ajax and Agamemnon and Achilles and Odysseus and Hector on the plain of Ilium. "He would come down in the evening and say, 'I've done three lines.' For him, having translated three lines was a triumph," Barnaby says. "Usually it was half a line, or no line at all. It was not being able to find the words in English."

Sally was an active partner in the enterprise. "She doesn't know Greek, but she surely knows English," Barnaby says. "They worked it out together, how to say it. And she proofread it and typed it.

"When my father finished something, he would read it out to us. For me, who loved to draw soldiers, *The Iliad* was much more wonderful than *The Odyssey*. The jealousy, the rivalry, the pouting, all mixed together with the sheer brutality! *The Iliad* is great stuff!"

While his parents were fretting over the Greeks and Trojans, little Barnaby was growing up Italian. "I became predominantly an Italian speaker," he says. "My parents had to revert to Italian to talk to me. They were afraid I was just not going to be able to speak English."

So when he was twelve, Robert and Sally decided to send him out of Italy to school. They chose Glenstall Abbey, a Benedictine boarding school in Shannon, Ireland.

"My parents were commuting from Italy to Cambridge, where my father was teaching his classes at Harvard," Barnaby says. "All the planes that went to Italy had to stop at Shannon Airport. They would visit me on their way back and forth."

Barnaby was learning English at last, but it was Irish English. He learned it well. His speech is soft, in complex sentences, with the deliberateness of a scholar. He chooses his words with care. He says he has been trying to get rid of his Irish inflection ever since he left Glenstall Abbey. But to a Texas ear, he has succeeded only in smoothing it into something more vaguely foreign.

"Glenstall Abbey stressed poetry," he says. "We had to memorize reams and reams of poetry. I still rock myself to sleep quoting those long, beautiful poems."

The art teacher at Glenstall Abbey told Barnaby he was a natural. "Learn to do this," he told the boy. "Don't bother with anything else."

That's what Barnaby did. He studied printmaking at the Instituto Statale D'Arte in Urbino, Italy, and received its Diploma di Magistero. He came home and studied printmaking and drawing at the Boston Museum School, and earned a Bachelor of Fine Arts degree from Boston University. Then he returned to Italy, where he had seen and loved the art of many centuries. "So many of those old paintings are still wonderful," he says. "They still work. Even minor painters had such a level of sheer seriousness and accomplishment in their paintings. Just dogged seriousness. Just getting things right."

For six years, he lived in the family's house in Umbria and painted landscapes and played piano in a rock band. He married an Italian woman. His daughter, Giulia, was born.

"I was fairly successful," he says. "I sold, I lived. But I was dying artistically. I wasn't getting any critical input. I realized that for most of my public I could have been painting little big-eyed boys with tears on their cheeks and it would have been exactly the same. The level of criticism was deplorable. Despite what Americans think, Italy has lost it. Just lost it."

So he came back to the United States and went to Yale. It was a delight to him. "I needed to be around people who were struggling with the same things I was," he says. "I stuffed myself with conversations, with critiques, happy to be bitched at, happy to be ground down. The more people tried to grind me down, the more alive I felt."

His son, James, was born in New Haven. But his wife was unhappy, and soon after he got his Master of Fine Arts degree and was hired by SMU, she returned to Italy. "She just couldn't stand the United States," he says. "It was too lonely for her. I'm sure she couldn't stand me as well. The move to Dallas was the last straw. There's so much human contact in Italy. There are crowds of people everywhere you go. And there's so much solitude in Dallas. People are locked up in their cars and their houses. Being a painter who works in solitude, I don't mind it. But she couldn't take it."

Mr. Fitzgerald, on the other hand, fell for the city. "The world isn't designed for this kind of comfort and this kind of space and this kind of opulence," he says. "I just love it. And I love the light in Dallas. The only place where you get this kind of late afternoon light in Italy is on top of a hill. You've got to be aristocracy to live up there. Here the light is democratic. Everybody can enjoy it."

He reared his children alone and fantasized of breakfast in bed. Giulia, now nineteen, is going to SMU and wants to be a physician. James, now seventeen, is in his last year at Subiaco, a small Benedictine school in Arkansas. He's interested in marine biology.

Most summers, Mr. Fitzgerald goes back to the family house in Italy and paints landscapes. One year while on sabbatical there, he met the live-in babysitter of a family who was renting some of the rooms in the house. Her African name was Essi. Her Christian name was Sylvie. She was of the Ewe people of Togo, and studying communications at a nearby university.

She posed for him. They became friends. The friendship developed into a courtship. Two years ago, they married. She's now an advertising intern with the Richards Group and finds the Dallas traffic "very scary."

"But I like the Texas people," she says. "I connect with them more easily than with people from other parts of the United States, even those who have moved to Dallas. The Texas people don't seem threatened by strangers."

For her husband, she says, art is all. "He talks about just that one thing," she says. "But he's so much fun. He likes to work around the house, cleaning up and cooking. He's a great cook. He likes being at home. I like that."

☆

Mr. Fitzgerald signs all his work "Barnaba," the Italian form of his

Christian name. It's the way he was called when he was growing up. It's the way he still thinks of himself. "Fitzgerald" is too long to write on a canvas, he says. It would take up too much space.

"Italy informs his whole life—its colors, its food, its people, its warmth," says Cheryl Vogel of the Valley House Gallery in North Dallas, where many of Mr. Fitzgerald's works are exhibited and sold. "He's really an Italian peasant at heart. But an intellectual one. His mind is a classical mind. He remembers books he read twenty years ago, even the names of the characters. The way he lives his life is a story, and all the things that he has read have become part of his personality."

Ms. Vogel has hung five exhibits of Mr. Fitzgerald's work. Over the ten years she has known him, she has sold more than 100 of his works. He also is represented by galleries in Houston and New York.

"From the very first painting of his that I saw, I wanted to exhibit him," Ms. Vogel says. "Barnaby is a complex man, and his work is complex. It's intriguing. There are always mysteries and so many metaphors in his paintings. They're really visual poems."

A Barnaba landscape, she says, is certain to have been painted in Italy. His paintings of nude and semi-nude figures just as certainly were done in Dallas. "The Dallas landscape isn't as inspiring as Italy's is," she says, "so in Dallas he makes the human body his landscape."

The people in his paintings often are eating or drinking or playing music. These activities, Mr. Fitzgerald says, are "the essentials of life." He likes to paint animals, especially cats. "I love their freedom," he says. "I like the fact that they don't grovel."

He speaks of "the poetry of subject matter," and makes no apologies for the old-fashioned, even archaic feel of many of his paintings and drawings. In a painting called *Europa,* the kidnapped lady lounges peacefully on the back of the white bull, flying serenely through the sky while the sea below is in turmoil and women on the land scream in terror. In *Bath,* black and white slaves relax in a ruined Roman bath in Pompeii. In *Black Cat,* the little beast lies cozily against the legs of a nude, sleeping woman, keeping watch.

"I'm a representational painter," he says. "My paintings have a kind of narrative in them. I like stories."

Another large painting, which Mr. Fitzgerald calls *Never Expect Power Again*, portrays a group of nude and almost-nude women washing clothes in a stream and hanging them on a line. The stream appears to flow away into a narrow tunnel in a hillside. A naked child is climbing in a nearby tree, reaching toward the hanging laundry, which is impossibly far away. On a low hill above the women, several nude men are gathered around a table, drinking, shouting, perhaps singing. In the upper left-hand corner of the canvas, in the distance, smaller than the other figures, a man clothed in black stands on a ladder, which is leaning against a tree. Mr. Fitzgerald tells the story he had in mind when he painted the picture.

"As a young boy in Italy, I used to help prune the olive trees every year. The man on the ladder is old. His name is Gustavo. He's the old man I helped when I was young. He's pruning away some of his memories so that he can concentrate his mind on something else. He's choosing to forget parts of his own youth, to get ready for a new season in his life. Some of his memories are of drinking, eating, and women. The painting is about youth and age. The little tunnel where the water is going is like a vanishing point. The old man is about to enter that tunnel. Also, there's the whole idea of washing away sin, of cleansing the soul. It's an allegory."

Noticing the bemused look on his listeners' faces, Mr. Fitzgerald smiles. "Of course, someone looking at it might come up with a story that's completely different from mine. People bring their own minds and lives to it."

The great foundation of all Mr. Fitzgerald's work is drawing, which has been his passion since childhood, but which many artists no longer bother to learn because it's tedious. They take photographs of subjects that they'll paint later. But Mr. Fitzgerald makes pen-and-ink drawings, an unforgiving medium that requires a keen eye and a sure hand and can't be erased. And drawing requires time. Lots of time.

"Generally speaking, painters get better as they get older," he says, "because it takes so much commitment to do it well and to keep doing it well. Very slowly, I feel myself moving in my work into territories that I can't predict, doing new kinds of things. It's not necessarily a campaign to get famous. That might be nice, but I'm not even sure it would be. It's a campaign to make things that stick, to get things really, really right.

"In the end, you have to be heroic. You've got no choice. There's no other way to do it. You have to grit your teeth and follow those impulses that are directing you.

"Barring ill health or some other catastrophe, there's no reason why I can't get good at this."

Thanks

In Greek mythology, ambrosia was the food of the gods who lived on Mount Olympus. I don't recall its ingredients ever being mentioned in the old tales. It was just the stuff the gods ate.

But more than forty years since I last tasted it, I still remember the ambrosia that my great-aunt Helen contributed to our Thanksgiving table every year, and everything she put in it. Whenever I think "Thanksgiving," the next thought to follow is "ambrosia." Which is strange, considering my mother's superlative cornbread dressing and buttermilk pies.

Every holiday was a big event when I was growing up because there were so many of us: my mother, my grandmother, we five kiddos, I being the eldest. And Aunt Helen.

Aunt Helen was my grandmother's youngest sister. She had had a brief, mysterious marriage that ended in divorce back in the dim past and remained single thereafter. She was the cosmopolitan member of our family. She had lived in Boston, New York, and Washington. She had traveled around the world several times, returning with small gifts for all of us from exotic places.

She practiced law in Alpine, a half-hour drive from our house in Fort Davis, and was moderately wealthy. But she was a lonely, unhappy, self-centered person—the opposite of her generously loving sister, my grand-mother—and had no children and few real friends.

So she always had Thanksgiving with us. My grandmother would make the ritual phone call inviting her, and Aunt Helen would accept and say, "I'll bring my ambrosia," and my grandmother would make loud clucking noises of glee and enthusiasm.

Whenever she and Mother were discussing the Thanksgiving menu and which of them was going to make what, my grandmother would say,

"And Helen is bringing her ambrosia." Then she would look at us kids and make a face that said she could hardly wait.

On Thanksgiving, Aunt Helen always arrived holding the same large crystal bowl before her as if about to place it on an altar. She would say, "And here's my ambrosia!"

We would flutter about her, exclaiming. My grandmother would accept the bowl and place it with great ceremony in the center of the table. During the meal, all of us would ask for two or three helpings of ambrosia, praising it all the while.

Aunt Helen's ambrosia was only a fruit salad. A mixture of coconut, grapes, slices of orange, and chunks of canned pineapple. It couldn't have required more than fifteen or twenty minutes to prepare. Compared to the succulent turkey, the melt-in-your-mouth dressing, the sweet potatoes, vegetables, gravies and sauces, breads, and pies that my mother and grandmother had spent days making, it was nothing.

So why did we make such an ado about it? Why, so many years later, does Aunt Helen's ambrosia flash into my mind first when I remember those Thanksgivings?

Because my grandmother's enthusiasm persuaded us that her unhappy sister's tiny contribution was special. So it became special, and bestowed upon us—and Aunt Helen—a happier feast, fit for gods.

Pioneers

One day in 1944, Lieutenant Julian MarDock of the U.S. Army Air Corps piloted a courier flight to Cambridge, England, to deliver the mail and two generals. While hanging about the Cambridge airfield, he saw a man in a western hat talking with a bunch of GIs. Lieutenant MarDock recognized the fellow.

He was J. Frank Dobie, the famous Texas writer and folklorist. He was teaching at Cambridge University that year.

The lieutenant joined the group of soldiers and introduced himself to Mr. Dobie as a fellow Texan. "Where are you from, young man?" Mr. Dobie asked him.

"Tyler, sir," Lieutenant MarDock replied.

"Your father was one of the Chinese laborers who built the Southern Pacific Railroad across West Texas, wasn't he?" Mr. Dobie asked.

Lieutenant MarDock's father, Sam MarDock, had died at age 80 two years earlier. He had been a prosperous businessman and farmer. He had lived in Tyler since 1890. He was a leading citizen, one of the town's benefactors. He had never mentioned to his son that he had once helped build a railroad.

"It was the first time I had ever heard about that part of my father's life," Julian MarDock says now. But Asians were so rare in Texas in the 1940s that Mr. Dobie knew a Chinese-American pilot from Tyler was probably the child of a former railroad laborer.

Asians and Asian Americans are no longer exotic in Texas. Even many smaller towns now have recent arrivals from Vietnam, Cambodia, Laos, Korea, Taiwan, India, Pakistan, and the Middle East living in them. They or their forebears came here for many kinds of reasons, usually in search of some opportunity they didn't have in their native lands. Customs, accents, costumes, and religions that once seemed strange to the Anglo, Hispanic and black Texans who arrived here earlier don't seem so unusual now.

But Sam MarDock and his wife were Texas pioneers in a time of pioneers. A few years ago, when Julian MarDock, now a retired Dallas physician, wrote a book about his family, he called it *The First of Many.* "My father was the first Asian man in Tyler and one of the first in this region of Texas," he says. "My mother was the first Asian woman. My brother and my sister and I were the first Asian children."

Also, the young Lieutenant MarDock that Mr. Dobie encountered in England was the first Chinese-American military pilot in U.S. history. And the pilot later would become the first Chinese-American doctor to practice in Dallas.

Mr. Dobie's remark had surprised Lieutenant MarDock. He always had thought of his father as a middle-class businessman and civic leader. Apparently there was more to the history of Sam MarDock than he knew. "After much study and research, and talking with my mother and Poppa Sam's old friends, I have come to know him better," he wrote in his book.

Sam began life in 1862 as a peasant named Mar Yum Eh in a Cantonese village called BokSha. "MarDock is a name he made up later," says the doctor. It was customary in BokSha for the village elders to choose strong young men to cross the sea to the Land of the Gold Mountain—as they called America, because of the California gold fields—to get work and send money home.

In 1875, the elders chose Mar Yum Eh, who was thirteen. He had never been to school. He had never learned to read or write Chinese. He didn't know numbers. In California, when labor brokers decided which workers would be hired out as house servants and which as farmhands, Mar Yum Eh was put with the farmhands.

But he had an aptitude for languages. During one of his farm jobs, his employer's wife taught him to speak, read, and write English. She also called him Sam, which would be his name for the rest of his life.

Later he got a job on a large ranch, where he was put in charge of the horses. He loved them and became an expert rider and wrangler.

When Sam heard that the Southern Pacific Railroad was looking for Chinese laborers to build its track from California to a tiny frontier village on the Rio Grande called El Paso, he signed up. The wage was better than ranch work, and it was rumored that land in Texas could be bought cheap. Sam hoped to buy some someday.

The crew worked its way across the deserts of Southern California, Arizona, and New Mexico, enduring torrid sun, poisonous snakes and insects, and hostile Indians. Sam taught himself to use a surveying transit and became the engineer's assistant, helping level and grade the railroad bed. He no longer worked with shovel and sledgehammer. His new job allowed him to learn numbers and improve his English.

In May 1881, the Southern Pacific reached El Paso and the construction contract was complete. The crew was paid off and dismissed. Sam saddled his horse and rode into town. It would be his home for ten years.

Unlike most men in that wild and dangerous place, Sam didn't drink. But he liked to gamble in the saloons. He carried a Colt on his hip, worked in laundries, in restaurants, and on ranches as a cowboy. He learned Spanish so well that he could hire himself out as an interpreter. He became a horse trader.

In 1885 he made a brief visit back to China and handed out gold coins to the elders of BokSha, and was admired as a successful man. But he had decided that his future lay in the Land of the Gold Mountain.

Back in El Paso, he learned that the Southern Pacific was hiring men to extend the railroad on eastward. Because of his knowledge of English and numbers, he was hired as a foreman.

The rails inched across the desert again, leaving Marfa, Marathon, and other new towns along their route. Over the Pecos River near Langtry, the Chinese and Irish laborers built the High Bridge, 321 feet above the water line, the highest bridge in America at the time.

Sam quit the railroad at Del Rio and rode horseback to San Antonio to seek his fortune. He worked as a government interpreter for a while, traveled to Houston, Galveston, and Dallas.

In the summer of 1890 he caught a train to Tyler. He liked the look of the town. Some businessmen there told him Tyler needed a good restaurant and offered him financial assistance to open one. Sam sent to El Paso for some Chinese cooks and waiters and opened the Grand Star Café. "Business was good," Dr. MarDock wrote in his book. "Waiters wore white coats and bow ties. Waitresses wore white dresses and little caps sort of like nurses."

By 1893 Sam was prosperous enough to return to China again, wearing gold coins as buttons on his coat. He hired a marriage broker to search for a suitable wife for him, and he built a large three-story house in BokSha for his family and future bride. Then he returned to Tyler.

Sam noticed that an area called the Levee, on Common Street, next to the Cotton Belt Railroad tracks, was one of the busier places in town. It was a neighborhood where many immigrants lived.

"The Levee spoke eight languages," Dr. MarDock wrote in his book. "These people had come from the four corners of the world because there was a need for them in this little corner of the new world. They had been rejected in the old country because they were poor and not from the ruling class. They had been rejected because of their religious differences with the majority. They had been rejected because there were too many people in the old country and not enough work."

Crowds gathered at the Cotton Belt depot several times a day to meet the trains. Train crewmen needed places to eat. So in 1897 Sam opened the Cotton Belt Restaurant across the street from the depot. "He got the spot right in the middle of the block," Dr. MarDock says. "He was pretty clever in doing business."

Sam's new restaurant served grub that the railroad men liked: steaks, ham, chili, bacon and eggs, roast beef and gravy, with lots of coffee. Sam also sold gloves, socks, tobacco, handkerchiefs, caps, soap, and other things the men and the neighborhood needed.

His two restaurants gave Sam the legal status of merchant, which under U.S. immigration law would allow him to leave the country and return with a wife. So as soon as the Cotton Belt Restaurant was running smoothly, he went to China to marry the bride that the marriage broker had chosen for him.

She was Wong Shee, daughter of a goldsmith. The wedding took place in BokSha in the house that Sam had built. He lived there several months with his bride. But when Sam was ready to return to Tyler, Wong was pregnant and unwilling to leave the familiarity of her home. Sam returned to Texas without her. Wong bore a son, but he died within a couple of years. His father never saw him.

"I knew that Sam wanted me to come to America and join him in Texas," Wong told Julian many years later. "Entry into the U.S. was difficult and at times impossible for the Chinese. The laws were always changing. There was the Chinese Exclusion Act of 1872. Then the act was extended. Sam was able to comply with this law by achieving the status of merchant. And he knew lawyers and judges in Texas. Still, the procedure took time and money."

And Wong was still fearful.

Finally, in 1911 Sam returned to BokSha and persuaded Wong to accompany him to the Land of the Gold Mountain. They had been married for fourteen years. Wong was now thirty-five years old.

When she stepped off the train in Tyler, she was dressed in traditional Chinese clothes and wore tiny slippers on her bound feet.

More than 400 people came out to greet her, the first Asian woman they had ever seen.

☆

Wong kept her Chinese ways. She raised Chinese vegetables in her garden, imported other ingredients from San Francisco, and cooked Cantonese food for her family every day.

"My mother didn't have any education at all because they didn't educate the girls over there," Dr. MarDock says. "But she got along pretty well with people on the block, speaking pidgin English. Texas was a very strange place to her. But my father took business courses by correspondence. He had a leadership personality. He ended up with restaurants in Tyler, Longview, Kilgore, and Gladewater."

For ten years, Sam and Wong lived in an apartment in the back of the Cotton Belt Restaurant. During those years, three children —Lucille, Sam Jr., and Julian—were born. When the family outgrew its quarters, Sam bought a cotton farm at the edge of town and built a home there.

"Some people still regarded our parents as foreigners," Dr. MarDock wrote in his book. "That gave us the push to correct our English and to do well in school. We admired our parents and wanted to succeed for their sake, having known of the sacrifices that they had made for us."

Unlike the black children who grew up in Tyler, the MarDock children didn't go to racially segregated schools. They joined the white Methodist church. They heard no racial slurs so long as they remained in their hometown.

"But when we got outside of Tyler, it was a different story," Dr. MarDock says. He recalls a certain high school football game in another East Texas town. "When I went on the field, the yelling started, 'Hey, Chop Suey! Hey, Chow Mein!' The other school had a real hotshot player. I tackled him a couple of times for a loss. The whole stands were yelling and yelling at me, all through the game.

"I ran into that hotshot years later. He said he didn't remember that game."

All three MarDock children graduated from high school. Lucille, the eldest, attended Tyler Junior College and then a business college. She became a secretary and an office manager for an oil company in Tyler. Sam went to Dallas Aviation College to become a pilot. He later ran a store in Tyler. Julian spent a year at Tyler Junior College, then in 1939 transferred to the University of Texas at Austin as a pre-med student.

In 1940, Julian began dating another young pre-med, Ruth Wilhelm of Fort Worth. She would become his wife, but not yet. They were still at UT when the Japanese attacked Pearl Harbor.

Julian immediately joined the army as an aviation cadet. A month later, Sam Jr. became a cadet, too. Julian won his wings as a fighter pilot. His brother would pilot small planes and gliders.

"A deep, hurting, demeaning indignity happened in January 1942, when it became necessary for aliens to register with the federal government," Dr. MarDock wrote in his book. Eighty-year-old Sam MarDock put on a suit and tie and the big black hat that he wore only to church and to funerals and went to the post office to register.

"It was all sort of bewildering," Lucille wrote later. "Here we had two fellows in the U.S. Army Air Corps—two blue stars on our door—and we had to register."

Sam died three months later.

When the army sent Julian to a field in Massachusetts for more training, Ruth got a job in New England as well, and they decided to marry. On the day she went to the courthouse for their marriage license, Julian's plane developed engine trouble during a training flight and crashed near Pittsfield, Massachusetts.

Civilians pulled him from the wreckage and took him to a hospital. He was in a coma for four days. His skull and several other bones were fractured. He and Ruth had to postpone their wedding for two months, but on January 9, 1943, they married. The Army offered Julian a medical discharge, but he refused it.

Eventually he was assigned to the 33rd Photo Reconnaissance Squadron of the 9th Tactical Air Force and went to Europe. He flew 100 missions in his P38, including one on D-Day and another on Christmas Day during the Battle of the Bulge.

To the Europeans they encountered, the Chinese-American flyer and his buddies were curiosities. "What a gang!" Dr. MarDock wrote in his book. "Flight jackets on at all times. No ties or coats at dinner. They polished their own shoes. None of them had an orderly. Few of them had ever known a servant at home. . . . They were the descendants of the pioneers who built America. Many of the pilots were first-generation children."

The army awarded Lieutenant MarDock the Distinguished Flying Cross for a mission over Berlin. He won the Air Medal with ten Oak Leaf Clusters.

After the war, Julian enrolled in medical school at Cornell, while Ruth worked to support them. He graduated in 1949. "Ever since high school, I had wanted to be a doctor," he says. "Our money was limited. But Ruth and I just plowed on and did it."

After an internship at Baylor Hospital in Dallas and a residency in Houston, Julian and Ruth lived in San Angelo for a year, then decided to open a clinic in Oak Cliff. "We chose Dallas because it was close to Ruth's family in Fort Worth and mine in Tyler," Dr. MarDock says. "At the time, we had absolutely nothing."

In 1955, the MarDock children decided to seek U.S. citizenship for their mother, who had lived in Tyler for fifty years. Although the local congressman and many of the leading citizens of Tyler and East Texas wrote letters supporting the request, the government turned it down.

Wong never saw China again. She died twenty years later, still an alien.

To make ends meet during the early years of his practice, Dr. MarDock served as jailhouse physician for Dallas County. Among the prisoners he examined was Jack Ruby, who had just shot Lee Harvey Oswald. Dr. MarDock remembers Ruby as "really pretty dumb."

Dr. MarDock practiced at his clinic for forty years, with Ruth as his office manager. They reared three boys and two girls.

Julian is eighty-two years old now. Ruth is eighty-one. They've been married for fifty-eight years.

A number of models of the young lieutenant's P38 are scattered about their house. He can still explain the mechanics and aerodynamics of his beloved plane in which he fought for the Land of the Gold Mountain.

"All I have to do now," he says, "is think about these things that happened in the past."

Bullet

"Why didn't I lock the doors, if my presentiment was so strong? Or just throw my arms around his neck?"

This is Jan Reid, doing what we all do after something terrible and sudden happens to us, something that changes us in cruel and irrevocable ways and reroutes our lives to tracks we never dreamt of. We think, "If only . . ." and "Why didn't I . . ." We retrace the chain of events in our minds. We marvel at how a series of such small choices led to such catastrophic results. We wish we had heeded the uneasy premonition that we seem to remember. We wish we could rewind the crucial minutes or hours and edit them toward a different conclusion.

The doors that Mr. Reid wishes he had locked were on a taxicab in Mexico City. The neck he wishes he had grabbed belonged to a robber holding a .38-caliber revolver. Instead, Mr. Reid threw a punch at the robber, and the robber shot him. Mr. Reid didn't quite die, but he still lives with the painful result of the choices made during that April evening in 1998.

He describes his second guesses about that night in his memoir, *The Bullet Meant for Me.* It's the story of the trip that Mr. Reid and three Austin friends took to Mexico City to see a boxing match in which superfeatherweight Jesus Chavez was fighting. Mr. Reid had met Mr. Chavez at an Austin boxing gym, and they had become close friends. But Mr. Chavez was an illegal immigrant. The government deported him to his native Chihuahua. He no longer could box in the United States.

So Mr. Reid and his friends went to Mexico. After Mr. Chavez won his fight, the Americans spent a day and a night bar-hopping and wound up in a taxicab whose driver had a sideline: robbing gringos. He drove his tipsy passengers to a dark, empty street and stopped. Two confederates flung open the car doors and brandished revolvers. Mr. Reid wound up with a bullet in him and screaming.

But he doesn't replay that horrible scene in his head anymore. "If there's a reason for doing this book, maybe that's it. To let it out of my system," he says. "But I think about the *consequences* of it." Four years later, he still walks with a cane and takes painkillers.

Jan Reid's name is a familiar one to Texas readers. In 1973 he was among the first free-lancers to publish in a new magazine called *Texas Monthly*. His story was about a couple of losers who held up an icehouse in San Antonio, ran a red light, and got into a chase with more than twenty cops. "By the time they got to New Braunfels, there were helicopters and shooting," Mr. Reid remembers. "The losers rolled their car in front of the high school, and that was the end of it." The driver's door alone had 122 bullet holes in it.

Mr. Reid was the sports editor of the New Braunfels *Herald-Zeitung* at the time. He later quit the newspaper and wrote for *Texas Monthly* pretty much full-time. He wasn't on the staff, but his stuff was in the magazine so often that many readers thought he was.

Another early *Texas Monthly* piece was about the countercultural music scene in Austin, where in the early 1970s a joint called the Armadillo World Headquarters was becoming the center of a new kind of song. That story eventually grew into Mr. Reid's first book, *The Improbable Rise of Redneck Rock*. The small Austin house that published it soon went out of business. But Texas music scholars revere the book as the classic account of Austin music's Golden Age, when such unique giants as Willie Nelson, Jerry Jeff Walker, Kinky Friedman, and Michael Murphy walked the Travis County earth. These days, a used copy of *Redneck Rock* in decent condition can cost $150 or more.

Over the years, Mr. Reid has published three other books: a novel called *Deerinwater* (his favorite); *Vain Glory*, a book about Texas football in its high-school, college, and professional manifestations; and *Close Calls*, a collection of his best magazine work. Its title was inspired by his Mexico City catastrophe.

In the introduction to *Close Calls*, Mr. Reid calls himself "an accidental journalist," because of the tortuous and unsystematic way in which he stumbled into the trade.

He was born in Abilene in 1945, but his family soon moved to Wichita

Falls, his father's hometown. His father was an oil refinery worker, "a good, blue-collar union man." His mother's family were tenant cotton farmers.

"Dad bought a house in a working-class neighborhood just four blocks from where he grew up," Mr. Reid says. "He wanted my sister and me to grow up just the way he had. But because of the vagaries of school boundary lines, I wound up going to school with kids who were incredibly rich." He still remembers his embarrassment at climbing into his father's old car while his classmates were riding away from school in Cadillacs.

After high school, Mr. Reid enrolled in his hometown college, Midwestern University—now called Midwestern State—and majored in history. He was the first of his family to go beyond high school.

Meanwhile, the oilfields around Wichita Falls petered out, the refinery closed, and Mr. Reid's father was transferred to another plant at Mount Pleasant, Texas.

"I was a slightly better than mediocre student," Mr. Reid says. "I didn't know what the hell I was going to do with my life. I thought about going to law school. I thought about becoming a football coach."

The summer before his senior year, he was living with his family in Mount Pleasant and working on a highway crew. Out of boredom during his off time, he began writing a short story. He worked on it all summer.

"My last semester at Midwestern, I had to take some course that wasn't in my major or minor," he says. "I signed up for Jim Hoggard's writing course, the first time he ever taught it." Because Mr. Reid wasn't an English major, Professor Hoggard—now a well-known Texas poet, novelist, essayist, and translator—had to grant him permission to enroll.

"The first story I wrote, Jim told me, 'You ought to publish this,'" Mr. Reid says. "His remark was a pretty heady experience for me. It fired me up. But it took me a while to do anything."

He graduated in 1968 and went to work for a Dallas insurance company as an underwriter. He hated it. "It seemed what I did most of the time was cancel people's car insurance, which was kind of awful. Then I was promoted up to work on commercial liability stuff, which I didn't understand. I was completely lost." After two years, he quit. "My boss, long after I was gone, still referred to me as 'the history major that didn't work out,'" he says.

Like many people who are unhappy in their jobs, Mr. Reid worked on a novel in his spare time. "But I discovered that I hadn't read enough to be a writer," he says. "So I came down to Austin and went to graduate school for two years. I thought about getting a Ph.D. and teaching, but that never really seemed real. Mostly, I just wanted to get an education so I could write."

He earned a master's degree in American studies at the University of Texas at Austin. "So I had two useless degrees," he says, "which is how I wound up being a journalist."

He applied for jobs at the big Dallas and Fort Worth newspapers, but he was told that without experience he couldn't get hired. So he went back to Mount Pleasant and wrote for the local *Daily Tribune* for several months, then moved to New Braunfels and the *Herald-Zeitung*.

By 1977, he was highly enough regarded as a magazine writer to win a Dobie-Paisano Fellowship from the Texas Institute of Letters. The institute pays the fellow a stipend to live on J. Frank Dobie's ranch outside Austin and write. There he did the early work on *Deerinwater*. "Things turned around," Mr. Reid says. "I started getting something done."

Mr. Reid's work has appeared in *Esquire, GQ, Men's Journal, Mother Jones, The New York Times Magazine,* and other publications, but *Texas Monthly* has always been his home base. Once during the nineties, *Texas Monthly* even hired him as a staff writer. Then, after a year, he was laid off during a "downsizing."

"The editors quickly established that we worked a lot better together if I wasn't around the office all the time," he says. "It felt an awful lot like getting fired."

Mr. Reid and his wife Dorothy, who has worked on the staffs of various state officials and agencies over the years, made a pleasant life for themselves and their dogs in a pleasant house on a pleasant street in Austin.

Then he went to a boxing match.

"My stepdaughter Lila didn't even know I was in Mexico when it happened," he says. "All of a sudden she gets a call that Jan has been shot in Mexico City. The phone rings, and your life is thrown way off into another orbit. It was as hard on Dorothy and Lila as it was on me."

He holds up his thumb and forefinger, almost touching. "The bullet missed my aorta by that much. I would have bled to death. It missed my spinal cord by a fraction. In many ways it was almost miraculous. There are so many ways it could have left me dead or in a wheelchair."

The pain comes in surges, he says. One day he counted them. There were twenty.

"The thing that often sets them off is mundane stress," he says. "Lost car keys, ordinary little upsets."

Five-and-Dime

From time to time, a customer comes into Bewley's five-cent-to-five-dollar store on the Bonham courthouse square and wants to buy something but doesn't know its name. Some customers get embarrassed about that, John Bewley says.

One day, he says, a cowboy's wife came in and described a kitchen tool that her husband had given her. She said he paid fifteen cents for it, and it was shaped like a stirrup turned upside down. When her husband presented it to her, she asked him what it was, but he didn't know. He had forgotten to ask the store clerk.

Now, fifty years later, the wife was needing another one of those things, and she didn't know what to ask for. It was embarrassing.

She said, "Do you know what I'm talking about?"

Mr. Bewley said, "Yes, ma'am, I know what you're talking about."

She said, "Do they still make them?"

Mr. Bewley said, "Yes, ma'am, they still make them."

She said, "Well, do you know the name of it?"

Mr. Bewley said, "Yes, ma'am. I've known it for many, many years."

She said, "What do I want?"

Mr. Bewley said, "You want a pastry blender."

She said, "And you've got them here, and I can buy one?"

Mr. Bewley said, "You can buy several."

The woman raised her hands over her head and shouted, "Lord, thank you!"

Another time, a man came in who lived in Dallas. He said he was looking for a pocket comb with a clip on it that would clip to his shirt pocket.

"There's not one in all of Dallas," he said. "I was in a store there, and a lady heard me complaining about that, and she said, 'You can get a comb with a clip on it in Bonham on the west side of the square.'"

So he drove seventy-five miles to Bonham and bought half a dozen pocket combs with clips from Mr. Bewley.

Back in the first half of the twentieth century, if you wanted a pastry blender or a comb with a clip on it, you knew exactly where to find it. Almost every little town and every city neighborhood had a store like Mr. Bewley's. Over its door might be a sign with the name of a big mercantile chain on it: Woolworth, Kress, Ben Franklin, W.T. Grant. Others bore the names of local, independent merchants like Mr. Bewley. Whoever owned them, the customers called them "five-and-tens" or "five-and-dimes" or "variety" stores.

They were where you went when you found yourself in need of the essential small items of life: thread, buttons, zippers, elastic, ribbon, knitting yarn, safety pins, iced-tea pitchers, iron skillets, can openers, curtain rods, ice trays, oilcloth, light bulbs, greeting cards, smoking pipes, laundry baskets, key rings, hummingbird feeders, electric fans, mouse and rat traps, ice picks, lamp chimneys and wicks and oil.

For the kid with a birthday dollar or a couple of dimes burning holes in his pocket, there was the glorious toy counter, its bins heaped with painted wooden tops, glass marbles, jacks, red rubber balls, glass piggy banks, slabs of modeling clay, dominoes, card games, cap pistols and caps, toy trucks and cars, stick horses, board games, dolls, tea sets.

The candy and bubblegum were on low shelves near the cash register, where the kids could reach them. Out on the sidewalk, especially around Christmas, stood genuine red Radio Flyer wagons in several sizes, and maybe even bicycles.

Bewley's is still like that. But stores like Bewley's are rare now. Like mom-and-pop grocery stores and gas stations, they've been bulldozed off the map by big business, by huge we-sell-everything chains of supermarkets and discount stores.

"Variety stores are disappearing because they're too much work and too little pay," says Mr. Bewley's wife, Annabel. "Not many young people want to do something like this. They want to do something big."

"This is the only variety store in Fannin County," Mr. Bewley says. "I have one in Commerce. These two, they tell me, are the only ones left in this part of the state. I did have one in Cooper and one over in Oklahoma, but we just couldn't take care of all of them. Help is very difficult to find in this type of business. Some people think they would like to get into it after retirement, but I advise them not to. It's difficult if you didn't grow up in it."

Mr. Bewley, who's eighty-four now, grew up in Cooke County and graduated from high school in Gainesville, where he also worked in a variety store. He served in the infantry and the air corps during World War II. After his discharge, he went back into the variety store business.

"I was with Duke & Ayres, out of Dallas, for nearly thirty years," he says. "They were one of the first variety store chains in the Southwest. Mr. Duke and Mr. Ayres, they started out in Bowie, Texas.

"I operated a store here in Bonham for Duke & Ayres from '46 until '53, then I moved away. This store I have now was put in by a gentleman in 1937. He was my competitor, but he was my friend. In 1970, he called me. I was living in San Marcos at the time. He said he was going to retire. He asked if I would be interested in his 'little bird nest.' That's what he called it."

Mr. and Mrs. Bewley bought the store and moved back to Bonham. They've run the place by themselves, with a little part-time help when needed.

"You stay in business by selling merchandise that other stores don't stock," Mr. Bewley says. "When you're the only store in town that sells that one item, it can be a pretty good seller."

Mr. Bewley roams the store, showing off his unique wares. "We let the ladies pick out their ribbon and bring it up to the front, then we measure and cut it," he says. "Every spool tells how much it costs for a yard. And here's a line that's really coming back: embroidery. The doctors say that it's great therapy. We sell a lot of Rit dye. We have handkerchiefs for ninety-nine cents. We sell lots of pins, needles, safety pins. We still sell oilcloth and lace by the yard. At Wal-Mart, they don't do that. You've got to buy whatever is in the package, because it takes a lot of time to measure out and cut a piece of oilcloth. And time is money.

"But I work a lot cheaper. And I have lots of time."

"John doesn't get down here as early as he used to," Mrs. Bewley says. "But he doesn't take many days off. He takes off Christmas and Thanksgiving and doesn't open on Sundays until after church."

Mr. Bewley unlocks his store about seven o'clock every morning. "If people don't see my pickup here by a certain time, they'll call my wife and ask, 'Is there something wrong with your husband?'" he says. He stays until dark. So long as there's still a car on the courthouse square, he won't close.

"There's something about the things we had when we were young that we hate to give up and not have anymore," he says.

He holds up a tiny heart-shaped bottle of Blue Waltz perfume, priced at $1.99.

"I sold this item when I went to work in a variety store in 1938," he says. "It sold for ten cents back then. It was a top seller at Christmastime, for schoolchildren to provide a gift for their teacher. Now the ladies come in, and they remember that they bought it as a child, and they buy it. A lot of retired teachers buy it."

A customer, Sheila Etnes, sets her purchase beside the cash register. It's a package of hairnets. She's a cook at the nutrition center over at Honey Grove.

"There really are things you can get here that you can't get anywhere else," she says. "Hairnets. Can't get hairnets anywhere else. Not with beads."

A few days ago, a man ten years younger than Mr. Bewley came in to buy a new tip for his crutch.

"So I went and got him one," Mr. Bewley says. "And he said, 'When you get to be my age, you won't be able to move around like that.' And I said, 'Well, tell me your age, so I can prepare for it.' And he said, 'I'm seventy-four.' And I said, 'Thank you. I'll remember that.'

"People ask me if I've thought about retiring. I kind of feel like I'm retired now. I like what I do. I got into this business as a way of getting out of the cotton patch, and I'm still out of the cotton patch."

Art

Joanna Rowntree hunkers on the terrace, holding a cup of green paint in her left hand and a brush poised in her right. She gazes appraisingly at Anthony Caro's *Sculpture Three*, then reaches out and touches it with the brush, lightly. Tap. Like that. She dips the brush and touches the sculpture again. Tap.

She's the conservator at the Nasher Sculpture Center, a doctor whose patients are the 350 modern sculptures in the collection that Dallas real estate developer and his late wife Patsy spent half a century assembling. "It's my job to make sure they're all as healthy as they can be," she says.

She wants them especially robust by Monday, when the $70 million museum—Mr. Nasher's gift to his home city and the art world—opens to the public.

For Mr. Nasher and architect Renzo Piano and landscape architect Peter Walker, the ribbon cutting will celebrate completion of a unique museum for the display of modern sculpture by the likes of Rodin, Picasso, Calder, and Giacometti, a jewel to which the world will come. For the general contractor, for about forty subcontractors and another forty consultants and the hundreds of workers who have labored since January 2001, it's the finish of a difficult and exhausting job done well.

For *Sculpture Three*, an assemblage of heavy iron pieces bolted together at various angles, Ms. Rowntree's delicate touches of paint are the end of a major overhaul to put it in shape for the grand occasion.

"It's from the sixties, and the original paint color has been slowly modified over the years," Ms. Rowntree says. "It has been repainted and repainted and repainted. So over the summer I spoke with Anthony Caro's assistant and got the correct color match information and took the sculpture apart and repainted it. When we brought it outside, some of the bolts had to be replaced. Now I'm touching up all the bolts that got chipped during installation and painting the new ones."

During the last few days before the museum opens, she has a lot still to do. "I'll be washing and waxing Magdalena Abakanowicz's *Bronze Crowd* over there by the wall," she says. "I'll be doing a little bit of touch-up on Miró's *Moonbird* . . ."

She won't hurry. It all has to be done right. Every detail must be complete and perfect. Elsewhere among the sun-flooded glass-and-travertine exhibit pavilions and the vast green sculpture garden, knots of workers stretch and bend in unhurried desperation, trying to make everything right in the little time they have left. Each group has a puzzle to solve: getting a door to fit right, getting a pedestal in just the right position for the right piece of sculpture to be set upon it, getting a tree planted in the right spot, getting a light fixture installed in the right place to give the right kind of light.

Along the garden walk below the terrace, electricians perch atop ladders like fruit pickers, plucking bulbs from the fixtures that have been attached to the new-planted trees. They're replacing the bulbs with new ones. Again.

The mounting pressure toward opening day is pushing the workers to the edge of exhaustion. "I was here till eleven-thirty the last two nights," says Durango DeFrance, the man in one of the trees. "We put in the lights and shine them on the sculptures and ask, 'Is this what you want?' And they say, 'Well, no, I need a wider lens. No, I need a 20-watter. No, I need a 50-watter. Turn it this way, turn it that way, turn it there.'"

He tilts back his hard hat and adjusts his mirror sunglasses. "We've got a lighting engineer that wants to do it one way and a lighting architect that wants to do it another way and an owner that wants it another way. Tomorrow they may want something different from what they want today. It just depends on who can persuade who to go with what."

Finally it's Mr. Nasher who must be persuaded. Natty in pinstripe suit, striped shirt, and red tie and handkerchief, he meets each morning with the contractors and prowls the site, stopping now and then to look, to consider, and give orders.

As he steps onto the terrace one morning, a landscaper in the garden recognizes him and murmurs to the man beside him, "El jefe."

"Ray is a hands-on owner. There's nothing in this building that he hasn't touched," says Vel Hawes, whose sculpture center business card identifies him as "owner's representative." He's the lightning rod to whom all suggestions, problems, and complaints come. "Ray's a perfectionist," he says. "He makes up reasons for being here as much as he is, but the real reason is, he just wants to be here. He tells me, 'If you need any decisions, call me.' Being translated, that means, 'Don't do anything I'm not involved in, because I want to have fun, too.'"

Mr. Hawes, an architect who practiced in Dallas for forty-two years, says he has worked with Mr. Nasher—now at eighty-one a patriarch among the city's real estate developers and philanthropists—on nearly every building he has built. Three years ago, Mr. Hawes was sixty-four and thinking of retiring. When Mr. Nasher found out, he phoned Mr. Hawes, who still remembers the conversation:

"I have something I want you to do," Mr. Nasher said.

"You don't understand. I'm trying to retire," Mr. Hawes said.

"Wait. You haven't heard the job yet," Mr. Nasher said. "I want you to build the sculpture center."

"Where do I report?" Mr. Hawes said.

Since then, he has been Mr. Nasher's man on the ground at 2001 Flora Street, responsible for design and construction. "Not to design it," he says, "and not to build it, but to be on the owner's side and to be his representative through it all.

"A shorter description of my job would be 'ego management.' There's quite a lot of that around here."

On a particularly hectic morning, Mr. Hawes has gotten a call from a representative of Mr. Piano, who's in Italy. The architect says he needs a helicopter photograph of the center. Now. Today. The weather in Dallas is overcast, threatening rain. Mr. Hawes sets someone looking for a helicopter, but even Mr. Piano will have to wait for the weather to clear.

"Renzo's a genius, a sheer genius," Mr. Hawes says. "And he's a lot of fun to work with right up until the time you tell him no. Then he turns into a gorilla. Boy, he can throw a tantrum!"

In the museum auditorium, workers are about to take down all the track lighting they've just installed. The fixtures were painted white to match a white ceiling. Mr. Piano decided to paint the ceiling gray instead, so white fixtures will no longer do.

"The lights will be sent back to the factory to be painted gray," Mr. Hawes says. "They won't be back for six or eight weeks." Theatrical lights must be rented and installed temporarily. They're black. "The original lights were black before they were painted white," says Mr. Hawes.

Meanwhile, the director of a video documentary is complaining about the bright light streaming into the auditorium from the glass wall overlooking the sculpture garden. "It won't do!" she's saying. "Everything will be backlit! We'll need some kind of scrim."

"This is what always happens," Mr. Hawes says. "Whenever an artist comes in, whenever a video person comes in, whenever a food person comes in, they want us to remodel the building all over again."

The museum has been an unusual job, says Neil McGlennon, senior manager on the project for Beck, the general contractor. It has been harder because most of the pieces that he has been fitting together in Dallas—the slabs of travertine, the great glass walls, the curved glass and beams and the unique aluminum screen that comprise the ceiling and roof, the heavy glass doors—were designed and made in Italy.

"It's an entirely custom building," he says. "There are no standard details. Everything about it is unique. Plus having to deal with Italian designers and a lot of Italian subcontractors. It's a challenge to say the least. With most projects, you work backward from the final design. But this design was always a work in progress. We never stopped designing. The only way to stop it was to get the work in place."

Impossible to get into place, it seems, are the glass entrance and exit doors, about 250 pounds each, that workers are trying to install on the four sides of the building. A typical American-made door may be tweaked in half a dozen ways to make it fit correctly after it's hung. But these Italian doors must be already adjusted perfectly before they're hung on their spindles. Otherwise they must be lifted down, readjusted, and lifted again, some as many as ten times before they're right.

"Hold on, men! Hold on!" Bill Rector urges his crew, again taking down the doors that lead from the boardroom to the terrace. "Come on! Come on! Get under this!"

"This type of design is like a new automobile," he says. "Once we get all the bugs out, we've got it made. But until then we have to play with it, find out what's working and what's not."

On another side of the building, four men are lifting down another door yet again, moving the heavy glass slab away from its opening, straining. "Swing your partner, do-si-do!" calls their leader. "Swing your partner, here we go!"

But slowly, slowly the jobs and the men who have done them disappear. For three years the cacophony of trucks, cement mixers, power drills, saws, and hammers has enveloped this block of Flora Street. Now in the final days of the museum's creation, its noises slide at last into whispers of paintbrushes, razor blades scraping glass, trowels digging in soft earth, the small knock of broom handles against dustpans, finally into the silence of hands in gloves lifting precious treasures to their pedestals.

In time for its opening day, the Nasher Sculpture Center rests in serene purity.

"It seems really simple when you look at it," says Mr. McGlennon. "But the most difficult thing in the world is making something look simple."

Game

All right, I'll say it right here at the beginning: We lost. The Strawn Greyhounds beat the Fort Davis Indians for the Texas State Six-Man Football Championship. The score was Strawn 67, Fort Davis 62. More points than that have never been scored in a Texas six-man championship game. During the last three minutes and nine seconds, Strawn scored two touchdowns and Fort Davis scored three. If the game had lasted another 45 seconds, I'm pretty sure we would have won.

The fans set a record, too. The combined populations of Fort Davis and Strawn total about 1,700 people. The official attendance at Odessa's Ratliff Stadium on that cool, clear December evening was 6,101. Judging from the size of the crowds in the opposing grandstands, two-thirds of them came to root for my Indians.

"I think the Methodist preacher's wife is the only person in Fort Davis tonight," said Indian fan Carry Huffman.

Neither Strawn nor Fort Davis had ever played for the state championship before. The Greyhounds were a fine, tough team, and maybe even deserved to win. OK, probably deserved to win. One pre-game poll favored them by seventeen points. But the Indians were the only far West Texas team still alive in any classification of the state football playoffs. And Strawn, well, it's about halfway between Abilene and Fort Worth, practically in East Texas.

So all the towns between El Paso and the Pecos River embraced the Indians as their own. Odessa people came. Hundreds drove from nearby Midland, Kermit, Andrews, and Wink, and from Marfa, Alpine, Pecos, and Fort Stockton, and from Balmorhea, Valentine, and Marathon, even from El Paso, nearly 300 miles away.

Alma Aranda said she had intended to spend Christmas with her family in Fort Davis, but changed her mind. "Christmas comes every year, but

Fort Davis has made the state playoffs for the first time," she said. "So I bumped my plans ahead and came for the game instead."

She lives in Maine. But she's a 1989 grad of Fort Davis High and "still an Indian all the way."

Sam Cauble flew in from California in the afternoon and would fly back the next morning. "I knew people would be coming out of the woodwork for this," he said. "How often do you go to state?"

Well, Fort Davis won a girls' volleyball state championship in 1980. A girls' doubles tennis team won state in the 1970s.

Sam played six-man football for the Indians in the seventies, "a long time ago," he said. His brothers—Freddy, Frank, and George—played, too. All were starters. George still lives in Fort Davis. He came to Odessa wearing the green-and-gold letter jacket he won in 1968.

"It was tough in those days," he said. "Let me tell you, it was tough. It was tough all the way around. Everybody was tough. Balmorhea, Marathon, Sierra Blanca, Toyah, Barstow, Pyote, Fort Hancock. Six-man was big then, and I'm glad we've gone back to it. I've always loved it."

Six-man football is for tiny schools. Under state rules, schools with 100 or more students can't compete in it. But Marathon, which won two state championships in the 1970s, didn't have enough boys even to field a team this year. Toyah, Barstow, and Pyote lost their schools years ago. They've almost disappeared even as towns. Not long ago I stopped by Toyah and found the boarded-up school and its sad football field, gone to weeds, its scoreboard rotting. But Toyah and Barstow, and Pyote were ferocious foes once. Tough, as George said.

In the 1952-53 Fort Davis High School yearbook, I'm crouching. My right-hand knuckles are firm against the ground. My left arm is laid across my thigh. That dark object near my right hand appears to be a football, but it's the shadow of the photographer's head.

I'm wearing the green-and-gold uniform of the Indians and a metallic gold helmet. (Metallic-painted helmets were new in West Texas. Very cool. Not many teams had them yet.)

I'm trying to look tough and aggressive, but I'm six foot tall and weigh 120 pounds. I'm awkward and slow. By the end of this, my sophomore season, I know I'll never be good at football. I don't go out for the team again.

But 1952 was a good year for the Indians. Four of our players—Van Kountz, Johnny and Rudy Granado, and Joe Webster—made All-District. We won the district championship. Barstow and Toyah and Marathon were among our victories; we tied Pyote. We won bi-district and went on to regional, which was the end of the championship road back then for six-man football. There was no state crown for the tiny schools.

Christoval was our foe for the regional trophy. They had a big fellow named Jack Pardee, who would become an All-American linebacker for Texas A&M, a two-time All-Pro for the Rams and the Redskins, and would someday coach the Houston Oilers.

Christoval beat us, 80-52. I barely got into the game.

More than fifty years later, I'm "still an Indian all the way," like Alma Aranda.

At Ratliff Stadium Coach Gerry Gartrell said I could watch the game from the sidelines, with the team. Everything seemed familiar. The green uniforms, the gold helmets, the substitute players, achingly young, roaming up and down the sideline, shouting hope to their teammates. One boy, tall and skinny, was a mirror image of me a half-century ago. The game's constant running, the long passes, the scoring, scoring, scoring that makes regular football look so lumbering in comparison. . . Yes, this was the real thing.

It was where my Indians should always have been. But in 1976 the Fort Davis High School enrollment inched past 100. The Indians had to switch to the eleven-man game. Fort Davis was the smallest school in a powerhouse district. It always had the fewest, always the youngest players. They got beat up a lot. During a quarter century the Indians made the playoffs only twice, and never lasted long there.

Watching their games became discouraging. Their fans grieved. Their crowds shriveled, even at home. In the 2000 and 2001 seasons they won not a single game. They lost twenty.

But by last year the enrollment had dropped into the eighties, and Coach Gartrell persuaded the school board to return to six-man. "Not everybody was for it," said George Cauble. "Some thought it would diminish the town and the school. They thought it would make us less."

The opposite happened. Last year, my Indians won second place in their district and a slot in the playoffs. This year, they won district, bi-district, regional, and area championships. They beat both the teams that had played in last year's finals. Now they had missed the state championship by five points.

It was a hard game to lose. There were a few manly tears. Then the Indian cheerleaders and the people in the stands started clapping, chanting, *We-are-proud-of-you. Hey! We are proud of you! We-are-proud-of-you! Hey! We are proud of you!*

On the field, Trini Granado, his forehead sweating, his leg bleeding, faced a TV reporter. Trini had scored five touchdowns for the Indians, including the last one with eleven seconds left to play.

"I'm not down about this game," he said. "This is as far as we've ever come. I can't be down about that. We were nothing two years ago, and now we're somebody. I'm glad to be here."

So was I.

Editor

María Eugenia Guerra is talking about her past. "Maybe I wasn't an out-right hippie," she says. "Sometimes my blue jeans were pressed at the cleaners. My parents had opened an account there for me. But certainly I was an earth mother and rabble-rouser, an organic farmer, a chicken-raiser. My son was raised on whole grains and raw milk."

She's talking about the late sixties and early seventies. Meg, as everybody calls her, was bouncing from one university to another because of bad grades. She owned a no-chemicals plant nursery called Jungle Stores in Austin for a while, was married "about five or six years," had a baby. After her divorce, she worked for a botanical company called Sweetheart Herbs and lived in bucolic Wimberly with her toddler, George Altgelt.

"I raised him by myself," she says. "I hated being his mother when he was a teenager, but everything worked out. Now he's twenty-eight and married to a wonderful woman. He's a law student at St. Mary's University in San Antonio. He's a real smart boy. He's a wonderful surprise."

The rabble-rousing that Ms. Guerra did in those long ago days was about Vietnam. The war was a subject of heated discourse around Austin and the University of Texas, one of the schools where she was a sometime student between "forced withdrawals." The war was a hot topic at home in Laredo, too. "My father was chairman of the draft board," she says. "My sister's husband was a pilot in Vietnam. But I believed the war was wrong. I believed we shouldn't be there."

She remembers it as a rich time, she says. "The friendships I made, the way I felt things so deeply, I loved that time. I think that time helped me find the ethic that I've always tried to push through in my work."

Ms. Guerra is almost fifty-four years old now, but she hasn't mellowed much. Rousing rabble is her principal occupation. She owns, publishes, and writes much of the copy in *LareDOS*, a butt-kicking monthly tabloid that she and an erstwhile partner cranked up in December 1994. In the spring of 1996 she bought out her partner and "pretty much started over," she says. She rented the bottom floor of a turn-of-the-century duplex that a bank was managing for an estate and moved *LareDOS* into it. When the building came up for sale, she bought it.

The paper comes out about the middle of every month. Ms. Guerra prints 5,000 copies, most of which are stacked beside the cash registers in Laredo restaurants and given away free. "They fly out of there," she says. "They go like hotcakes." She sells enough advertising to publish sixty-four to seventy-two pages most months.

"I've stopped at nothing to keep it going," she says, "finding ways to sell more ads, doing the kinds of stories that need to be written." She and her editor, Tom Moore, write most of them.

Her paper is subtitled *A Journal of the Borderlands,* and the *DOS* is capitalized because there are, of course, *dos* Laredos, the Texas border town of 185,000 and its more-than-three-times-larger Mexican sister, Nuevo Laredo, just across the narrow Rio Grande.

That's really too much territory for Ms. Guerra and her staff of four to cover. She acknowledges that the Texas Laredo occupies nearly all her time and attention. "I've always been interested by public corruption," she says. "How dare they, with taxpayer money, enjoy themselves to the extent that they do?" So for seven years she has dogged the school board, the county commissioners, the city council, and various law enforcement and social services agencies with notebook and camera and telephoto lens, exposing the sins committed at the public trough.

From time to time, her efforts result in a "shakeout," she says. "But it's a shakeout in the Laredo way. Nobody gets fired. People get reassigned. People decide to retire. There's a certain degree of decorum used in Laredo. They always soften the blow."

Ms. Guerra's main passion is the Rio Grande. Laredo's bridges over the river are glutted with NAFTA trucks carrying goods up and down Interstate 35. The river also is Laredo's water supply. The U.S. government's role in its environmental deterioration, the unbridled development along its banks, and Laredo officials' seeming indifference to the river's condition all infuriate her.

"The federal government, in its zeal about drug interdiction and illegal visitors from Mexico, has peeled back the riverbank. They've taken away the bank and made a road where they can four-wheel drive. The border patrol doesn't do anything very well. They're not stopping the flow of drugs, and they're plucking people off the landscape who really just want to work. They should put all their money into drug interdiction. That's the real crime."

Even worse atrocities are committed against the river, in Ms. Guerra's opinion, by American developers building end-to-end warehouses along its banks, and pell-mell development on the south bank in Nuevo Laredo, which has no apparent plan to include a sewage treatment plant. Ms. Guerra fears that raw sewage in the river—already a huge problem along the Rio Grande—will increase.

"The water quality in Laredo isn't good," she says. "I don't drink it. I know a lot of people who don't drink it. It's laden with heavy metals. Every study done on the river says Laredo has major problems. But city officials don't read the studies or don't understand them or don't believe them.

"We try to let people know that gravity will prevail. What we do to the watershed ultimately will end up in our water. All those chemicals people use to make their yards look not like part of the Chihuahuan Desert but like a golf course, those they will someday drink.

"And we still have people on the city council who say, 'Conserve water for what? So that McAllen can get it?'"

Despite her constant surveillance and rolling volleys of journalistic buckshot, Ms. Guerra says she gets along pretty well with Laredo's public officials. "I'm not sure they like me a lot," she says. "I don't know what they say when I'm not there. But in Laredo everybody kisses everybody on the cheek. It's the custom."

Maybe the hearty doses of satire and humor that she includes in *LareDOS* soften the bite of her criticisms and crusades. "We poke fun at City Hall," she says. "We make sure they don't take themselves all that seriously. And we bop them when they misbehave."

When the mayor and city council were beating the drums for a new arena to house a minor-league hockey team, a *LareDOS* cover was a doctored full-page photograph of the local politicos in hockey garb, on the ice and wielding sticks. The smiling mayor appeared to be missing a front tooth.

When the fire chief resigned after allegedly ridiculing the religious beliefs of one of his firemen, *LareDOS* superimposed the chief's mug shot on a picture of a martyr standing in flames.

Ms. Guerra especially enjoys spoofing the Society of Martha Washington, a group of Laredo socialites that celebrates President Washington's birthday every year with a pageant and ball at which everyone dresses as an officer in the Continental Army or a colonial dame.

Another debutante society called the Princess Pocahontas Council dresses in American Indian costumes and stages another pageant "designed to recreate the lives and values of our first Americans." In 2001, the theme was "Legends of the Totem Pole Through Indian Eyes."

"That's pretty strange stuff for a town on the Mexican border to do," Ms. Guerra says. "But every year Laredo outdoes last year's celebration. I really try to understand what this is about, but I can't."

So *LareDOS* proposed an alternative "Colonia Ball" and suggested that everyone come dressed as a social or environmental or political issue.

"The Marthas laughed," Ms. Guerra says. "They thought it was hysterical. We're good friends with the Marthas. They advertise with us."

The first of Ms. Guerra's western hemisphere ancestors arrived at Veracruz in 1602, only eighty-three years after the Spanish conquered the Aztecs. Over the centuries the family moved northward until they reached the Rio Grande, crossed into Texas in the late 1880s, and settled in the Laredo area.

Ms. Guerra's father was a Laredo businessman. Her mother's family worked a ranch near San Ygnacio, a small town south of Laredo.

"As my family had always done, I moved north, too," she says. "I went to Austin, I even went to Dallas, but I came back." (Her first attempt at college had been at the University of Dallas, then UT-Austin, and then Southwest Texas State University at San Marcos, where, in her forties, she eventually graduated with a journalism degree.)

When she moved south again something over a decade ago, she went to work for the *Zapata County News*, one of two rival newspapers in the tiny South Texas town of Zapata. Then she hired on to run its competitor, the upstart *Zapata Weekly Express*, for a couple of years until it went out of business. Then she was the first director of the Rio Grande International Studies Center, an environmental organization that monitors water quality in the Rio Grande and tries to be a voice for the river. Then *LareDOS* happened.

Meanwhile, she had moved into the old house on the ranch near San Ygnacio and had taken over management of the place for her family. "My parents were horrified when I told them I wanted to live there," Ms. Guerra says. "It's very primitive. But I filled it with books and made it comfortable. It's not splendid, but it's a wonderful, beautiful place."

So, at the end of a long work day on the streets of Laredo, she climbs into her Ford F-250 four-wheel-drive pickup, shoves a CD into the player, and heads the forty miles south toward home while Dwight Yoakum sings "Cattle Call." There she feeds her free-range chickens, gathers their eggs, and worries about the next issue.

"There are deadline nights when we're still wondering what's going on the cover," she says. "Sometimes we're too loose. We don't plan ahead a lot. And it certainly doesn't make much money. It's always on the edge of overdraft."

In December 1999 she published a special issue of *LareDOS*, celebrating her paper's fifth anniversary. "Anyone versed in the publishing business knows that in newspaper years five years is practically a lifetime," she wrote. "Little papers don't have a life past a couple of years."

Then she wrote, "I love this place. I love the faces of this town. I love the scoundrels that run for public office and sometimes get there. . . . I love the principled ones, the compassionate ones. I love the ordinariness of this place, but I love, too, our penchant for pomp and circumstance. . . . I love the goodness of us, this town of pretty children."

Maybe that's why she and her edgy tabloid are still around.

Vet

Dr. Charlie Edwards remembers the day he started thinking about retiring. It was 1991. He was standing in some ramshackle shipping pens at Presidio, medically testing a herd of cattle that was about to be delivered over the Rio Grande into Mexico. He was sixty-six years old. The temperature in the shade of the scale house was 112. Dr. Edwards was in the sun.

The pens were some six inches deep in dry, powdered manure, which reflected the heat and the sunlight and, from under the hooves of the cattle, rose into nose-clogging clouds. "The only shade I had was a three-foot-tall dead cottonwood tree," Dr. Edwards says. "Not a breath of air was stirring. Even the flies were looking for a hole. My pickup was so full of them that there was no room in it for me."

So when he finished the day's job, Dr. Edwards stretched himself on the ground under his truck to rest. He awoke later to find men shaking him and calling his name. He thinks he had passed out.

A few days after that, when Dr. Edwards had more work to do at those pens, he and the cowboys who were helping him decided to do the job at night. "The thermometer showed 114 degrees in the shade when I arrived at six P.M.," he says. "When we finished up at two-thirty the next morning, it was ninety-nine. That doesn't sound much better, but there was no sun blazing on me and not many flies."

That day under his pickup was one of several times in recent years that the sun, the heat, the relentless pace of his work, and his unwillingness to pause for enough swallows of water had put him under.

"My lungs got bad on me, and my thermostat burned out," he says. "When the temperature would get above seventy, I melted, and when it would get below seventy, I froze. The doctors think it was because of the heat exhaustion."

So in 1995 he retired, sort of. "I didn't go out in the country and rassle cattle anymore," he says. "I did some consulting, peddled some pills, and treated dogs and cats." A couple of years ago his fragile health forced him to give up that, too. "With my lungs and my heart, I don't even buy green bananas anymore," he says.

So he wrote his memoirs. The book is called *Up to My Armpits: Adventures of a West Texas Veterinarian.* If you have to ask what the title means, you probably don't want to know.

☆

In the cities, the practice of veterinary medicine takes place in a well-equipped air-conditioned animal hospital with clean examination rooms, nice boarding cages, and comfortable reception rooms. Nearly all the patients there are cats and dogs and, from time to time, maybe a rabbit or a cockatoo.

Dr. Edwards had an examination room and a few cages in his hospital, too, on the south side of Marfa. The hospital was part of the house where he and his wife, JoAnn, still live, more than fifty years after he hung his shingle out front, facing the highway to Presidio. The shingle is down now, and Dr. Edwards' old office is bare of instruments, medicines, and beasts.

For most of the days and nights between 1949, when he won his vet degree from Texas A&M and moved to Marfa, until his retirement, Dr. Edwards wasn't at his hospital much anyway. His patients were cows, horses, goats, and sheep scattered over some of the roughest terrain in America, and he was the only practicing veterinarian between the Pecos River and the El Paso County line, an area of ranch country about the size of South Carolina.

Getting to his patients often required driving 100 miles or more on narrow Trans-Pecos highways, then fifteen or twenty or thirty miles over rocky, bone-jarring ranch roads. Sometimes, if the sick or pregnant cow was off in the mountains somewhere, the rancher or a cowboy would then have to drive him up to find her.

"Some old cowboys that spend most of their time in the saddle can make a pickup ride down a ranch road a real adventure," Dr. Edwards writes in his book. "They don't really drive it, they just kind of herd it. Well, not that either exactly, it's more like letting a horse have his head to pick his way along. 'Course the dumb pickup doesn't watch where it's going, so the cowboy floorboards it and lets the chuck holes and rocks look out for themselves."

Dr. Edwards' trips to the distant, lonely ranches usually had a social side to them, as well as a professional one. Sometimes the rancher and his wife hadn't been to town for weeks. They were eager for news and gossip. And since that visit might take up Dr. Edwards' entire workday, the rancher and his wife would invite him to spend the night or stay for supper or at least have a little refreshment before hitting the road again.

Of a visit to the Reid brothers' remote ranch in Jeff Davis County shortly after he began practice, Dr. Edwards writes, "I had coffee and cake and a nice visit. You didn't just dash up and go to work, besides this was my first call and we needed to get acquainted. They were so congenial that I'm afraid I always spent more time than I should have. Some would say I wasted time, but this was a different era. It is sad to remember those nice, long visits and compare them with the way we now run around helter-skelter. Our clients are more customers now instead of friends."

Wade Reid drove Dr. Edwards to a sick cow in the mountains. She was foaming at the mouth and wouldn't eat. She might have rabies. But Dr. Edwards recently had removed a thorny mesquite limb from the throat of a similarly foaming cow and thought this might be a similar case.

He thrust his arm down the cow's throat and slowly extracted a big piece of deer antler. He keeps it on a shelf in his old office, amidst other souvenirs of his long practice.

"It seems I had my arm down a cow's throat half the time in the first part of my practice and up the other end the later part," he says. "But there are no teeth back there."

Iron Mountain Press, a tiny publishing house in tiny Marathon, Texas, published *Up to My Armpits* in 2002. The press concentrates on such local matters as the grasses and wildflowers of the Trans-Pecos, cowboy memoirs, and Big Bend folklore. Dr. Edwards' stories about his adventures as a ranch country vet are detailed and colorful and often hilarious. He also writes remarkable character portraits of nearly every man and woman who ranched in Trans-Pecos Texas during the second half of the twentieth century.

"J.M. Fowlkes was always called Manny," he writes of one well-known cattleman. "He may have signed his checks that way—I don't remember. He was known as one of the whispering Fowlkes boys. They had the most remarkable volume to their voices. A normal conversation voice in front of the Paisano Hotel could be heard a block away. I never heard him raise his voice. He didn't have to."

Dr. Edwards' account of his career seems so exact that readers assume he relied on diaries or journals to write it, but he didn't. "All this is from memory," he says. "Now, it's not my memory entirely. Ranchers would come in, and we would visit, and they would help me remember things. And I would share my joys and my triumphs and my traumas with my wife. She could remember lots of things that stirred my memory."

Mrs. Edwards remembers so many of her husband's adventures because she was there when they happened. He was on call twenty-four hours a day, seven days a week, and almost never took a day off. "I tried to go to church on Sunday morning," he says. "I made it about half the time."

Often after completing a big job on one ranch, he would climb into his pickup and drive immediately to another, perhaps three or four hours away. "When I was so sleepy and tired, JoAnn would drive and let me sleep," he says. "I was going some really ridiculous hours in those days. People shouldn't push themselves like that. But I felt an obligation to the public. There weren't any other veterinarians in the country. I felt I ought to take care of them."

He was used to hardship. The drought of 1917-18 had wiped out his rancher grandfather. The drought of 1932 had wiped out his rancher father. "We never had very good luck ranching," Dr. Edwards says, "but I wanted to do it anyway. I didn't have any money to get in the business, but I thought I could get my foot in the door by becoming a veterinarian and going from there into the cattle business. I never did that. But I got to spend time with the cows. That was as much fun as if they belonged to me."

His lack of cow ownership didn't spare him from the troubles suffered by the families who owned the herds. During the first decade of his practice, one of the worst droughts in history struck West Texas. From 1953 to 1957, most of the land got no measurable rain and could grow no grass. On some ranchers' land, no rain fell for seven years.

"When some of the cattle on a few ranches appeared to be doing fairly well where no animal should," Dr. Edwards says, "it was explained by saying the cattle had learned to crack open the rocks and get the kernels out."

Many cattlemen had to sell off their herds. Many went broke and abandoned the business or left the country. With fewer ranchers and fewer cattle, the vet had less work. "Finances became tight," he says. "Often, when JoAnn and I passed an ice cream place, we became silent."

In desperation he accepted a ranch job near Fort Stockton and was about to close his practice, when a group of six Big Bend cattlemen called him to a meeting at the Paisano Hotel in Marfa.

"They offered to buy all their ranch supplies from me if I would put in a stock of them," Dr. Edwards says. "And they would get their friends to. If I still couldn't make it, they would make up a kitty for me at the end of the year.

"Well, you can't leave people who are making you that kind of offer. So I managed to tough it out, and they were nice enough to go by their word. And they never had to get up a kitty for me."

But the big drought drastically reduced the number of cattle in the Trans-Pecos, and the land has never recovered completely.

Now it's in the grips of another drought. This one isn't as severe as the 1950s one, but it has lasted thirteen years so far.

"Really, the main compensation for my practice has been the wonderful people I've known and the visiting I've done with them," Dr. Edwards says. "Gosh, there's some good people out here! I just wish it had rained again."

Yodeler

Don Edwards remembers the day he first saw a cowboy. He was a young lad. He and his family were on a visit to relatives. One day, a 1946 Ford wood-paneled station wagon pulled up in front of the house next door.

"It had Arizona license plates on it," says Mr. Edwards. "This man got out and went up to Mrs. Briggs' front door. He had his hat on, and he was wearing boots and a plaid shirt and blue jeans with the cuffs turned up the way they wore them in that era. He was a sure 'nuff cowboy. I could tell that."

Mr. Edwards smiles. "It's funny that the first cowboy I ever saw wasn't out West. It was in Massachusetts."

Even before he saw a cowboy, he was nuts about them. "From my earliest times, I was eaten up with the cowboy deal," he says.

Like many kids growing up in the 1940s and fifties, he played cowboy with his friends and watched the Saturday B westerns at the movie theater. But his fascination with cowboys went deeper.

He devoured *Smoky, the Cowhorse* and *Sand* and *The Drifting Cowboy* and the other stories of cowboy author/artist Will James. "My parents gave me one of his books every year for Christmas," he says. "From Will James I learned what a *real* cowboy was."

His mother tried to get him to wear shoes to school like the other boys did, but he insisted on cowboy boots.

His father—a former vaudeville magician and musician—bought him a Sears Roebuck Silvertone guitar. Don began learning cowboy songs.

"I knew what I wanted to do with my life when I was nine years old," Mr. Edwards says. "My mind was already set."

But he lived in New Jersey. Nobody could be a cowboy there, even in the bucolic countryside of little Boonton, where he and his two sisters were growing up. There were no wide open spaces in New Jersey. What cows were there had to be milked.

When he turned sixteen, Don Edwards quit school and headed for Texas.

He's still here.

☆

The study in Mr. Edwards' country home near Weatherford is filled with the memorabilia of his forty-year career as a cowboy folk singer. There's a framed photograph of him with George W. and Laura Bush, taken after he had played for them at the governor's mansion in Austin. There's another of Mr. Edwards with Ronald Reagan and Gene Autry and Texas cowboy singer and poet Red Steagall, with two secret service agents glowering in the background. There's a framed program from the World Championship Rodeo with Roy Rogers' photograph on the cover. It's autographed, "Roy Rogers and Trigger." Over Mr. Edwards' huge desk hangs the framed original manuscript of the Western classic song, "Tumbling Tumbleweeds," written by Bob Nolan in 1932.

In a glass bookcase are early editions of books by Will James and other western writers. And on another shelf stands a collection of 78-rpm record albums that belonged to his dad the vaudevillian.

"Dad wasn't in the big-time like Milton Berle and Bob Hope," Mr. Edwards says. "He was on the rural, small-town circuit, all through New Jersey, New England. Besides his magic and his music, Dad was an actor in plays. He did a lot of summer stock.

"By the time I was old enough to appreciate what he was doing, he quit all that. He thought show business was a frivolous way to make a living. So, being a responsible father, he just gave it up when we kids came along. But sometimes he would play the grange hall on weekends."

On a shelf near his father's albums are arrayed the awards that Mr. Edwards has won for his recordings of traditional cowboy songs: the Cowboy Hall of Fame Wrangler Award for 1992 and 1996; the Indie Award for Traditional Album of the year for 1998; the Western Music Association Artist of the Year Award for 1997 and 1998.

"Traditional cowboy music is basically a part of folk music," Mr. Edwards says. "It's pretty much songs that were collected from among cowboys. When I say 'cowboys,' I mean working cowboys, not movie cowboys."

Not that he has anything against movie cowboys. Across the room from his awards, another framed photograph stands on a bookcase. It's of Mr. Edwards and his wife, Kathy, and Robert Redford. It was taken on location in Montana in 1997, when Mr. Redford was directing and starring in *The Horse Whisperer*. Mr. Edwards plays the part of Smokey in the movie. Smokey is a singing cowboy.

"Redford was introduced to my music by a fellow named Patrick Markey, who produced *A River Runs Through It* with him," Mr. Edwards says. "So one day my agent called me and told me Redford wanted me to read for the part of Smokey. I had never been in a motion picture in my life. I had never thought of trying to act.

"I thought I would be going to one of those cattle-call auditions. Big names in Nashville were pursuing that part with a vengeance. I read for the thing. They said, 'We'll call you.' I said, 'Yeah, sure,' and never gave it another thought.

"Then one day the phone rang, and they said, 'Bob wants you to play the part of Smokey.' It turned out that I was the only guy they auditioned for it. Redford had already made up his mind.

"I kept calling him 'Mr. Redford.'

"He kept telling me, 'It's 'Bob.'"

Mr. Edwards never worked on a ranch for wages. "When I first came down to Texas, I worked for nothing, just to be a part of it," he says.

He got a job with Fort Worth Pipe and Supply, hauling oil field stuff. This got him onto a lot of ranches. "Later on, I'd go back and help them gather cattle and brand them or ship them. I'd get to work with cowboys. But I was just passing through the lifestyle. I wasn't born into it. I wished I had been born into it."

When he wasn't hauling oil field pipe, he played street corners and bars with his guitar and banjo, singing the cowboy folk classics: "Little Joe the Wrangler," "The Streets of Laredo," "When the Work's All Done This Fall." Then in 1960 he saw an ad in *The Fort Worth Star-Telegram* and *The Dallas Morning News*. A new amusement park called Six Flags Over Texas was auditioning entertainers.

"They wanted somebody to sing in the Texas section of the park," Mr. Edwards says. He answered the ad. "I sang 'Cattle Call' and 'Strawberry Roan.' Then they asked me if I knew how to use a gun. I had never handled a six-shooter, but I said, 'Yeah. Of course.' So, lo and behold, I got the job.

"The major thing at Six Flags now is the rides, but back then it was the live shows. I would get out there and sing a couple of cowboy songs, then me and the other guys would get in a gunfight. We did that gunfight several times a day. They brought stunt people in from Hollywood to show us how to do it.

"That's how my career began. I stayed at Six Flags until 1965 or '66."

In 1964, he cut his first 45-rpm record, "The Young Ranger," at a studio in Dallas. It was a gunfighter ballad, a rewrite of a folk song called "The Dying Ranger."

"I took my records around in my little truck when I was driving for Fort Worth Pipe and Supply," he says. "I was in every oil patch in Texas, Oklahoma, Kansas, Nebraska. Every time I would see a radio station tower, I would drive over and introduce myself. I was selling a lot of records off the back of my pickup."

Then he took his guitar to Nashville, hoping for the big-time. He wasted a few years there, and didn't make an impression. "I didn't like commercial country music, and they didn't like cowboy songs," he says.

So he came home to Fort Worth and got a gig playing at a bar called Poker Flat, and later at the White Elephant Saloon in the Stockyards district. He met Kathy Davis, who also worked at the White Elephant. They've been married for twenty-three years now, and own an interest in the saloon.

Mr. Edwards has recorded fifteen albums over the years. His latest is *King of the Wind: Memories of Marty Robbins*. It's gunfighter ballads and other songs Marty used to sing. Mr. Edwards' smooth baritone sounds eerily like him.

After a stint with Warner Brothers, Mr. Edwards records for Western Jubilee Recording Co. now. It's an independent label that's owned by him and the other musicians who record on it. And he entertains at colleges and universities and cowboy and folk gatherings all over the country. Wherever an audience gathers for the music of the old West.

"It's a niche market," he says. "Nobody's going to get rich. I do it for the love of it. I believe in kind of a destiny thing. I think you're steered in a lot of ways. I've gone through life and been on the verge of hell and every place else and up and down and all around. But there's a feeling I get sometimes that says, 'Yeah, I'm supposed to be here.'"

Matador

David Renk shrugs into his jacket. He examines his image in the mirror. "It's like Superman coming out of the phone booth," he says. "I'm different now."

Earlier, he looked like any tall, skinny cowboy in plaid shirt and faded jeans and big buckle, slouching among friends, drinking beer and laughing. Now he's the gringo matador known as "El Texano," splendid in a maroon, gold-brocaded suit of lights, ready to step out and face the bulls again.

Beyond the thin walls of the trailer where he's dressing, canned bullfight music blares from a loudspeaker. Friends and strangers who have spent the afternoon eating barbecue and drinking are leaving the cover of the plastic awnings that have sheltered them from the brilliant sun. They're making their way to their seats at the Santa Maria Bullring.

The ring is only a few yards from the home of Fred Renk, David's stepfather and owner of La Querencia Ranch. Fred built the ring three years ago. The blood-red structure of wood and welded steel looms against the cloudless, hot sky and the flat acres of mesquite in the pasture beyond the fence.

This will be like no bullfight in Mexico or Spain or South America. There will be no spear-bearing picadors on horseback, no banderilleros running at the bulls with barbed sticks. There will be no swords. Because traditional bullfighting is illegal in all the fifty states, no bulls will be injured or killed. If blood is to be spilt, it will belong to the matadors.

El Texano is forty years old. He retired three years ago after nearly a quarter of a century as a professional matador, after 175 fights throughout Mexico. But today he and three fellow toreros will march into the Santa

Maria ring to offer the spectators an abbreviated, bloodless version of the ancient Spanish art.

"Bullfighting goes back 5,000 years," says Ed Cohn, an aficionado who has traveled from Walnut Creek, California, to preside over today's event. "We're talking caveman times. In caves in Spain, they've found murals of men fighting bulls. It goes as far back as history goes."

For generations, border Texans and tourists have crossed the Rio Grande on Sunday afternoons to watch bullfights in Matamoros, Reynosa, Ciudad Acuña, Ciudad Juárez, and other towns on the Mexican side. Among those fans was Fred Renk, a water conditioner salesman living for a time in Las Cruces, New Mexico. In the 1960s he would become a bullfighter himself. He started too old—in his late twenties—and never made the big-time of the taurine world.

But he never lost the *gusano*, the worm that aficionados say dwells inside them and never stops gnawing, the passion that makes them think or talk of little else but bulls and matadors.

Fred passed the *gusano* to his young stepson, David. David was a unique story. He was born with two clubfeet. Through painful surgery and years of training, he graduated from braces, special shoes, and wheelchair to the matador's suit of lights. On New Years Day 1978, he fought his first bullfight in Reynosa, across the river from McAllen, Texas. He was fourteen. Over the next twenty years he would carry his nom de guerre "El Texano" (a spelling that he and Fred prefer to the more usual "Tejano") into all the major bullrings of Mexico.

He was featured in *People* magazine. *Sports Illustrated* gave him a ten-page spread. He appeared on *The Tonight Show with Johnny Carson* and *Good Morning, America* and, more lately, in documentaries on NBC and A&E. He's only the sixth American to become a full-fledged *matador de toros,* a big-league star of the bullfight world. He's the only American to have that rank confirmed in La Plaza Mexico, the world's largest bullring. On the night before that ceremony, President Reagan phoned to wish him luck.

David also has performed in bloodless bullfights north of the border in such unlikely places as Dodge City, Kansas, and the Astrodome, and at the indoor rodeo arena at Gilly's honky-tonk in Pasadena, Texas. All those fights were attempts to infect American fans with the bullfight *gusano*.

On February 20, 2000—by then married and a father—David fought his last professional fight in Reynosa, where he had begun. At the end, the band struck up "Las Golondrinas," a song of farewell. David and Fred walked together to the center of the ring, and Fred removed the matador's pigtail from the back of his stepson's head. Then they walked together around the ring, acknowledging the crowd's cheers, and weeping.

☆

La Gloria, Texas, is a crossroads hamlet thirty miles northeast of Rio Grande City at the junction of Texas farm to market roads 755 and 1017. A few hundred yards east of the La Gloria gas station, there are two signs on the left side of the road. One advertises Renk Water Systems and Manufacturing International, the business that pays the bills. The other advertises the Santa Maria Bullring, named for Fred Renk's patron saint. From the road the ring looks like a Little League ballpark.

Across the cattle guard and down the dirt road are also the ranch house and the bullpens and chutes. In the pasture behind the house are fourteen cows, eight calves, and a nine-year-old seed bull named Pepete. They all are of the fighting Saltillo blood, the beginnings of a herd. Fred says he's the only breeder of fighting bulls in the United States.

"I built the ring in 2000 to have a place to teach students," he says. "Then I said, 'We might as well put some stands here, and then we might as well put some corrals here, then we need some chutes.' Once the welders were working, we just kept on going. Pretty soon we've got $150,000 sitting over there. We'd go out and hustle and make a buck and come back and put it right in that ring."

Fred and David and some visiting matadors teach four bullfight schools a year at the ranch. They comprise one to six students who come from Maryland, from New York City, from California, all over. The *gusano* is gnawing at their innards. They pay $950 for the week-long school, including room and board. During the first two schools that they attend, they learn cape work against a fake bullhead mounted on bicycle wheels and plunge their swords into a hay bale. If they return for a third school, they get to face a real bull in the ring. "Two of them are hoping to wear the suit of lights," Fred says. "That's pretty good for the fifteen or so who've come to our schools."

Like many things on the border, the scheduling of the schools is indefinite. "We kind of work around when the people can get off from their jobs and come down here," Fred says.

During the winter, Fred presents a bullfight in his ring about once a month for the snowbirds—Midwesterners and Canadians fleeing the winter, who arrive each year by the thousands in the Rio Grande Valley. The ring will hold about 1,200 spectators, he says, "and we fill it up."

Other times during the winter, lines of yellow school buses pull into the Santa Maria parking lot. South Texas intermediate schoolchildren pour out of them and into the bleacher seats. "They've never seen bullfights," Fred says. "We're trying to introduce them to the taurine world. It's one of their own Hispanic arts. It's their culture, and they don't even know about it."

Among the matadors they come to see is El Texano, who works for the family business and lives just down the road from his stepfather. "Driving three-quarters of a mile to fight is a hell of a lot better than going and sitting in some motel 300 or 1,000 miles away," he says.

This year Fred extended his season to the Memorial Day weekend and there "could be" another bullfight around Labor Day, he says.

Whether a bullfight is scheduled or not, Fred's home always is open to passing aficionados and toreros who drop by for a good meal and a little tequila or beer. A big room just off the covered patio is furnished with a pool table and a bar and tables where people can eat and drink and smoke. The walls are covered with bullfight posters and photographs from the careers of Fred and David and many Mexican matadors who have been their friends.

Some guests stay an afternoon, others for days. The bunkhouse behind Fred's house will sleep six. It's usually full, says Ed Cohn, who comes to La Querencia three or four times a year. For this Memorial weekend fight, it also houses the three matadors who will appear in the ring with El Texano, each to face one bull. They're Longinos Mendoza, a matador who is also a bank loan officer in Houston; Enrique Delgado, a popular matador from Monterrey, Mexico; and Bruce Hutton, a fifty-five-year-old San Diego businessman. For years he has been an *aficionado practico*, an amateur torero, but says he has never aspired to the rank of *matador de toros*. He'll wear a *charro* costume, not a suit of lights, to meet his bull.

Every time he goes into a ring, El Texano says, the same words move through his mind, 'What the hell am I doing here?'

"Before, it was for good reasons," he says. "Now it's for other reasons. I'm forty years old now. I'm married. I have kids. I don't need to be doing this. But I want to help out my dad. If we want bullfighting to survive, we've got to grow the crowds. We're losing people all the time, losing our fan base. Even the new generation of Latin Americans don't go to bullfights like they used to. They go to see soccer. So we're trying to do something to get more Americans to understand what bullfighting is and to appreciate it."

In the Santa Maria ring, when the matador has finished his cape work and the "moment of truth" arrives, he doesn't plunge a sword into the animal. He rushes at the bull and tries to grab a rose that's stuck with glue and Velcro between the beast's shoulders. "If this is what we have to do, then we've got to do it," David says. "It's not the traditional bullfight, but baseball's not the traditional baseball, either. That game has changed, too."

From a booth high above the ring, the announcer, Lyn Sherwood, explains to the local fans and the tourists what they're going to see and what they're not.

"Contrary to popular belief, bullfighting in the United States isn't illegal," he says into the microphone. "But the killing of bulls or the shedding of their blood in the ring is strictly forbidden. However, it's perfectly OK for the bulls to spill the blood of the toreros. . . ."

Then, to the stirring trumpet strains of "La Virgen de la Macarena" the four bullfighters march together into the ring. They salute the crowd.

A minute later, the red door opens. The first huge bull charges out, bellowing.

Captain

As the birdwatchers and tourists climb aboard the boat, dawn is just rising over Aransas Bay. A light fog sits upon the water. The water is gray, like the fog, and smooth, barely lapping at the dock pilings where seven gulls sit watching.

The passengers, bundled in jackets and sweatshirts, are grateful for the coffee and doughnuts that the deck hand offers them. They laugh and joke in Midwestern and Canadian accents. There are thirty-three of them. They slide into the bus-like arrangement of seats along the boat's windowed bulkheads and look for spaces to stow their cameras and binoculars.

Captain Ted Appell, the boat's owner and skipper, isn't feeling well. He has turned the wheel over to his associate, Captain Harold "Stoner" Jones. Captain Ted, as everybody calls him, will guide the tour from the second seat this morning.

He's wearing a white shirt with captains' epaulettes on the shoulders, a black gimme cap with "No. 1 Grandpa" on the front, and a green satin jacket with "Fitzgerald's Casino, Las Vegas" on the back. He sits down behind Captain Jones and looks at his watch. "We've got two minutes to wait for two more people," he says. He waits the minutes. Nobody else shows up. "Let's go," he tells Captain Jones. "We're wasting daylight."

At exactly 7:00 A.M. Captain Jones backs the boat away from its dock. Captain Ted picks up his microphone and goes to work. "When these clouds burn off, we ain't going to have nothing but sunshine and a pretty, pretty day," he says. "I ordered it special for you." Then he directs the passengers' attention to the birds on the pilings. "What you see there is pretty much laughing gulls," he says. "Laughing gulls."

This is the thirtieth year that Captain Ted has ferried people across the bay for a visit with the Texas Gulf Coast's most famous residents. In the marshes and bays of the Aransas Wildlife Refuge, 174 endangered whooping cranes pace with the solemnity of bishops, whiling away their winter in warmth and plenty. Sometime about the end of April, the great white birds will rise into the sky and depart again for their nesting ground in Canada's remote Northwest Territories, 2,500 miles away. Then, as they've done since time immemorial, they'll come back to Texas again when the Arctic winds begin to chill.

The Aransas refuge is the only place in the world where devoted bird-watchers and curious tourists can get close enough to the cranes to observe them in their natural habitat, even through binoculars.

Although he's only fifty-eight, this may be the last month of Captain Ted's last season as master of his beloved *Skimmer*, the boat he designed and built eighteen years ago for just this job. "I've been talking about retiring for five years," he says. "It looks like this time the good Lord is going to make me do it. I don't want to, but I've had a lot of heart problems lately. I've got to slow down."

He's advertising the *Skimmer* for sale in the Gulf Coast newspapers and on the Web. He's asking $375,000 for it. "Whoever buys the business, I'm not going to leave them out there wet," he says. "I'll work with them for a year and get them a good captain and make sure everything is going right."

Captain Ted says these things quietly, in a conversation. The always-cheerful captain never burdens his passengers with unpleasant matters.

"Aransas Bay is eight miles across and twenty-two miles in length," he says into the mike. "Its average depth is less than three-and-a-half feet. The *Skimmer* is usually operating in less than two feet of water. So if you fall overboard, just stand up and holler and I'll come back and get you. If you drown yourself in two feet of water, I'll be very unhappy with you.

"Over on the right side, you've got Pelican Reef. You've got white pelicans, you've got brown pelicans, you've got double-crested cormorants. Off Blackjack Peninsula over there, you've got pintail ducks."

The ducks appear to be floating on a foggy mirror against the background of low, dark trees along the edge of the peninsula. The *Skimmer* has entered the wildlife refuge.

"Whoa, looks like we've got a brown flathead mugwump sitting on that post over to the left of us," Captain Ted says. "That's a rare bird. Get your eyeballs on him. They're not often seen around here. We mostly find them up around Washington, D.C. It's real easy to identify that bird. Look at him. He's got his mug on one side of that post and his wump on the other."

The passengers groan at the joke. Then they get what they've paid for. "OK," the captain says, "we've got three whooping cranes. This is a family unit. Two adults, one juvenile. You all run up to the top deck and have yourselves a good time."

The birds are only about fifty yards away, wading majestically among the reeds and grasses, hunting their breakfast in the water. Most of the passengers grab their binoculars and cameras and bird books and clamber up the stairs. Captain Ted shifts into full lecture:

"The whooping crane is our tallest North American bird. Standing in a full erect position, it's almost five foot tall. It has a seven-and-a-half-foot wingspan. Its weight runs along fifteen to twenty pounds. They're red on top of the head, black on the cheek, white all over with black wingtips. . . ."

He tells how the plumage of the juvenile will change color as it grows up. He tells how the birds migrate and live together as family units, how the male establishes and defends his family's territory, how each family occupies its same exclusive territory every year. He tells of the cranes' courtship rituals and their mating, their Canadian summer home, the hazards they face during their migrations, their life cycle, their eating habits.

"What they're doing right now is what they do all day, just walk up and down and eat," he says. "They love berries, bugs, frogs, toads, lizards, snakes, eels, acorns, blue crabs, fiddler crabs, stone crabs, crawfish, shrimp, dead fish, small birds if they can catch them, small animals if they can catch them, mussels, and clams."

If Captain Ted wrote down everything he tells about his beloved whoopers and added footnotes to it, it could be a master's thesis. Certainly few ornithological scholars have known the subject as long or intimately as he. "They don't do too good getting their young birds down here," he says. "We had about fifty nesting pairs this year, two eggs each, and we got about eight chicks out of that. That's not good odds.

"Now this particular family right here, the male is twenty-eight years old this year," he says. "Mom out there is twenty-five. The first mate he had, she was a pretty little thing. She lasted about a year, then passed away of a massive coronary heart attack. It was really heartbreaking."

Birds and other wildlife have fascinated him since he was a kid growing up in Florida and Texas and Louisiana, he says. "We didn't know about endangered species back then, but we knew there was some things that needed to be helped out."

He started working on the water when he was nine years old on commercial snapper boats, deep-sea fishing boats, tour vessels, private yachts, three-masted schooners. He joined the Marines and served for four years, three of them in Vietnam, and returned to the Texas Gulf Coast in 1967.

He thinks it was about 1969 that he first saw the whooping cranes. "I was on a fishing trip in the preserve," he says. "The guy I was with says, 'Look over there. There's one of them whooping cranes.' It was quite an experience. We didn't know much about them back then."

There were only about thirty of them in the world that day. Now there are the 174 that he takes people to see, and about 200 more in zoos and experimental programs.

"I went into the birding business in the early seventies, working with Captain Brownie Brown," he says. "He was like an adopted father of mine. I had known him before I went into the service. He started the first whooping crane tours in 1964. His boat was called the *Whooping Crane*. It was a beautiful old wooden boat, but very slow.

"I worked for Brownie for fourteen years, then he passed away in '84 or '85, and I took over and ran his operation for a year or two. Then I designed and engineered the *Skimmer* and had it built. I wanted a high-speed boat with a shallow draft and maneuverability, to cut the length of time it took to get from point A to point B, so you would have more time for birding."

The *Skimmer* is all aluminum with a fourteen-foot beam, forty-five-foot length, and only an eighteen-inch draft. Captain Ted hired a man in Fulton to build her. They laid her keel in 1986, and had her in the water for the 1987 season. Thus was born Captain Ted's Whooping Crane Tours. "She's still a good old gal," says the captain. "She's doing her job."

He conducts the tours from November through April, the months the cranes are in residence at Aransas. In the off season, he goes looking for other birds in such places as Central and South America, Australia, New Zealand, Canada. Before she died of cancer three years ago, his wife, Bobbie, went with him. "She loved birding with me," he says. "She was the right hand of my business."

Suddenly the day has turned out as Captain Ted promised his customers. The breeze is still cool, but the clouds and fog are gone. The sunshine is warm and brilliant. The peninsula, the marshes, the water itself shine with a hyper-sharp clarity that seems unreal.

"Aw, look at this pretty sunshine!" he says. "You can't find anything closer to God's land than this right here. Beautiful! We've got some grackles bouncing around over here on the right-hand side."

The birds seem in collaboration with the captain to provide a better-than-usual show. He points out a killdeer, a tri-colored heron, an osprey, a fishhawk, a long-billed curlew, an ibis, two American oystercatchers, two great blue herons, more cormorants, and brown pelicans. He tells how DDT almost wiped out the brown pelican along the Gulf Coast and how it has come back since the pesticide was banned. "I'm happy to report that there are now well over 1,500 brown pelicans on the Texas coast now," he says, "and their population is increasing rapidly every year."

There are Caspian terns, willetts, a black-bellied plover, a common loon, more oystercatchers sitting on reefs in the bay, a reddish egret, and several Bonaparte's gulls. There's even a rare peregrine falcon, standing on a post in the water, posing for the birdwatchers' cameras. "There's the fastest animal anywhere in the world," Captain Ted says into his mike. "Peregrine falcons have been clocked at 220 miles an hour in a dive." He tells Captain Jones to steer in a tight circle around the post, to give the passengers a better view. "Isn't he fantastic?"

Four white pelicans fly over in a straight line, one behind the other. There are more great blue herons, a roseate spoonbill, a redtail hawk, a golden harrier hawk, various egrets, more cormorants, sandhill cranes, sandpipers, a group of juvenile whooping cranes hanging out, probably up to no good, some solitary juveniles, several family units of three. More than thirty whooping cranes in all. The birdwatchers are excited, writing in their books.

"We might get back late today, it's so doggone pretty," Captain Ted says. "I hope you don't have a doctor's appointment or something."

He directs Captain Jones to take the *Skimmer* almost to the end of Aransas Bay, where it opens into the adjacent San Antonio Bay, then reluctantly tells him to turn and head for home.

At precisely 10:30, the boat eases back into its berth at Fulton, thirty minutes later than usual. Captain Ted stands by the gangway and tells his passengers goodbye, then goes next door to the Sand Dollar restaurant for a cup of coffee. In two days, he says, he will go into the hospital for more tests on his heart. He talks again of retirement and his boat.

"I know I'm going to hate the day I sell her," he says. "This has been a good life for me. Every time I see those birds out there, I get just as excited as I did the first time I ever saw them. I've got no complaints."

Cowgirl

When Diane Masters was a child in San Antonio, she wanted to be a cowgirl. "I was a big Roy Rogers and Dale Evans fan," she says. "I lived in my cowgirl suit. My brother and I put on our pearl-handled cap pistols every morning when we got up. My bicycle was a white stallion named King."

While she was majoring in art at Texas Christian University, she started dating a football player named Chris Lacy. "We dated for a long time before I ever knew he had a connection to a ranch," she says. "Then he told me he wanted to come out here and help his grandfather."

Chris Lacy's grandfather was Herbert L. Kokernot, Jr., owner of the o6, a beautiful, historic, and famous ranch in far West Texas.

As Diane's father was walking her down the aisle to marry Chris, he said, "Well, your dream has come true. You're going to be a cowgirl."

"And I'll tell you what," she says. "From the moment we moved out here until this day, I haven't had one boring day."

On this bright, windy spring morning, Diane Lacy, now a fifty-three-year-old grandmother, is leaning against her red pickup truck near the foot of a mountain. She's wearing sunglasses against the glare. A red baseball cap covers her hair, but her blond ponytail blows anyway. She's holding a camera with a zoom lens, waiting. Her husband, her son, Lance, and a cowboy named Rod DeVoll have ridden up the mountainside and are somewhere on top, out of sight, looking for horses.

They may not be back for a couple of hours Ms. Lacy says. "It's hard to get up those trails. Sometimes you have to jump your horse up those boulders and just hope he doesn't fall. It's wild up there. The last of the wilderness."

The horses have been on the mountain all winter. Now they're needed for the spring roundup. "When they come down, they'll be kicking and bucking," Ms. Lacy says.

She isn't at the bottom of the mountain for snapshots. Over the past decade or so, Ms. Lacy's photographs have appeared in *The Cattleman, Cowboys and Indians,* and other western magazines, on the covers of books and the walls of galleries. They've won awards at western art exhibitions across the Southwest. Custom-made limited-edition prints of her work sell for hundreds of dollars at the galleries and on her Web site.

"I started shooting photographs when I was in high school," she says. "I had a little darkroom at home. My father was interested in photography, and I would help him. He bought me my first really good camera when I graduated from high school. I took photography in college. But when I came out here and saw this country, it was like, 'Oh my goodness!'"

Her constant subject is the rugged Davis Mountains country of the o6 Ranch and the life she lives there as wife, mother, grandmother, and, yes, cowgirl. Portrayed throughout her work are cowboys, horses, cattle, windmills, sunrises and sunsets, rugged mountain landscapes, thunderstorms and drought, green grass when it's there, brown dust when it's not.

"I just want to tell our story, what this ranch is about, what we're trying to do," she says. "There are so many wonderful moments when I'm out there working cattle with the others that I wish everybody I know could be with me. If I'm in the pens branding, I want them to be in the pens branding with me.

"They can't be there, so I try to capture that moment for them. If I could get smell and hearing and tasting into my photographs, it would be even better, because they're all part of it. And the bigness of this country. If I could somehow capture the vastness of the sky and the land. . . ."

The o6 cattle brand is older than the state of Texas. David L. Kokernot, a scout for Sam Houston during the battle of San Jacinto, acquired it in 1837. In 1883 it was brought westward from Gonzales County on the hides of his family's herds into the unfenced Davis Mountains. In 1912, when the open range was being fenced, David's grandson, Herbert L. Kokernot, established the o6 Ranch. Eventually it would comprise large swatches of Jeff Davis, Brewster, and Pecos counties.

Herbert L. Kokernot, Jr., succeeded his father as boss of the big spread.

He was a quiet, modest man, beloved throughout the Big Bend and Texas and the cattle business for his silent philanthropy and his love of people and the land and his animals. He served sixty-five years as a commissioner of Jeff Davis County, the longest tenure of any elected official in Texas history.

Chris Lacy, "Mister Herbert's" grandson and the sixth generation of his family to follow the cattle business, now manages the o6 for his family, which includes his mother, Mary Ann Kokernot Lacy, and his three sisters.

Like his grandfather and his great-grandfather, Chris Lacy runs the ranch in the traditional way more typical of the nineteenth and early twentieth centuries than of the present day. He's one of the few Texas ranchers who still do.

Fences are few across the o6 range. At roundup time—for branding in the spring and shipping in the fall—a crew of sixteen to twenty cowboys and a remuda of more than 100 horses move into the mountains and stay until the cow work is done. The hands sleep in teepee tents and eat off the chuck wagon for three or four weeks. They work ten to twenty sections of land a day, depending on the terrain. A section is 640 acres, a square mile.

"We've got a great cowboy crew that comes in every year," Ms. Lacy says. "At the end of the spring roundup, they sign up for the next one in the fall. There's a waiting list. We've had cowboys come from as far as Australia and Canada. Arizona, Wyoming, Colorado, New Mexico. But most of them are from around West Texas."

Ms. Lacy often goes with them into the mountains. "I photograph what's happening. I don't set up anything," she says. "If you try to set up cowboys, they feel self-conscious, and it always looks a little staged. I don't want that. When I'm on horseback, I'll be taking pictures and chasing cattle at the same time. Sometimes I have to change film while I'm riding. I have to just hope I get the right composition and the right light and the right focus.

"I'm always looking for what could happen. I don't want to miss the moment. Since I've worked out here all these years—thirty-two years—we've done sixty-four or sixty-five roundups, so I kind of know what the horses might do, what the cowboys might do, what the cows might do. I try to be mentally ready."

☆

Ms. Lacy refers to the ranch and the mountains and the quiet isolation of them as "our way of life." For a century, it was a way of life that few people outside the mountain counties of Jeff Davis, Brewster, and Presidio knew about. They were miles and miles from anywhere else, and roads leading into the Big Bend were few, narrow, twisting, and lightly traveled.

But during the past three decades, interstate highways have made them accessible. People from other states and regions have discovered the mountains' beauty and their salubrious climate and have moved there. Many of them try to change what they find.

Since her children are grown now, Ms. Lacy has devoted much time to trying to ensure that as little change as possible happens to her children and grandchildren and the traditional Big Bend way of life.

Her children, Lance and Kristin, grew up on the 06, and Ms. Lacy home-schooled them all the way through high school.

"I wanted them to learn the family business and appreciate the ranch and what we do," she says. "I didn't want them to miss the roundups, because that's the most educational and fun thing there is to do. It was a big job, but they went on to college and did really well."

Both went to Baylor University. Lance was an outfielder on the school's last Southwest Conference baseball team, just before the venerable league was dismantled. He graduated from Baylor and met his wife, Brandee, there. They are soon to have their second child. Lance's sister, Kristin Cavness, transferred back home and graduated at Sul Ross State University. She and her husband also have two children and own several business interests in Marathon and Alpine.

Now that Lance and Kristin are grown, Ms. Lacy has embarked on a public career apart from her photography work. She's president of the Davis Mountains Trans-Pecos Heritage Association, a grassroots organization of landowners, headquartered in Alpine, which does battle against the state and federal governments and against such environmental groups as the Nature Conservancy and the Sierra Club for control of the land.

"We believe in conservation through private ownership, not public ownership or some organization like the Nature Conservancy making the decisions how your land will be used," she says.

Last year, she was elected to the same seat on the Jeff Davis County

Commissioners Court that Herbert Kokernot, Jr., occupied for sixty-five years and her husband Chris occupied for twelve. Ms. Lacy is the first female commissioner in the history of the county.

"I hate politics," she says. "I am not a politician. I like to tell it like it is. I like to be up front with people. Half the people are mad at you all the time. You don't get paid. It's a very hard job. But I care very much about where we live. I care very much about our county. I care very much about all the counties out here. I want to keep the specialness of this area.

"A lot of people move out here because it's unique. But when they've been here a while, they want to make it like the place they came from."

There's suddenly a faint rumble up the mountainside. About thirty horses are making their way down the steep slope, through the boulders and the brush. Chris, Lance, and Mr. DeVoll are following, yelping, whistling.

The horses reach the bottom, then gallop down the dusty brown road and across the flat. A dun, a paint, a white, sorrels, bays, their winter coats still shaggy.

Ms. Lacy is shooting, quickly, quickly, as the beasts pass her lens, bucking and kicking. "Perfect!" she cries. "Perfect."

Execution

The witnesses to the execution lounge on the long veranda, eating sandwiches, drinking iced tea, and sweating in the high-nineties heat and humidity.

There are about fifty of them, art folks from Houston, from Austin, from Dallas. James Surls, the renowned sculptor and printmaker, invited them.

Mr. Surls, now sixty, has been prominent on the national art scene—especially as a sculptor — for a long time. His work is in the collections of the Whitney Museum of American Art, the Museum of Modern Art, and the Guggenheim Museum. He's especially admired in his native Texas. Nearly all its major galleries and museums have shown his work.

In 1981 Mr. Surls built this barn-like studio on the edge of the Big Thicket, thirty-five miles northeast of Houston, where for almost two decades he carved huge, highly original wooden sculptures from the steaming forest around him.

"Every poisonous thing on the North American continent lives near my house," he once told a Kansas City audience.

Yielding to his wife's pleas, he moved to Colorado in 1998, but still owns the huge studio with the veranda. He has come back for the execution.

To call what is about to happen an "execution," he says, is something of a joke. The event is an artistically serious one. "I am destroying a body of work as it was," he says. "It will be more in the realm of a carcass. The question is: What becomes of the carcass? I think it will be a new work of art."

Beyond the veranda's shade where the witnesses sit in T-shirts and shorts and sneakers, the early Saturday afternoon sun beats hot and blinding. Cicadas whir insanely in the trees. Somewhere behind the witnesses, invisible beyond the sweltering woods, the tiny town of Splendora (population about 750) drowses.

Mr. Surls' almost-waist-length gray hair is tied in a horsetail. His weathered face shows a few days' growth of whiskers, also gray. Sweat blotches his T-shirt as he and five strong helpers appear around the corner of the building. They're carrying a heavy table as pallbearers would bear a coffin. Clamped to the tabletop are two sheets of plywood. Sandwiched between the sheets is the entire second edition of a woodblock print called *Cut Hand/Hurt Eyes*. All fifteen numbered copies of it, plus several proofs, plus the carved block from which they were pulled.

Mr. Surls issued the original edition of the print in 1986. It's a large work, three feet wide and six feet tall, and a powerful one. Its primitive/mythic figure, apparently dancing in pain against a bloody-red background, with knife blades around him, seems simple. His pain seems pure. The image is unforgettable.

Mr. Surls made twenty prints, numbered them, signed them, and sold them. Ordinarily, after a limited edition is printed, the artist "strikes" the plate from which it is made, defacing it so that it can't be used again. But the plate of *Cut Hand/Hurt Eyes* simply disappeared into the clutter of the print shop. In 1999, the printer found the plate and gave it back to Mr. Surls.

"Looking back, I should have struck that plate the minute I saw it," he says. Instead, he decided to make a second edition using a different paper, a different ink, and a different printer. It's a common practice among artists, he says.

"It's not the same print," Mr. Surls says. "It's visually different. I never even thought about whether I should or shouldn't have done it."

Last spring, one of the second-edition prints was included in a big Surls exhibition at the Meadows Museum at Southern Methodist University. Ted Lee, a Houston lawyer who had bought a print from the original edition saw the second-edition version on display there and, in Mr. Surls' words, "He was very, very seriously upset. He felt that the existence of the second edition would devalue his first-edition print." He threatened a lawsuit.

"I did nothing wrong," Mr. Surls says. "It was clearly labeled a second edition. It was a different piece of art. But there are some very, very conservative collectors who believe it's unethical to make a second edition of a limited edition print. Period."

The artist phoned Mr. Lee. "What he wanted me to do was destroy the second edition," Mr. Surls says. "I told my dealer, 'My God, he just wants me to shoot the damn thing!' That's how shooting the prints came into the lexicon of the moment."

So instead of going to court, Mr. Surls told Mr. Lee he was willing to shoot the second-edition *Cut Hand/Hurt Eyes* with a gun. Kill it. Execute it. He says the upset collector agreed to that solution.

Asked to comment about the controversy, Mr. Lee replies, "Thanks for asking, but I choose not to."

"When you formally execute something, you are planning on something being dead when it's over with," Mr. Surls says. "The paradox of a political execution is that something is left. And it's not just the corpus itself. It's a stigma, an aura, something that you can't touch. That's what a martyr is. Something lives on in the minds of the believers. It really takes on a life of its own. I put this event into that realm."

So the six sweaty men carry the heavy table forward, turn it on one end, and stand it against the trunk of a storm-felled tree in the small clearing between the veranda and the woods. The witnesses see that a window has been cut through the top plywood slab, exposing part of the naked white back of one of the prints. On this surface, Mr. Surls has drawn nine small black ink dots in triangular groups of three.

The executioner is standing about thirty feet from his target, his back to the witnesses. Beside him stands a smaller table, covered with guns, cartridge boxes, and other shooting equipment.

When preparations are complete, he slides a clip into his .45 semi-automatic pistol, steps forward and shouts, "Fire in the hole!" and pulls the trigger. The pistol barks. Its slug drills a neat round hole where one of the dots had been. The witnesses clap their hands and whistle. "Unbelievable!" someone cries.

The executioner is Mr. Surls' friend David Bradshaw, fifty-eight, of Cecilia, Louisiana. Like Mr. Surls, he's a well-known artist. He's also a champion marksman and ballistics expert. He often uses guns in his art, and sometimes dynamite.

Mr. Bradshaw fires nine times in all. Each bullet strikes on or very near a black dot. When he has finished, there are three neat bullet-hole triangles across the exposed back of *Cut Hand/Hurt Eyes*, edition two. The witnesses stand and whistle and shout, "Wow!"

They step down from the veranda and gather around the executed art, marveling at the accuracy of Mr. Bradshaw's marksmanship. "Nice job!" they say. Mr. Bradshaw, a pleasant balding man dressed in a light blue shirt, khakis, and sandals, answers questions about his semi-automatic pistol and also the big .45-caliber revolver, lying holstered on his table, that he decided not to use.

Two or three witnesses work their way around the fallen tree and search for Mr. Bradshaw's bullets in the forest debris. They find none.

Mr. Surls shouts, "There are 800 pounds of sandwiches inside and fifty-two gallons of tea! So eat and drink up!"

He and his helpers carefully pick up the bullet-scarred table with the art clamped to it and carry it into the studio. There they undo the clamps, lift the plywood top slab, and turn over the first of the executed prints.

There's a bullet-hole triangle in each outstretched hand of the primitive/mythic figure, like crucifixion stigmata. The middle triangle is in the figure's face—a bullet hole under each eye and one between the eyes. The bullets penetrated the woodblock as well. Mr. Surls' plate finally has been "struck."

He signed the prints when he made them in 1999. Now, as each is peeled from the stack, Mr. Bradshaw adds his own signature and some data about the weapon and ammunition—"Les Baur Model 1911 .45 ACP." Also, "Splendora, Texas, 9 Aug. 03."

"There's a history of shooting something in the name of art," Mr. Surls says. "But I know of no other instance of an entire edition of a work being shot at the same time. Visually, the bullet holes don't change the work terribly a lot. Symbolically, they change it greatly. David is a true collaborator in this. He's the co-creator with me of a new piece of art."

So. Will the new work of art be given a new title?

Mr. Surls raises his eyebrows. "A good question," he says.

The witnesses make themselves another sandwich and drink some more tea, then disperse quickly toward their air-conditioned cars.

Letters

Oweda Shults came home on a Saturday afternoon in 2002 and found a family of strangers sitting at her kitchen table. Her husband, Babe, was standing beside the table, crying.

"I was kind of alarmed," Mrs. Shults says. "I was apprehensive."

One of the strangers stood and extended his hand. He was Ramiro Castillo, he said. He and his wife, Manuela, and his sons, Richard and Ramiro Jr., had driven to Stratford, Oklahoma, all the way from Pharr, Texas, more than 600 miles away on the Mexican border. Mr. Castillo said he had something that belonged to the Shultses, and he wanted to return it.

On the table lay a large ring binder full of photocopied letters enclosed in plastic sleeves, like an album. Reading the letters had made Babe Shults cry. Some were from his brother Lynwood, who was killed in action during World War II. The others, full of longing for the young sailor's safe return, were to Lynwood from his family and his sweetheart.

The Shultses vaguely remember that the letters used to be kept in a box in the attic of Babe and Lynwood's father's house. But they lost track of them many years ago, after the old man died and the house was sold. "We didn't even know they were missing until Mr. Castillo brought them to us," Oweda Shults says.

Mr. Castillo and his family had driven across Texas and part of Oklahoma on an impulse. They hoped to find some member of Lynwood's family, or maybe Margaret Lee Scott, the young schoolteacher who was his sweetheart. But Mr. Castillo had so little hope of success that he didn't bring the original letters with him. Just the album of photocopies he had made for his own use. Lynwood went to war sixty years ago. How likely were the Shultses to still be in the place where he had grown up?

Mr. Castillo had to try. The letters had become his obsession.

He found them at a flea market in the Rio Grande Valley town of

Donna in November or December of 2001. "They were in an old shoe-box, lying on a table with a bunch of other stuff," he says. "I noticed from the postmarks that they were from the World War II era. I picked one up and read it." But he decided not to buy them.

Mr. Castillo, fifty-two, teaches history at Pharr-San Juan-Alamo North High School. He's always on the lookout for interesting stuff to take into his classroom. "All that week, I kept thinking about that box," he says. "The more I thought about it, the more I wanted it. So I went back to Donna the next Saturday, hoping it was still there. It was. I pulled out another letter and read it. In it, the writer said he had been assigned to a submarine."

"Dear Papa, Audney, and kids," Lynwood had written, "Hello and how is everyone? I'm getting along just fine. At last I have made it. I've been transferred to a submarine, the U.S.S. *Gudgeon*. It is a good one plus a swell crew and officers which means a lot. Kinda lucky if you ask me. . . ."

That was enough for Mr. Castillo. He paid $10 for the box. Some of the letters had been pulled from their envelopes and were lying about on the table. He gathered them up, put them back into the box, and took everything to his car.

"As I was driving home, I pulled out another letter and was skimming through it," he says. "It was a condolence letter. Then I knew I had something on my hands. These were the letters of a young man who didn't come back from the war."

More than 100 letters were in the box. When Mr. Castillo got them home, he tried to put them all into their correct envelopes. He catalogued them and placed them in chronological order. He returned to the man who had sold them at the Donna flea market.

"He seemed to be one of those who come down to the Valley for the winter," Mr. Castillo remembers. "They bring their wares with them so they can sell and make money while they're here. I asked him where he got the letters. He told me they were part of a consignment from an estate sale. He said the consignment had come out of Weatherford, but I don't remember whether he said Weatherford, Texas, or Weatherford, Oklahoma."

As he studied the letters, Mr. Castillo got more and more involved in the lives of the people in them: Lynwood and his father, Jim Shults; Lynwood's stepmother, Audney; and his half-siblings, Harold, who was called "Son," Lorene, who was called "Sis," and John, the youngest, who was called "Babe"; and the schoolteacher, Margaret Lee Scott, whom Lynwood planned to marry when he returned. Lynwood had sent her a doll, and she would knit and crochet things for it. Sometimes she and Lynwood referred to it in their letters as "the baby." Margaret Lee named it Bozo.

"Dearest Lynwood," she wrote to him, "here goes about the third letter since I heard from you. I sincerely hope I get a letter from you tomorrow. Every time the mail comes I expect to hear from you. I don't care how long it has been since I heard, I'm always expecting and hoping to hear again."

"I wondered if they were still alive," Mr. Castillo says. "I visualized a sailor writing those letters home, and the people at home writing him. I visualized Oklahoma in my mind, and the little town. When I would wake up at night and couldn't sleep, I would pull out the box and read the letters. I checked maps to see where Lynwood's submarine had been. I would look at the picture of a young sailor that was in one of the letters and ask, 'Are you Lynwood?'"

Mr. Castillo decided to research Lynwood's submarine, the *Gudgeon*. It was based at Pearl Harbor, but was on patrol when the Japanese attacked the American fleet there. It was one of the first three subs to enter Japanese home waters and harass enemy shipping. In January 1942, it became the first U.S. submarine in history to sink an enemy warship. It received three Presidential Unit Citations for its many victories.

Lynwood didn't join its crew until August 1943. His younger brothers back home wondered what sailing underwater was like. "Son, I'm afraid I can't answer those questions you asked," Lynwood wrote back, "except the one about seeing the fish. You can't see the fish when you are submerged in a submarine."

If anything exciting was happening to him, he couldn't say. The military mail censors forbade communication about almost everything. Lynwood often expressed his frustration, "I will try writing a few lines about something today but really there isn't much to write about. Just think how it would be trying to write when you couldn't speak of your surroundings and most of the things you do."

On April 4, 1944, the *Gudgeon* left Pearl Harbor on its twelfth war patrol. Sometime later that month or in early May, Japanese planes apparently bombed and sank it as it was making a solitary attack against an enemy convoy. Its eighty-nine officers and crew were declared missing in action. A year later, they were declared killed in action. Lynwood was twenty-two when he died.

Among Lynwood's personal effects that the navy shipped to Stratford from his locker at Pearl Harbor were several letters he never got to see. One was from his dad. "I'll be glad when this war is over and all you boys get to come home," Jim Shults had written. "Well, will close for this time. God be with you wherever you may be and guide you safely home is my prayer. With lots of love. I hope I can be with you in heaven."

Lynwood and three buddies had joined the navy on September 1, 1942, at Phoenix, Arizona. They had been working in a copper mine and were exempt from the draft, but they joined up anyway.

When Jim Shults got the telegram telling him his son was missing, he was working in a magnesium plant at Las Vegas, Nevada. "It was during the war, and times was hard," says Harold "Son" Shults' widow, Marjorie. Babe was fourteen when they got word. Harold was sixteen. He quit school and went to work in a grocery store so he could help make a living."

After he heard that Lynwood was missing, Jim Shults decided to move his family back to Stratford. "He thought, 'If Lynwood comes back and we're out here in Nevada, he won't know where to find us,'" Marjorie Shults says. Jim got a job as a butcher at a Stratford grocery.

As soon as Margaret Lee Scott heard of Lynwood's death, she moved to California and never returned.

"Lynwood's daddy turned white-headed in a year," Oweda Shults says. "He didn't sleep. He walked the yard. He used to talk about Lynwood all the time. He never got to buy him a suit of clothes, he never got to buy him anything. He never got to bury him. He said that was what was breaking his heart. He was struggling and poor all of Lynwood's life, and when he got to where he could do something, Lynwood was gone. That grieved him bad."

Kenneth Bundy, a cousin who lives in Arkansas, remembers Lynwood as a shy boy. "You kind of had to prod him to get him to talk," he says.

"But even when he was a kid, grownups treated him kind of like he was a grownup, too. They didn't treat me that way. They treated me like a kid. But they always treated Lynwood with respect. I don't know why."

Mr. Bundy's sister, Cloma Martin, who lives in Irving, was only five or six years old when Lynwood went off to war, but she has one memory of him, "I looked up at him—he was a big guy—and I remember black, beautiful, big eyes and black hair."

"Everybody liked Lynwood," Mr. Bundy says. "The girls made over him."

Jim Shults put the letters that Lynwood had saved in Hawaii and the letters that he had sent home into a shoebox together and put them in his attic. "He died about fifteen years ago, and everybody forgot about the letters," Oweda says. "How they got out of the house and almost down to Mexico, no one knows. It's a mystery."

As Mr. Castillo neared the end of his trek up Interstate 35, he stopped at the police station in Pauls Valley, Oklahoma, only sixteen miles west of Stratford. He asked if any Shultses still lived in the area. Someone checked the phone book, and a Babe Shults was listed in Stratford.

"When we got there, my son saw that the American Legion was open. We stopped and went in. They were having a birthday party for somebody. They said, yeah, they knew Babe Shults. They called him and then took us down to where he lives.

"I asked him if he knew who Lynwood Shults was. He said it was his brother who had died in World War II. I showed him the picture I had found in one of the letters and said, 'Who is this?' And he said, 'That's Lynwood.'"

When Mr. Castillo was satisfied that he had found the right family, he told them he would come to Stratford again in a few days with the real letters. And he did.

"They were very grateful," he says. "They wanted to pay me for the letters and for the effort, but I said no. I told the Shultses that a higher power must be involved in this."

That feeling is strengthened, he says, by the fact that he found the Shults family on July 20. It was Lynwood's birthday. He would have been eighty-two years old.

Moccasins

The moccasins came to me in 1987, while I was working on a story at the Apache reservation in New Mexico. I had gone there to observe the naming ceremony for a baby. The ceremony would be done in the Catholic church on the reservation, but it would include elements of the Apaches' native religion, such as sage smoke and eagle feathers and prayers spoken in the Apache tongue.

My story was one of a series my newspaper was doing about efforts of the Catholic clergy to incorporate elements of non-European cultures—Asian, African, American Indian—into church rituals in congregations where the parishioners weren't of European heritage. Texas was more interested than usual in Catholicism in the summer of 1987 because Pope John Paul II was coming to visit San Antonio in September.

The naming ceremony was a simple one, done at dusk with sunlight streaming in the big windows. The baby lay on a blanket on the stone floor before the stone altar in the beautiful stone church while the sage smoke and the prayers swirled around her. The Catholic priest and the Apache shaman and the little girl's parents and their friends in the congregation all had their parts.

It was beautiful and dignified, a perfect thing to be done by those people among their magnificent pine trees and mountains. Afterwards, there was a dinner, prepared by the Apache women. When the dinner was done, the Catholic priest invited me and the photographer who was working with me to come to his quarters for a drink and a visit.

He was a young, soft-spoken Franciscan friar, dressed in the brown robe and cowl of his order. In his comfortable living room, we spoke of history and Apaches and saints and popes, and he showed us some beautiful objects of native art that he had collected during his time on the reservation. I was able to tell some things he didn't know about the four Apache warriors—Geronimo, Victorio, Cochise, and Nana—whose oil portraits hung on the back wall of his church.

As the photographer and I were saying goodnight and leaving for our motel, the friar invited us to have breakfast with him in the morning, then he would give us a tour of the reservation.

I remember how beautiful that morning was. Cool. Sun shining through the pines, brightly dappling the ground with its light, us bouncing over the dirt roads in the priest's old pickup, and him pointing out places where important things had happened over the years.

As the photographer and I were about to leave for the city to catch our plane back to Dallas, the priest said he had some little going-away gifts for us. He gave the photographer a key ring with a long beautifully beaded buckskin fob. He gave me a small white cardboard box. Inside it, wrapped in tissue paper, was a pair of tiny doeskin moccasins, decorated with orange and brown beads. They were moccasins for a baby.

The priest told me that an Apache woman who lived on the reservation had made them. He said he hoped I would enjoy having them.

His gift puzzled me. There was no infant in my house. My sons were teenagers. Why had he chosen such a gift for me? Was it because of the baby's naming ceremony that I had watched? Or had he just liked the beautifully crafted little shoes and thought I would, too? Or was he wishing me grandchildren?

I took the moccasins home and showed them to Isabel. She loved them in the way women love baby things. We rewrapped them in their tissue paper, nestled them back into their box, and stowed them in a corner of a remote bookcase.

From time to time, when a search for a book brought us to their vicinity, we would take the lid off the box and visit briefly with the lovely little moccasins. A couple of times over the years, when Ted and Pat and Chris were visiting, we took down the box and said, "These moccasins will belong to our first grandchild."

Our sons' schooling and careers and long-term relationships continued apace with no mention of children. Meanwhile, Isabel and I were growing older. In time the moccasins became a kind of shorthand hint of our aspirations. "Remember the moccasins," we would say. Our sons would smile and look away.

Then one night about a year ago, the phone rang. It was Ted in California. "Dad," he said. "I'm calling to collect the moccasins."

"Ted's calling to collect the moccasins!" I hollered to Isabel.

The news spread like fire through our huge extended family. Among our generation, only Isabel and I were without grandchildren. One couple already had great-grandchildren! The jubilation intensified when word arrived that our new arrival would be a girl, a rarity among my family's throng of progeny.

Then the U.S. Air Force inadvertently added to my joy by transferring Captain Ted and his wife, Captain Kim, to San Antonio. My granddaughter would be a native Texan!

In the wee hours of September 17, 2002, Samantha Peace Woolley arrived in our world.

"Yo!" said Chris in New York. "Ted wins the moccasins!"

"So," e-mailed Pat, traveling in Australia, "I guess I am out of the running for the moccasins, huh?"

If you're a grandparent, you know the rest: Yes, she's the most beautiful child ever born. Yes, we're spoiling her rotten. Yes, she's bringing more hope and light into more fading lives than she can ever know.

In October, I drove down to San Antonio and named Samantha the princess of our tribe and placed the tiny moccasins on her feet. They were too large and kept slipping off. By Thanksgiving, they fit perfectly. By now, they're probably too small.

But the moccasins belong to Samantha now. And they still belong in some mysterious, pine-scented way to the Apache woman who made them, and to the Franciscan friar who gave them to me, and to the baby who was lying on the stone church floor with smoke and prayers around her, receiving her name.

Someday Samantha will give them to somebody else.